POWER
AMBITION
GLORY

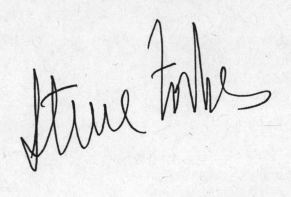

POWER
AMBITION
GLORY

THE STUNNING PARALLELS BETWEEN

GREAT LEADERS OF THE ANCIENT WORLD AND TODAY...

AND THE LESSONS YOU CAN LEARN

STEVE FORBES
&
JOHN PREVAS

THREE RIVERS PRESS

NEW YORK

Published in the United States by Three Rivers Press, an imprint of the
Crown Publishing Group, a division of Random House, Inc., New York.

Three Rivers Press and the Tugboat design
are registered trademarks of Random House, Inc.

Originally published in hardcover in the United States by Crown Business, an imprint of the
Crown Publishing Group, a division of Random House, Inc., New York, in 2009.

Library of Congress Cataloging-in-Publication Data

Forbes, Steve, 1947–

Prevas, John, 1943–

Power ambition glory / Steve Forbes and John Prevas.

1. Leadership—Case studies.   2. Power (Social Sciences)—Case studies.

3. Civilization, Classical.   I. Prevas, John.   II. Title.

HD57.7.F665 2009

658.4'092–dc22

2008052008

ISBN 978-0-307-40845-7

Printed in the United States of America

Design by Leonard W. Henderson

10 9 8 7 6 5 4 3 2

First Paperback Edition

To Leila and Winston,
future leaders
—*Steve Forbes*

CONTENTS

Rem tene verba sequentur.

(Get hold of the matter and the words will follow.)
—Cato

FOREWORD

by Rudy Giuliani

This is a complicated age for Americans. At times it feels like we are alone in history, suffering through a unique set of trials that leaders have never faced before. A book like *Power Ambition Glory* serves as a testament to the cycles of history and reminds us that nations and leaders have survived grave challenges. It's also a reminder that nations and leaders have overreached and failed. If the fragile balance of power, ambition, and glory is disrupted, then empires are lost.

The challenges we face today are certainly historic. The global economy is crumbling, and all of us are wondering how our new leaders will actually lead. Will they follow the example of a leader like Alexander the Great, whose grand vision was colored by an insatiable need for flattery? Will our leaders look to Cyrus, who boldly added to his vast empire but struggled to make all the far-flung parts function together in harmony?

It is the obligation of any leader to try to learn from the successes and failures of the past. In taking us on a fascinating tour of the principles, habits, styles, and results of leaders of the past, Steve Forbes and John Prevas draw clear lessons that today's readers can put to work in their own lives.

Reading this book, I was reminded of a problem I faced after I became mayor of New York City in 1994. Our tourism industry was on life support. No one wanted to drive into New York because they were accosted at the tunnels, and no one wanted to stay in New York because the hotel taxes were exorbitant. People who were inclined to spend money in New York City—money that would provide good jobs and support New York families—were afraid of being confronted by a "squeegee man" wielding a filthy wiper and demanding a handout. And if they chose to stay overnight, they faced a hotel tax of 21.25 percent—a burden that was about triple the average of the country's busiest cities. The result was predictable. Businesses staged 50 percent fewer conventions in New York in 1993 than they had five years earlier—the Professional Convention Management Association in effect boycotted the city.

New Yorkers had been told that both these problems were intractable. The squeegee men supposedly had a "right" to wander into traffic and intimidate visitors. The hotel tax was high because the city and state desperately needed the revenue. My administration was determined to tackle both of these problems, not only to solve these two problems, but more important, to show New Yorkers that progress and reform were possible, that actual results could be achieved.

As one of my first actions as mayor, I sent a letter to the governor asking for a repeal of the state's 5 percent hotel tax. And I cut the New York City tax from 6 percent to 5 percent. This was a small step, but important symbolically—no one could remember any tax ever being reduced in New York City. Since the leader of any large enterprise cannot speak directly to each constituent, symbols are significant. I wanted to send a powerful message that I believed that lower taxes would stimulate more than enough business to offset any immediate loss in revenue. That's exactly what happened with the hotel tax. Within months, net revenue from the hotel tax was actually higher at 5 percent than it had been at 6 percent, since far more visitors were coming to the city.

At the same time, we began to tackle the "squeegee man" problem. Estimates had generally placed their numbers at a couple thousand, but we had the police study the situation; we were astonished to discover that they identified only about 180. Rather than tangle with First Amendment issues, we took the novel—and fully legal—approach of ticketing these men for jaywalking. After all, running in between moving cars was dangerous for drivers and for the squeegee men themselves. In the process they were identified and often found to be wanted for other violations and crimes. They were removed, and that very visible success set the stage for a series of dramatic improvements in New York City. An early victory set the tone for the next eight years.

More than most authors, Steve Forbes understands the power of symbols. As the leader of one of the publishing world's great brand names, Steve understands that large organizations must set clear goals and hold themselves accountable. If someone representing Forbes does something irresponsible, then to the public—and to the rest of the Forbes organization—it is as though the action were made by Forbes itself.

By the same token, a powerful idea can be broadly transmitted by a leader, who can use his position to communicate ideas throughout the organization. Steve Forbes himself has been a forceful advocate of the idea that the American tax code is far too complicated and has greatly strayed from its revenue-collection mission, becoming a force for social engineering. In communicating that idea—and offering a postcard-sized alternative—Steve entered the public debate and emerged as a leader of the movement to make taxation fairer and simpler.

John Prevas also exhibits impressive initiative. By going into the field, John frequently observes one of my principles of leadership—"see things for yourself."

For example, there had been a centuries-long controversy over what route Hannibal took over the Alps. John actually explored the various possibilities, and in his book on Hannibal made an incontrovertible case as to the route Hannibal actually used. John has also visited various parts of the world that were the old stomping grounds of Alexander and other figures of classical times. Some of these areas are not particularly hospitable to Americans, yet John found ways to see what needed to be seen to help understand the past.

Leaders set the tone for those under their sway. Their priorities must be established and communicated if they are to achieve the support of the people they hope to lead. It is too soon to tell what will happen in our country as we enter a time of new leadership and unprecedented economic turmoil. *Power Ambition Glory* serves as a remarkable historical guide. It's both a reference guide to the rise and fall of empires, as well as a fresh look at modern business leaders and how they fit into the framework of history.

INTRODUCTION

How the Past Can Guide Your Future

A couple of years ago while browsing in a local bookstore in Naples, Florida, for something interesting to read, I* came across *Hannibal Crosses the Alps* by John Prevas. It's the story of the ancient Carthaginian commander who accomplished something that neither his allies nor his enemies thought possible: He led an army, including horses and elephants, over the Alps in winter and then defeated his Roman adversaries in their own backyard.

As I reviewed the book in *Forbes* magazine, two thoughts occurred to me about leadership: (1) Anyone who accomplishes something great, something unique, whether in business or in politics, often does so by defying the conventional thinking of his time. (2) Even though more than two thousand years have passed since Hannibal crossed those Alps, the elements of what it takes to be a successful leader have not changed. They are simple and obvious, or should be: motivating those who follow you to share your vision; inspiring through example; a sense of duty and responsibility to those who trust and depend on you; the capacity to see a problem and the skill to fix it; developing and maintaining a proper perspective on yourself in the face of success or adversity; setting and achieving goals; understanding people's limits and knowing when to drive hard and when to ease up on both subordinates and competitors.

The ancient Greeks tell us that nothing is more important than

---

*Coauthor Steve Forbes

good leadership for the harmonious functioning of society and nothing hurts more than the lack of it. Our times cry out for leadership—political, financial, and even ethical. Many people are asking today, "Where have the good leaders gone?" In a recent *New York Times* column about global gridlock entitled "Missing Dean Acheson," David Brooks posed this question, noting that Americans are about to enter their nineteenth consecutive year of Truman envy. Ever since the Berlin Wall fell in 1989, Brooks observed, people have yearned for a return to a time when leaders such as Harry Truman and George C. Marshall were able to create successful, forward-looking global institutions and policies to confront the challenges that faced America at the end of the Second World War. Brooks asked, "Why can't we rally that same kind of international cooperation to solve our current economic crisis, confront terrorism, slow down global warming, limit nuclear proliferation and a host of other pressing problems today?"

Ours is a complex and stressful time. We face the most serious financial crisis since the Great Depression of the 1930s and foreign policy issues that if left unsolved could bring us to the brink of nuclear war. Rising new powers in the world today, such as China and India, are changing traditional Western ways of conducting worldwide politics and business. Old powers such as Russia and the members of the relatively new European Union are seeking to advance their influence in the international community. Responses to these developments require effective leadership. The financial crisis and America's recent foreign policy setbacks can be traced directly to a failure of leadership. But where do we turn for leadership, and what do we want in our leaders? History is one place to look. The past is filled with leaders who possessed extraordinary capabilities, enjoyed tremendous success, and directed societies that experienced problems similar to our own. Their successes and failures as leaders can help us develop a valuable perspective as we grapple with our problems and try to prepare for the future. Similarities between those who ruled the empires of the ancient world and many of today's corporate and political leaders are remarkable. Times and circumstances may change, but the principles of sound leadership do not.

Leaders in today's corporate world pursue the same goals that energized their ancient counterparts: wealth, accomplishment, recognition, and prestige. They are motivated by the same things—power, ambition, and glory—and they often use the same tactics to achieve their ends. They also suffer the same setbacks and reversals. Why, then, do we rarely consult history to help ourselves understand the present and guide us into the future? We make the same mistake the ancients did: We assume we will go on forever at the top because our prosperity, technology, and know-how make us unique, and the experiences of those who came before us seem to have little or no relevance.

We seem to forget that America's time as a superpower—only since the end of World War II—has been relatively brief, and it is questionable how long we will remain at the top. What is certain is that as we advance into the twenty-first century the parameters of power will be changing around us and our place in the world will be redefined with or without our compliance. We have to be prepared to face new challenges—who knows what the long-term social and political ramifications of the financial crisis that began in the summer of 2007 will be—and we can do that only with effective leadership.

The parallels between ancient and modern leaders are fascinating, and their relevance is what brought John Prevas and me together to write this book. As John and I got to know each other, I discovered that the man who wrote about Hannibal crossing the Alps was no armchair professor of classics lecturing students about places he had never seen. He has spent years climbing in the southern French Alps, looking for the pass the ancient Greek and Roman historians describe as the one Hannibal used.

After writing about Hannibal, John turned his attention to Xenophon and Alexander the Great, whose accomplishments have fascinating and relevant parallels in our own times. In the course of his research, he followed in their footsteps, traveling through the mountains of eastern Turkey, into Iran, onto the plains of Afghanistan and Uzbekistan, through the Khyber Pass, and into the troubled tribal areas of northwestern Pakistan. With nothing more for protection than his Greek passport and his ability to move quickly without drawing attention to himself, John went to dangerous places and took risks to try to understand why and how leaders from the ancient world were able to accomplish what they did.

In our search for examples, we selected six leaders from the ancient Mediterranean world to profile: Cyrus the Great, Xenophon of Athens, Alexander the Great, Hannibal of Carthage, Julius Caesar, and Augustus. Each was unique in his way of doing things and brought an array of talents to the realm of leadership. Each had faults and shortcomings. All were warriors capable of showing generosity and compassion toward the vanquished, but at times they all committed acts of inexplicable cruelty. If there is one common thread that ties them together, it is their astounding capacity for getting things done. Their lives—occasionally embellished and glamorized by Hollywood—contain some of the best and the worst examples of leadership.

There are interesting parallels as well between many of today's multinational corporations and the empires that the ancients led and in some cases created. Like their counterparts in the modern corporate world, the empires of the past existed to create wealth. They extracted wealth and exploited manpower from those "under management" through a combination of trade and conquest, but unlike today's businesses they did not have to worry too much about pleasing customers.

In today's free-market economies, businesses succeed only when they meet the needs and wants of their customers. In the ancient world, things were a little different when it came to "customer service." Management's mentality back then was more of a "do what we want—or else!" policy. Still, in some important ways, such as providing security and infrastructure, ancient leaders had to keep the people they ruled satisfied. Like many of today's corporations, the empires of Persia, Greece, Carthage, and Rome spanned continents and affected, for better or worse, the lives of millions. Each enjoyed a period of unrestricted expansion and unrivaled prosperity, followed by decline and finally extinction at the hands of more aggressive and efficient competitors. It was a form of survival of the fittest, not much different from today's business climate, but without a federal bailout system to rescue those who falter.

●   ●   ●

Cyrus the Great (576–530 BC) put together the Persian Empire, and what set him apart from other leaders of his time were his extraordinary vision and his willingness to build an empire based on tolerance and inclusion of other cultures. With Cyrus, leadership was more than just conquest; it included vision. Even in his early years as a nomadic tribal chief, he was able to see beyond the parched deserts of Iran and recognize the potential of an empire situated at the crossroads of the lucrative trade routes that ran between China and the West. Then he went out and built it.

Ray Kroc, the genius behind the fast-food industry, was a like-minded visionary. In the 1950s, he was selling milkshake mixers to restaurants, and among his customers were the McDonald Brothers, who owned a hamburger stand in southern California. Kroc saw society being transformed by affordable automobiles and cheap gas. Americans were falling in love with their cars, and he suspected they would be looking for a place to combine this love with food. The drive-in was born.

That hunch or insight became the foundation of Kroc's vision. Back then, the idea that you could create a restaurant empire on the shifting sands of consumer tastes was seen as preposterous. Restaurants were like nomadic tribes, here one day and gone the next. Even today, some sixty years later, nearly two-thirds of all independent restaurants fail in the first two years. But Kroc believed standardization could transform a notoriously precarious business with a narrow profit margin and high mortality rate into a resilient, fast-growing, and profitable empire. He was right, and the rest is history. Kroc not only created the fast-food industry but his vision transformed the motel and hotel industries as well.

●   ●   ●

Xenophon (435–354 BC), a young scholar from Athens, is an example of a reluctant leader who came forward in a time of crisis to fill a void. He found himself in command of an army of Greek mercenaries—mostly Spartans—trapped in the middle of the Persian Empire in the region known today as Iraq. Xenophon's mission was to organize these soldiers, motivate them, and get them home alive.

What complicated Xenophon's task and challenged his leadership were not just the Persians who surrounded him but the Greeks who followed him demanding their right to express their opinions and vote on how things should be done. Faced with an enemy that out-numbered him probably a hundred to one, some of the most difficult terrain in the world to cross, and a constituency that demanded the right to question every one of his decisions, Xenophon was in a seem-ingly no-win situation as a leader. But he succeeded. He brought the Greeks out of Persia because he was able to forge a common purpose from dissent and build a consensus that gave those who followed him the strength to endure what it took to make their way home.

The relevance of Xenophon's leadership skills for our time be-comes apparent when we compare the intrepid Athenian with execu-tives of similar nature, like Finbarr O'Neill, the former head of Hyundai and Mitsubishi. Both Xenophon and O'Neill demonstrated the same successful approach when facing a leadership vacuum in their organizations, dissension from within the ranks, and threats from hostile competitors surrounding them. Both leaders filled the power vacuum, built consensus, and inspired followers with their sense of vision. They succeeded because they continually adapted to devel-oping circumstances and held together their coalitions of diverse fac-tions. For both Xenophon and O'Neill, leadership was about what it would take to accomplish a mission, not just about personal ambition, glory, or wealth.

•   •   •

Alexander the Great (356–323 BC) needs no introduction. Everyone knows his name, and he is often regarded as the standard by which leaders are measured when it comes to strategy and tactics. Alexander, however, embodies the "my way or the highway" brand of leadership, something very different from Xenophon's style. With this manage-ment approach, you are either an ally or an enemy; there is no middle ground. Alexander confronted his competitors head-on in a direct at-tack and took no prisoners. Friends and colleagues either agreed with his view on how things needed to be done or soon found themselves nailed to the cross.

Alexander had extraordinary success on the battlefield and was able to conquer vast parts of the ancient world, but in the end he proved incapable of consolidating and ruling what he controlled to extract its maximum potential. With Alexander, leadership was about conquest, and he was ultimately destroyed by his inability to set limits for himself and manage his success. Alexander's head was turned by vanity, and he remains the classic example of Aristotle's warning that it is more important for a leader to conquer himself than to conquer others.

Modern parallels to Alexander's style and examples of its consequences abound, not only in the corporate world but in politics, sports, and entertainment. Examples of business leaders who rise to the heights of corporate power only to be brought down by their egos include Dennis Kozlowski, the former CEO of Tyco, and Carly Fiorina, former head of Hewlett-Packard. As leaders of corporate empires, both failed because they focused on what flattered, instead of on what mattered.

•   •   •

Hannibal (247–183 BC) was a leader caught in a conflict between two ancient superpowers for control of the western Mediterranean. Carthage and Rome were vying for power when Hannibal seized the initiative and turned the ancient world upside down. He accomplished what everyone thought impossible at the time: crossing the Alps with an army in winter and bringing war to the Roman backyard. Hannibal was successful because he was able to innovate and turn the tables on his larger and more powerful adversary. Like Alexander the Great, Hannibal was the boss on and off the battlefield, but unlike Alexander, he had nothing personal to prove, no ego at work here. For him, fighting was a means to an end, and leadership was about outsmarting your adversary and moving methodically closer to accomplishing your objective. It was not about winning glory and amassing a personal fortune.

Sam Walton, founder of Wal-Mart, was the Hannibal of the twentieth-century retail wars. In the early 1960s, Kmart, formerly S. S. Kresge, was the retail equivalent of Rome. It was fifty times the size of Wal-Mart, but

Walton leveled the playing field by using computer technology in a way no other retailer had ever tried. He was able to manage inventories and improve productivity while lowering prices from his suppliers. He made money by moving into markets that competitors had written off as too rural or too small to bother with. Kmart could not compete in Walton's new world of retail and subsequently was forced into bankruptcy and reduced to a mere shadow of its once formidable self. Today Wal-Mart is the Rome of the retail world and employs over a million people in the United States and 2 million worldwide.

•   •   •

Julius Caesar (101–44 BC) and Rome are synonymous. Caesar came to power at a time of political turbulence, civil war, and tremendous opportunities. He was the consummate politician, able to master the most unfavorable of circumstances, turn adversity into advantage, and continually push the limits to achieve his goals. As a military leader, he conquered more territory than Alexander the Great, and he fought more battles.

But, unlike Alexander, Caesar stepped back from conquest to consolidate his holdings and undertake a radical reform of Roman government and society. Although Caesar, like Alexander, took a "my way or the highway" approach to leadership, he was much more forgiving toward adversaries, especially Romans who were willing to acknowledge the error of their ways and enter or reenter the fold. But like Alexander, Caesar came to believe that his success was the result of his divine status, and he became a dictator with aspirations to rule Rome and the world as a king. Ego blinded him to the plots developing behind his back and brought an end not only to his career but his life.

In today's corporate world, leaders are dispatched by less gruesome means than the daggers of their shareholders, but there are many examples of CEOs who, like Julius Caesar and Alexander, achieve great things only to be brought down suddenly by their own hubris. Maurice "Hank" Greenberg of AIG and Sandy Weill of Citicorp immediately come to mind as powerful leaders who made their marks but in the end were destroyed by their egos.

•   •   •

We conclude with the Roman leader Augustus (63 BC–AD 14), arguably the most successful of all our ancient examples when looked at from a leadership perspective. He ruled the biggest and most profitable empire in history for over forty years and yet, in spite of his success and power, modestly referred to himself as no more than Rome's *primus inter pares,* or "first among equals."

Over the years, Augustus kept a sane perspective on himself. Even though he became the undisputed ruler of millions and the richest man in the ancient world, he listened to others and understood the value of moving cautiously and thoughtfully on everything from building roads to conducting wars. His favorite expression was *festina lente*—"make haste slowly"—and this approach, coupled with a degree of personal humility rarely found in powerful leaders, put Rome on the sound footing that made it the largest, richest, and most powerful force in the ancient world.

While Julius Caesar put Rome on the road to empire, Augustus kept it moving in the right direction and at the right pace. He made the empire profitable by building a solid political and financial infrastructure that enabled it to prosper for years. Augustus understood limitations, both personal and corporate. He surrounded himself with competent people to help him keep Rome on a steady course of development while setting limits to how far the empire could expand. It's rare today to find a leader who doesn't measure personal success solely by his or her ability to make an organization bigger simply for the sake of getting bigger. Augustus is proof positive that real leadership and success come from being able to strike a balance between power, ambition, and glory.

When it comes to successful administration and establishing lasting infrastructure for a company, Alfred Sloan is the corporate equivalent of Augustus. In the early 1920s, General Motors was a poorly run collection of auto companies on the verge of bankruptcy. Sloan turned the company around through a combination of innovative administrative practices and brilliant marketing and sales breakthroughs. He built GM into a worldwide automotive empire, which now, nearly a hundred years later, is again in serious financial trouble. With worldwide competition and a vehicle line in the United States that is, like it was in the early 1920s, too unwieldy and unappealing, GM is on the verge of bankruptcy, barely kept alive with bailout money from Washington. Can GM find another Alfred Sloan to come forward in its time of crisis to save it?

●   ●   ●

Of course, parallels between ancient leaders and modern executives will never align perfectly, but there is definite value in making the comparisons. Ancient leaders obviously operated under different conditions and lacked many advantages that modern-day CEOs take for granted, but they ran their empires by utilizing similar styles of leadership. And, although our world is very different from that of the ancients, life and the essentials of human interaction, especially as they pertain to who gives orders and who obeys them, have not changed that much.

By examining the experiences of leaders like Cyrus, Xenophon, Alexander, Hannibal, Julius Caesar, and Augustus, and the lessons to be drawn from them, we might be able to gain a little better perspective on where we are going today, how we will get there, and what shape we will be in when we arrive. Examining ancient leaders won't give us point-by-point guides that guarantee success, but it will give us real-life lessons and examples that can make us more effective in guiding our organizations and meeting our responsibilities.

●   ●   ●

Power Ambition Glory is divided into four chronological sections, each one covering one or two of these prominent leaders from ancient Persia, Greece, Carthage, and Rome. Each section is introduced by a short chapter providing an overview of the geography, history, and politics of the empire at hand, to give you a feel for the times in which these leaders moved. There follows a more detailed treatment of their lives and comparisons with modern corporate leaders in the subsequent chapters. Our hope is that we can make the connection for you between what constituted great leadership in the ancient world and what we need today as we move into the most complicated, fearful, yet promising time in history: the twenty-first century.

part ■

1

THE PERSIAN EMPIRE

Cultural Diversity, Self-Determination,

and the Art of Making Money

The Persians are a mysterious and remote civilization often confused in the popular imagination with the modern-day Islamic theocracy of Iran. We know less about the Persians than we know about the Greeks and Romans because the important archaeological sites are scattered throughout Iraq, Iran, Afghanistan, Uzbekistan, and Pakistan, where alternating periods of war and political dislocation over the last few decades have hampered efforts to conduct extensive research. The governments of those countries have shown little interest in the periods of their history that predate Islam and have made little effort to preserve many of the fragile and vulnerable sites within their borders.

Another thing that makes learning about Persia difficult is that what we do know has come to us through Greek writers—much of it from one man, the fifth-century-BC historian Herodotus. The freedom-loving Greeks referred to the Persians as "barbarians," because their language to Greek ears sounded like "bar bar." They viewed Persia as a land where "everybody is educated to be a slave and nobody stands up for himself." The Greeks viewed the Persian king and his aristocracy as contemptible parasites with few interests beyond "eating, drinking and sex." This perspective has framed the traditional Western view of Persia, although in recent years historians have tended to become more skeptical of Greek objectivity.

Modern historians have concluded that there was considerable cultural, political, and economic interaction between Greece and Persia and that the relationship might not have been as hostile as the Greeks made it out to be. There were brutal conflicts, to be sure; history records a number of them. For example, in the fifth century BC, the Persians looted and burned Athens, and in the fourth century BC, Alexander the Great looted and burned Persepolis, the Persian capital. But as our own experiences in postwar Japan and Germany have shown, conflict alone does not always provide an accurate and definitive perspective on the true nature of relationships, nor does it totally derail cooperation when prospects for mutual economic gain are at stake.

The earliest Persians were nomads from central Asia and most likely trekked into Iran around 1000 BC from the bleak plains of Turkistan and Uzbekistan looking for more hospitable surroundings. They first settled in the deserts and mountains then moved into the fertile area between the Tigris and Euphrates rivers known as Mesopotamia. There they established themselves among the older but declining empires of the Medes, Babylonians, and Assyrians, taking over many of their more populated centers and eventually blending them into the people who became known in history as the Persians.

Even the powerful Egyptians came under Persian domination as the conquering armies of the Iranian kings reached the Nile River and Sudan. By the middle of the fifth century BC, the Persian Empire reached the height of its power, and the lands of the "king of kings" stretched from western Turkey to Pakistan and from Egypt to Russia, encompassing nearly 2 million square miles and an estimated 10 million people.

The history of Persia is the history of its kings. Everything in the empire was oriented toward the support and exultation of the ruler who became the center of the universe for his people. According to the Greeks, the king's subjects were driven "under the lash," and punishment for transgressions against his person, his family, his property, or his representatives could be swift and severe. Everyone in Persia was subject to the death penalty. Flogging, mutilation of hands and feet, and blinding were lesser penalties that remain today in many parts of the Middle East and central Asia.

More recent interpretations of Persian history tend to portray the kings as less repressive and more tolerant of the cultures they ruled than the Greeks would have us believe. Current thinking tends to suggest that although the king was the center of the empire, as long as tribute was paid and subjects remained loyal, he was inclined to afford them considerable latitude and even self-determination in cultural, religious, and political matters.

Within the climate of toleration developed several of the world's most significant religions and codes of ethical behavior. Zoroastrianism, for example, proclaimed the existence of one god and promised reward or punishment in an afterlife, five hundred years before Christianity. Jewish scholars living in exile in Babylon were allowed to refine the laws and beliefs of Judaism, and the Jewish people were freed from bondage and allowed to return home. In the Persian-controlled part of ancient India (present-day Pakistan), the Buddha—the "Enlightened One"— began to preach a doctrine of universal brotherhood and peace.

In spite of its inclination toward cultural diversity and self-determination, the Persian Empire was still all about making money. The Persians developed new and for the time enlightened techniques for administering large areas and diverse cultures. Repression and enslavement alone, techniques employed by the earlier Assyrian, Babylonian, and Egyptian empires, could never have held together an enterprise as large as Persia became. Fear, intimidation, and exploitation certainly played their part in building and maintaining the empire, but in general, the Persians seem to have followed a policy of interfering as little as possible in the daily lives of their subjects as long as tribute was paid. Each spring, in celebration of the Persian New Year, ambassadors from all over the empire came to Persepolis bearing tribute for the king.

Within this vast empire, Persian kings provided economic opportunities for their subjects. A policy of inclusion resulted in an improved

standard of living for many along with increased levels of revenue for the aristocracy. Historians view this policy as a conscious effort by the Persians to improve the organization of their society. The policies of inclusion and tolerance, however, might have been practical accommodations to the size of the empire and the slow pace of travel. Tight administration from the center might have been impossible.

A royal family known as the Achaemenids ruled the Persian Empire for more than two hundred years. Their dynasty appears to have been successful because each king accepted an obligation to contribute to the well-being of the empire either by expanding its holdings through conquest or by increasing its wealth through competent administration. Each king up to the last managed to improve on or expand what had been passed down to him by his predecessor. No one in the ancient world had ever controlled so much territory or so much wealth as the eleven kings who successively sat on the Persian throne from the rise of Cyrus the Great in 550 BC until the destruction of the empire by Alexander in 330 BC. The pharaohs of Egypt, the kings of Mesopotamia and Asia Minor, the nomad chieftains of the eastern deserts of Iran and Afghanistan, the rajas of

India, and even the Greeks all paid tribute to the Persian rulers. No other empire became as big or as wealthy until Rome nearly five centuries later.

Cyrus the Great (reigned 550–530 BC), the first of the Persian kings, is credited by historians with laying the foundation for the empire through his conquests of Iran, Afghanistan, Iraq, and Turkey. When Cyrus died, the crown passed to his eldest son, Cambyses, who proved to be the equal of his father even though he ruled for a much shorter period (reigned 530–522 BC). While Cambyses conquered Egypt and added the island of Cyprus to the empire, it was Darius I (reigned 521–486 BC), the third king, who rivaled Cyrus in greatness.

Darius became surnamed the "worker" and undertook to bring the coast of Asia Minor under his control, a move that would eventually lead to war with the Greeks. Darius, however, was less concerned with conquest than his predecessors, and focused on improving the administration of the empire, which had become so large that even the "king of kings" could not rule it single-handedly. He skillfully balanced the need for local self-determination with the necessity of centralized control by retaining the *satrapies,* or "provinces," into which his predecessors had divided the empire. In an effort to ensure consistent and fair administrative practices as well as efficient and clear lines of authority between the center and the provinces, he issued what he called his "Ordinance of Good Regulations." Darius took pride in his new code and compared it to the one drafted more than a thousand years earlier by Hammurabi, the Babylonian king best remembered for his dictum "An eye for an eye and a tooth for a tooth."

To provide for his personal security, Darius established an elite military unit known as the "immortals," because their replacement due to retirement or death was so swift and seamless that people had the impression they neither aged nor died but remained perpetually young.

To facilitate the flow of commerce within the empire, Darius created a single monetary unit, the Daric, and instituted a uniform system of weights and measures. The coins were minted in both gold and silver and became not only the monetary unit for the empire but an accepted and widely circulated currency throughout the ancient world.

Under Darius, the Persian Empire became a marketplace for the ancient world. Spices, gold, pearls, and gems, came from India, while silver, copper, iron, flax, and papyrus came from Turkey and Egypt. Textiles were shipped from Carthage and Corinth along with rare purple dyes from Phoenicia. Carpets came from Iran, along with shields and swords from workshops in Greece. Timber to build homes and palaces came from the Black Sea coast, Lebanon, and Thrace in northern Greece. As the empire prospered, a strong demand developed at the center for luxury goods, and the benefits of free trade even trickled down to the poorer classes.

A network of roads allowed for the rapid and safe transport of goods and people as well as the deployment of troops in time of crisis (the same motive propelled construction of the U.S. interstate system in the 1950s and 1960s). The main road, known as the royal highway, was approximately 1,700 miles long and stretched from Sardis, the Persian administrative center in the western part of Turkey, to Babylon, the commercial heart of the empire. East of Babylon, the highway divided as one branch led to Iran and the most distant provinces of the empire in Afghanistan and Pakistan, while the other led south to the capital at Persepolis. A second route led from Babylon, through Palestine, to Egypt.

Because tribute was the lifeblood of the empire, Darius restructured the tax code. Under the prior kings, states subject to tribute had paid either in gold or in some form of produce. Those collections, however, tended to be haphazard, and the sum required often bore no relation to a region's ability to pay. Some sections of the empire that could least afford it overpaid, while other, more prosperous provinces underpaid. To remedy the situation, Darius ordered his officials to accurately estimate the revenue potential of each province and set the tax rate accordingly.

Other revenues accrued to the imperial coffers from mining tariffs, port duties, water- and land-use fees, commercial fees, and sales tax. Babylonia paid its taxes in silver and gold, while India paid in gold dust and the Arabs in frankincense. Huge plantations, or *latifundia*, worked by serfs and slaves in the rich floodplains of Babylonia and Egypt, yielded bumper crops of wheat, barley, flax, millet, sesame, and dates. Persian engineers built irrigation systems to increase productivity, and estate owners experimented with new farming techniques.

More than any other Persian king, except Cyrus, Darius increased the empire's material well-being by taking an interest in the details of administration and economics. As the empire prospered, he felt the need for a new capital and selected a site in a wide and fertile valley 50 miles southwest of Cyrus's old capital and named it Persepolis.

The city took nearly fifty years to complete, and at the entrance, a triumphal arch known as the Gate of All Nations was flanked by two massive stone bulls and opened onto a broad plaza. The centerpiece of the city was the Apadana, an elaborate audience hall of a hundred columns, each of which soared nearly 65 feet and carried the weight of an elaborately vaulted, gold-leafed roof of timbers. Darius built a magnificent palace for himself in the city that became the symbol, though not always the center, of Persian power for the next two centuries.

When Darius died, his son Xerxes I (reigned 485–465 BC) succeeded him. Although his name in Persian means "the warrior," the Greeks referred to him derisively as "the weak-minded and effeminate." Yet Xerxes proved sufficiently strong-minded and manly to invade Greece in 480 BC at the head of the largest army the ancient world had ever seen. Supported by their navy, the Persians crossed the Hellespont, the narrow body of water that separates Asia from Greece, by means of history's first pontoon bridge. As the Persian army moved south, a small contingent of three hundred Spartans managed to keep them at bay in a narrow defile known as Thermopylae, or the "hot gates," until they were betrayed by a fellow Greek.

The Spartan sacrifice bought the rulers of the Greek city-states the time they needed to move a large army into position at Corinth, though not before the Persians looted Athens, sending vast amounts of its treasure and art back to Persia as the spoils of war. Athenian naval forces caught the Persian fleet in the narrow strait of Salamis and in the ensuing battle destroyed most of their ships. On land, a coalition from the Greek city-states defeated the Persian army, and Xerxes was forced to return to Asia. No Persian king would ever again set foot on Greek soil.

Xerxes was succeeded by his son Artaxerxes I (reigned 464–425 BC), known as "the great warrior." The new king ended hostilities with the Greeks and turned his attention to the Egyptians who had taken advantage of the Persian conflicts with the Greeks to stray. Egypt was too wealthy and strategically important to be allowed out of the fold, so Artaxerxes in a particularly repressive campaign brought the country once more within the empire.

When Artaxerxes died in 425 BC, his son, Xerxes II, succeeded him but was assassinated while sleeping off the effects of a drinking bout. Xerxes' half brother, Darius II (reigned 424–405 BC), came to the throne. Darius was known as *nothus* (the bastard) because he was the product of a dalliance between his father and a Babylonian concubine. But in spite of his lack of a full royal pedigree and his insulting nickname, he managed to outmaneuver seventeen of his siblings to take power and, with the assistance of a competent and strong-willed wife, developed into an able administrator who ruled for nearly twenty years. Using generous amounts of gold, he became a power broker among the Greeks and influenced the outcome of a brutal series of internecine conflicts between them known as the Peloponnesian Wars (431–404 BC).

Darius's successor was his eldest son, Artaxerxes II (reigned 405–359 BC), who ruled the longest of any Persian king, forty-six years, and administered the empire largely from Babylon. When Artaxerxes died, his son, Artaxerxes III (reigned 359–338 BC), ruled until he was poisoned by his eunuch. His successor, Artaxerxes IV (reigned 338–336 BC), was poisoned by the same eunuch, who finally was executed by the last Persian king, Darius III (reigned 336–330 BC).

Darius III was perhaps the most tragic of all the Persian kings. A competent and kindly man, he ruled until Alexander the Great overran Persia in 330 BC, forcing him to flee into the great desert of Iran, where he was killed by his satraps. The death of Darius III brought to an end what had been at the time the largest and richest empire in the world. Never again could the Persians boast that their empire "extended so far north that men could not live there because of the cold and so far south that they could not live there because of the heat."

2

CYRUS THE GREAT

Lessons in Tolerance and Inclusion

"He turned and granted mercy in all lands everywhere."
—THE CYRUS CYLINDER

Cyrus the Great is not a name recognized by many modern readers. At best, he may be recalled as the shadowy figure from the Old Testament who freed the Israelites from bondage in Babylon and allowed them to return to their promised land. Yet there is considerably more to Cyrus and his empire. He is one of history's most gifted leaders, and his accomplishments are worth a deeper look—especially by anyone interested in learning what it takes to build and manage a great enterprise. In fact, a picture of Cyrus should be on the desk of every expansion-minded CEO—or at least hanging on the board-room wall.

What sets Cyrus apart from most empire builders is the political infrastructure he created to unite his acquisitions and the tolerant policies he devised to administer them. His policies were forward-looking and struck the right balance between centralized and local control. His achievements were extraordinary, given the era he lived in and the fact that he had none of our modern advantages in technology and communication. Cyrus had no Internet, computers, satellites, corporate jets, or worldwide media to help him develop the image so necessary for success today. The Persian king did most of his work sitting either on the back of a horse or within a tent. But using his innate leadership abilities, and fueled by a driving ambition to succeed, he built an empire that eventually touched the lives of millions and controlled a piece of nearly everything that had value in the ancient world.

What made Cyrus unique among warrior-kings of his time was his "Charter of Human Rights." Inscribed in cuneiform on a clay tablet now known as the Cyrus Cylinder and housed in the British Museum (a replica is displayed at the entrance to the United Nations), the charter is one of the earliest documents to recognize basic rights and the value of cultural diversity. It became an operations manual for holding together a vast empire of diverse cultures by pledging not to force people into a single mold of conformity.

From a modest beginning as a tribal leader in the Zagros Mountains of Iran, Cyrus systematically brought vast areas of the Middle East and central Asia under his control, establishing what became the Persian Empire, the largest, richest, and perhaps most efficiently run empire in the ancient world. At its height in the fifth century BC, the empire stretched east from Turkey's Mediterranean coast to the banks of the Indus River in Pakistan and south from the coast of the Black Sea in southern Russia to the banks of the Nile in Egypt. As the Greek historian Herodotus wrote, "It became the meeting ground of the great cultures of the ancient world."

At the beginning of the sixth century BC, when Cyrus was born, four kingdoms dominated most of the eastern part of the ancient world: the Medes, Chaldaeans, Lydians, and Egyptians. The Medes occupied the northern half of the Zagros Mountains and had built their capital at Ecbatana (the modern Iranian city of Hamadan). The Chaldaeans occupied central Mesopotamia (Iraq); their capital was at Babylon (a few miles south of modern-day Baghdad). The Lydians controlled Asia Minor (Turkey); their capital was at Sardis, near the Aegean coast. On the periphery of these four kingdoms were the Greeks, who had established colonies along the coast of Asia Minor but were not yet major players in the game of empire building. From what historians have been able to piece together, these kingdoms seem to have coexisted in relative peace by developing spheres of influence that balanced their shifting economic and political interests.

The king of the Medes was Astyages, who, in what must have been a political arrangement to increase his power, married his daughter to Cambyses, the leader of a large nomadic tribe from the southern half of the Zagros Mountains known as the Pasargadae. Cambyses came from an elite family within the tribe known as the Achaemenidae, and the marriage produced a child, Cyrus. In later years, a romantic tale about Cyrus's birth and childhood developed, following a well-known paradigm of stories about heroes from the ancient world, such as Moses in the bulrushes, the infant Hercules strangling serpents, or Romulus and Remus raised by a wolf.

According to this legend, just before Cyrus was born, Astyages had a dream in which a monstrous vine grew from his daughter's womb and strangled Asia. Alarmed, the king consulted his high priests, the Magi, and they warned him that the dream signified that the unborn child would one day rule all of Media. Concerned that his grandson might seize his throne, Astyages ordered Cyrus taken into the mountains shortly after his birth and killed.

The odious task was assigned to one of the king's advisers, who, moved by compassion, placed Cyrus in the care of a shepherd whose own newborn had recently died. Cyrus was raised in the isolation of the mountains and led a simple life, where he learned to ride a horse, draw a bow with skill, and tell the truth.

When Cyrus had nearly reached manhood, he struck the son of a local nobleman during an argument and was summoned to the court of the king. As soon as Astyages saw the young man, his suspicions were aroused. Cyrus's royal bearing and his intelligent and even arrogant responses to questions caused the king concern. The shepherd who had been posing as Cyrus's father and had accompanied him to court was tortured until he revealed the boy's true identity.

Again, Astyages turned to the Magi for advice, and they assured him that Cyrus was no threat. The young man's life was spared, and he was sent to live with his parents in the south of Iran, where he eventually succeeded his father as ruler of the Pasargadae.

HOW CYRUS BUILT HIS EMPIRE:
TRANSFORMING VISION INTO ACTION

Not content to remain the ruler of a nomadic tribe in the southern mountains of Iran, Cyrus had visions of exciting possibilities for his people. Profitable trade routes linking China, India, and the west ran through Iran, and Cyrus believed an empire strategically located there could become the dominant power in the eastern half of the ancient world.

To sell his vision, Cyrus assembled his people and ordered them to spend a day digging holes. They complained the entire time that the work was tiring and served no purpose. The next day, Cyrus ordered them to spend their time eating, drinking, and dancing. When he asked which they preferred, their response was predictable. Cyrus told his people they could enjoy leisure and wealth by building an empire, or they could remain in the mountains and spend the rest of their lives digging holes. He observed that complacency sometimes makes people so comfortable with traditional ways of doing things that they are blind to the advantages that can come with change.

●   ●   ●

Cyrus is one of the earliest leaders we know of to employ homespun wisdom to make a point. In our own time, no corporate leader parallels Cyrus in this regard better than Warren Buffett, probably the richest man in the world. Known as "the Sage of Omaha," Buffett would appreciate Cyrus's notion that all a man needs to know to succeed is how to ride a horse well, shoot a bow accurately, and tell the truth.

In a 2008 *New York Times* op-ed piece on what investors should do, given the current debacle in the financial markets, Buffett suggested being "fearful when others are greedy and greedy when others are fearful." One of the most successful investors ever, Buffett dispenses similar observations on the economy and financial pearls of wisdom to a rapt audience each year at the annual meeting of his holding company, Berkshire Hathaway. Unlike most annual meetings, this one is standing-room-only because of Buffett's casual yet successful approach to achieving financial success.

Forbes magazine first wrote about Buffett in 1969, when he was an unknown money manager. What sparked interest back then? Buffett had cleared out of the stock market, and *Forbes* was curious to find out why. Buffett was going against the conventional wisdom and the crowd. But he sensed stocks were ready to plunge, and he was right. Five years later, *Forbes* came back to Buffett as Wall Street was experiencing its worst decline since the Great Depression, and pessimism reigned supreme. What was he doing now, he was asked. Buffett was eagerly buying. Never had he seen such bargains—"I feel like a sex-starved maniac in a harem"—and time proved him right as equity markets increased in value twentyfold before their current plummet. In 2008, when stocks crashed again, Buffett, true to his philosophy, was once more out there in the market hunting for bargains and making spectacular investments, in Goldman Sachs, General Electric, and the legendary motorcycle manufacturer Harley Davidson.

HOW LEADERS BUILD LASTING EMPIRES

The first step for Cyrus was to expand his area of control in southern Iran by unifying the nomads who lived in the deserts east of the mountains. Once that was accomplished, he began to cultivate allies among the larger kingdoms in nearby Mesopotamia. The more successful Cyrus became at building his strategic alliances, the more paranoid his grandfather in the north grew. Finally, in 550 BC, Astyages sent an army to show his grandson who was boss. But the old king had become increasingly dictatorial, and many of his advisers and military commanders were fed up with him. Once the army left Media, its commander deserted to Cyrus, taking his entire general staff with him.

Responding to the defection, Astyages put a second army in the field and personally took command. But no sooner had he passed outside the boundaries of Media than his officers placed him in chains and turned him over to Cyrus. The old king had become complacent and lost touch with his subjects. Instead of ruling in the interests of his people, Astyages ruled in his own interests, and it cost him his throne. Cyrus, showing the tolerance that made him famous, spared his grandfather and allowed him to live out the remainder of his years in comfortable, but isolated, retirement. The people of Media were invited to join Cyrus as equals in a partnership for building a future.

Conquest followed by inclusion became the template for Cyrus's successful pattern of empire building. Cyrus integrated the Medes into the empire he was building with full rights of citizenship and participation. He displayed remarkable tolerance for their customs and religions, and in return he benefited from their support, experience, and wealth. Over time, the words *Persian* and *Mede* came to be used synonymously throughout the ancient world to refer to the same people.

●　　　●　　　●

John Chambers, CEO of Cisco Systems, the leading supplier of networking management and communications technology for the Internet, is one corporate leader who would get Cyrus's seal of approval when it comes to following a policy of inclusion. Much of Cisco's growth has come through acquisitions, and Chambers has never been a victim of the "it must be invented here" mentality. If there's a company with a product that fits in with Cisco's strategy, Chambers doesn't hesitate to go after it, even as Cisco pours considerable sums into its own research and development efforts. Cisco has a constant need for new technologies and refinements of its existing technologies for new markets. If it can't develop them, it goes out and acquires them— almost like putting the pieces of a puzzle together. Like Cyrus, Chambers is an integrator.

When the high-tech market crashed in 2000, rapidly growing Cisco suddenly "hit the wall." Chambers reacted aggressively by firing 15 percent of his workforce and cutting his own salary to $1 a year. At the same time, he kept on building his empire through acquisitions and by remaining innovative and aggressive. This strategy accounts for Cisco's success today in dominating the pathways through which the world's data travels. Cisco, however, is something of a rarity in the corporate world. Too often, companies achieve successes, like those of Cyrus, but then stagnate or are upended by competing innovators.

HOLDING YOUR EMPIRE TOGETHER

As Cyrus built his empire, he saw that the loose system of tribal organization no longer sufficed. He developed a new, more efficient system of administration based on the organization of conquered territories into *satrapies,* or provinces. Media became the first of these administrative units, which would grow to twenty-three, and remain the organizational foundation of the empire for two centuries.

Each satrapy had a governor, or *satrap*—a "protector of the kingdom." The king provided the satrap with a staff to carry out civil administration and collect taxes, and with a military garrison to ensure compliance with the satrap's decrees. From all outward appearances, each satrap was autonomous and local systems of government and law remained in place. Cyrus, however, pulled the important strings from the center. Failure or disloyalty by satraps could be severely punished, just as success and loyalty were generously rewarded. The sons of each satrap were kept at Cyrus's court, ostensibly to be educated for future leadership roles, but really as hostages to ensure the loyalty of their fathers.

As a further check on his satraps, Cyrus appointed individuals to serve as the chief financial officers and generals to command the garrisons. Both had the authority to circumvent their immediate boss— the satrap—and report any irregularities in the administration of the provinces directly to the king. Two centuries later, Alexander the Great would adopt this same strategy when he built his new empire on the ruins of Persia.

The Persian kings who succeeded Cyrus later established a second layer of control over their provincial governors. Agents who became known as the "king's eyes and ears" made a careful annual inspection of each satrapy, including an audit of records, to be sure nothing that was due the king was failing to reach him.

●   ●   ●

The Gannett Company, the largest newspaper publisher in the United States, is an empire based on principles that Cyrus would have appreciated and related to. It publishes eighty-five dailies and nine hundred nondaily papers in the United States plus seventeen dailies in the UK.

In addition, Gannett counts twenty-three television stations among its assets.

Frank Gannett bought his first paper in 1906, the *Elmira Gazette*, and by 1957 when he died the number had grown to twenty-two. The patient but persistent acquisition of family-owned newspapers throughout the United States allowed Gannett and his successors to build a large and successful empire. The two-fisted acquisitions approach of an Alexander or a Julius Caesar wouldn't have worked in an industry where owners of local newspapers hated to give up their "babies." The tortoise-like approach of Gannett and some of his CEOs, such as the late Paul Miller, paid off.

Unlike William Randolph Hearst, Henry Luce, and other print tycoons, Gannett never issued any directives about what editors were supposed to write. Editorial freedom was something that the owners of the papers valued, and it facilitated many of his acquisitions. But although Gannett respected editorial freedom, he expected expenses at each newspaper to be tightly controlled and revenues to grow. His expectations were not all that different from Cyrus, who gave his satraps autonomy as long as they filled his treasury with the expected tribute each year. The Gannett Company did not use its "tribute" only for acquisitions or dividends; in 1982, then-CEO Al Neuharth invested considerable capital to expand the empire by launching *USA Today*, a national daily that became a staple for frenetic business travelers seeking access to a quick source for news. Today, Gannett, like most newspaper publishers, is facing severe pressures as the Internet threatens to do to its empire what Alexander the Great did to Persia.

WHEN EXPANDING, BE METHODICAL

With the conquest of Media completed and the foundation of his empire in place, Cyrus moved west against the smaller kingdoms of Armenia, Assyria, and Syria. This alarmed Croesus, the powerful king of Lydia, a wealthy kingdom that encompassed most of present-day western Turkey. According to the ancient sources, Croesus had so much gold in his treasury that his name personified luxury.

Concerned about the Persian threat, Croesus traveled to Delphi in Greece to consult an oracle revered throughout the ancient world. Prophecies were expensive, and Croesus paid a large quantity of gold, including most of his wife's jewelry, for information regarding the future of his kingdom. The oracle told him that war with Cyrus was coming and would result in "the destruction of a great empire." The overconfident Croesus heard only what he wanted to hear and returned to Lydia certain he would prevail against Cyrus.

Cyrus crossed the Tigris River north of Babylon and continued moving west through the deserts of northern Syria toward Asia Minor. His army moved into Cilicia, on the southeastern Mediterranean coast, and then through an opening in the Taurus Mountains known as the "Cilician Gates" onto the great plains of central Turkey, known as Cappadocia.

In the autumn of 546 BC, the armies of Cyrus and Croesus clashed, but Croesus broke off the engagement and returned home to Sardis. He sent ambassadors to the Egyptians, the Babylonians, and the Spartans in Greece with requests to join him in a major offensive against Cyrus the following spring.

Warfare in the ancient world tended to be seasonal. Armies usually mobilized in the spring, fought all summer, and then disbanded in autumn so soldiers could return home to their families, tend their flocks, and plant their winter crops. Cyrus, however, was not a slave to tradition. Taking the initiative, he marched his army across the plains and appeared unexpectedly in the countryside outside Sardis well before spring.

Croesus sent a large force of cavalry to stop Cyrus before he got too close to the city. The Lydians were renowned for their skill as horsemen and their courage in battle. Faced with the prospect of heavy casualties among his infantry and even the possibility that his army, tired by the long winter march, might break, Cyrus devised a way to neutralize the Lydian cavalry.

The Persian army had thousands of camels to carry its baggage, so Cyrus ordered the animals outfitted to carry riders instead. When the camels galloped into battle, their appearance and smell panicked the

Lydian horses. Many of Croesus's men were thrown from their mounts, and the force of their attack was effectively broken. Finding himself surrounded by the Persian army, Croesus understood the full meaning of what the oracle at Delphi had told him. Unfortunately, it was his own "great empire" that would be destroyed.

Sardis fell to Cyrus in fourteen days. As the last of its walls was breached, Croesus retreated to the highest ramparts of the citadel, where his attendants had prepared his funeral pyre. The Lydian king reclined on a couch atop the pyre and quietly waited as the flames worked their way up toward him. Then, suddenly, the heavens unleashed a torrential downpour that extinguished the fire and saved him. Cyrus was so impressed by what he interpreted as an act of the gods, as well as by the personal bravery and demeanor of the defeated king, that he spared Croesus and welcomed him into the royal entourage as an adviser. The kingdom of Lydia became the Persian satrapy of Sardis, and Cyrus showed another facet of sound leadership: make your enemy your ally and put him on your payroll.

The conquest of Lydia brought the Persians into contact with the Greeks, whose colonies lined the western edge of Cyrus's empire. But neither Persians nor Greeks could have anticipated the role each would play in the destiny and politics of the other. In the next century, Darius I and Xerxes I would invade mainland Greece, and a century after that, the Greeks, led by Alexander of Macedonia, would destroy Persia.

Cyrus and the Greeks were not impressed with each other. Cyrus characterized the Greeks as a "depraved and dishonest" people who spent most of their time in their markets trying to cheat each other. Fearing that commercial interactions with the Greeks would corrupt his own people, he banned the Greek open-air markets from his empire. The Greeks on the other hand considered the Persians effeminate barbarians living under a form of Oriental despotism abhorrent to anyone who valued political freedom and free enterprise.

The Greeks, who had rebuffed Cyrus when he approached them with an offer to become his allies against Croesus, now demanded the same favored status and political independence they had enjoyed under the Lydians. When Cyrus refused, the Greeks who lived along the coast of Asia Minor appealed to Sparta for protection. Sparta, the most powerful military power on the Greek mainland, sent a delegation to Sardis to warn Cyrus to keep away from the Greeks of Asia Minor. He quizzically inquired, "Who are these Spartans?" and then sent his armies to subdue the coastal cities, most of which surrendered or quickly reached an accommodation with him. Over time, Cyrus found that the Greeks, especially the Spartans and Athenians, were excellent, disciplined fighters but, like members of a dysfunctional family, could not set aside their differences long enough to cooperate; nor could their leaders resist bribes to betray each other. The Greeks of Asia Minor were placed under the jurisdiction of the Persian satrap at Sardis, but they continued to pose a growing problem on the borders of Cyrus's empire.

Cyrus returned to Iran, postponing a confrontation with the Babylonians, and turned his attention to the conquest of the nomadic tribes along the shores of the Caspian Sea. Then he moved farther east into what is today Afghanistan and crossed the Hindu Kush Mountains into the vast steppes of central Asia (Turkistan, Uzbekistan, and Tajikistan). On the steppes Cyrus found small cultivable oases inhabited by nomadic tribes and put his engineers to work improving the productivity of the area through a massive irrigation system. When the task was completed, he moved north and east, capturing the city of Maracanda (modern Samarqand), an important stop along the profitable Silk Route from China to the West.

Near what is today the Uzbek capital of Tashkent, Cyrus established the northernmost limit of his empire by building a protective line of forts. He was reluctant to advance farther into the steppes, which were the domain of a fierce nomadic tribe known as the Massagetae, a people who, according to the ancient sources, shared their wives in common and devoured their old. Once his northern frontier was established, Cyrus moved through the Khyber Pass into what is today Pakistan, where he set the eastern limit of his empire along the banks of the Indus River.

Now Cyrus controlled all the trade routes leading from China and India to the West, but he found success could be a double-edged sword. The more he controlled, the more he was compelled to conquer. Unless the empire continued to expand, it risked lapsing into a state of stagnation followed by decline. In less than ten years, Cyrus had doubled his holdings; his reach extended halfway across Asia, but he had conquered vast areas of wasteland that were expensive to hold.

An interesting modern parallel to the methodical Cyrus is Rupert Murdoch. As a very young man, Australian-born Murdoch inherited a daily newspaper when his father—a legendary editor—suddenly died. After battling executives who thought they could push "the kid" aside, much as Astyages thought he could push young Cyrus aside, Murdoch built a media empire first in Australia and then in Britain. He entered U.S. markets with a series of splashy acquisitions in the mid-1970s, which included the *New York Post* and *New York* magazine. With a nod to King Kong, a cover of *Time* caricatured Murdoch climbing the Empire State Building.

The established media regarded Murdoch as an uncouth parvenu, but despite a few temporary setbacks, he stitched together a media colossus as impressive in size and influence as the Persian Empire. Unlike many of his competitors, Murdoch was early in recognizing the threat—and the opportunity—of the Internet. For example, he acquired the social networking site MySpace. Today, other media empires are breaking up or shrinking, but Murdoch's News Corporation continues to expand. In 2007, he acquired Dow Jones and a crown jewel, the *Wall Street Journal*, which he is working to reshape as a competitor to the *New York Times*.

BABYLON AND BUSINESS

Babylon, the most important commercial and cultural center of the eastern part of the ancient world, lay right in the middle of the empire Cyrus was building. It was a magnificent city located on a narrow strip

of land between the Euphrates and Tigris rivers, and its most famous
king, Nebuchadnezzar (reigned 604–562 BC), had enclosed it within
walls so thick that a row of houses and a paved street wide enough for
chariots to pass were constructed atop them. Nebuchadnezzar's palace
is reputed to have been the most magnificent structure in the city, and
its fabled hanging gardens became one of the seven wonders of the
ancient world. The royal engineers built terrace upon terrace contain-
ing trees, vines, and flowers of every type, which flowed from one level
to the next. Even the Greeks, who set the standard for architecture in
the ancient world, were amazed at the beauty, size, and splendor of
Babylon.

Today, a few miles south of Baghdad, there is little left of the magnificent city referred to in the Old Testament as "the mother of all
whores and earth's abominations." What centuries of war and the rav-
ages of time did not destroy, the late Iraqi dictator Saddam Hussein
did. He ordered the remnants of the great walls to be dismantled and
the bricks used to build a palace to celebrate what he thought would
be his own immortality. A small museum that housed the few artifacts
that survived the centuries was looted during the Gulf War, and many
of its most treasured pieces disappeared into the lucrative black market for artifacts that has developed in the West.

Babylon was important to Cyrus because it controlled the trade
routes into Arabia as well as those through Syria and Palestine to the
Mediterranean coast. He realized that if he could take the city, he would
control a sizable percentage of the ancient world's wealth. Babylon was
a formidable obstacle, but Cyrus had an experienced army, ample resources, and confidence to take on what he knew would be his biggest
challenge. Surprisingly, though, Babylon turned out to be the easiest
of all his acquisitions.

The Babylonian economy was based on what sociologists call a *temple culture*, which means that the priests had developed an extensive
system of lending and borrowing based on the wealth of their treasur-
ies and augmented by the private holdings of merchants. After the
death of Nebuchadnezzar, Babylon began a slow but steady decline.
The new king, Nabonidus, was not interested in the commercial life

of the city and spent most of his time immersed in the mysteries of religious cults from the East, and alienating the conservative priesthood of the traditional god Marduk.

Cyrus's first move was to launch a propaganda campaign against Nabonidus centered on the discontent of his people. There was so much corruption and graft in Babylon that civil authority had begun to disintegrate, and conditions became nearly chaotic. Disaffected Babylonians began to pave the way for Cyrus. The profligate lifestyle of the king's son, the infamous Belshazzar mentioned in the Old Testament, added fuel to the fires of discontent. One night during debaucheries at his palace, the young prince and his followers were terrified when a severed hand appeared and wrote an ominous warning on the wall: "You are found wanting and your kingdom is finished." Nabonidus and his son were finished as Cyrus and his forces were approaching the city, and its once formidable wall was ready to collapse.

SUCCESSFUL LEADERSHIP MEANS ADAPTING, NOT STAYING BEHIND THE WALL

The wall that enclosed Babylon provides an excellent metaphor about management—or, more accurately, mismanagement. Examples abound of corporations developing a "Babylonian wall" mentality, believing they are immune to attack or takeover. The wall that surrounded Babylon led the king to believe his city was impregnable, and frequently, a successful product, service, or corporate strategy results in similar complacency or overconfidence in a company: Threats to the corporation from outside are ignored or fundamentally misjudged. New and perhaps better ways of doing things are ignored because the corporate mind-set is to stay securely behind the wall. Protected by its wall and properly run, Babylon would have been an impregnable barrier against Cyrus or anyone else. But catastrophic mistakes by Babylon's management—the king and his family—undermined the city more quickly than any besieging army ever could.

Even companies that think they are wide awake and on top of

things in their various fields can misjudge conditions and competitors. Goodyear's top managers stayed behind their corporate wall, thinking they were secure, and their overconfidence cost them. After World War II, Goodyear was the world's largest and most profitable tire maker, easily outdistancing its nearest competitors. Then Michelin assaulted its walls with a radical advance in tire technology—the radial tire, which was far more durable than the traditional belted tire produced by Goodyear.

From 1964 to 1973, the CEO of Goodyear was a gruff-talking character named Russ DeYoung, who dismissed radial tires as a passing fad and growled that Michelin survived only because French automakers gave it business out of a sense of national pride. But suddenly the American consumer market—truckers, farmers, motorists—took to the new product. Radials were better tires than what Goodyear had to offer, but DeYoung and his management team woke up to that reality only when their wall was breached.

Even entrepreneurs and CEOs in the rapidly changing, trendy, and sexy field of high technology frequently get stuck in their ways. They hide behind their respective Babylonian walls, then wind up blindsided by earthshaking innovations going on outside their view. IBM provides a perfect example. Kenneth Olsen, an engineer who founded a company called Digital Equipment in 1957, foresaw that small computing machines—which came to be called minicomputers—could break the dominance of mainframe computers.

Since the early 1950s, IBM had ruled the mainframe world. Numerous competitors, including RCA and Xerox, had fallen by the wayside, and those that remained had a minuscule share of the market, usually in specialized areas—for example, Burroughs in commercial banking and Cray in so-called supercomputers. In those days, corporate buyers knew they were safe going with IBM but could easily end up in trouble if they dealt with one of Big Blue's smaller competitors.

So Kenneth Olsen didn't take on IBM directly by producing mainframes. Instead he—and others—hit its flanks with smaller, more versatile machines. These minicomputers expanded the market for computer technology. Since they were smaller than mainframes and could easily and cheaply meet specific needs, more and more customers in the corporate and government worlds were willing to take the plunge and buy them. The rule of thumb on "minis": 75 percent of the power of a mainframe at 25 percent of the price. By the 1970s, Olsen's company was a major player in corporate America as enthusiastic investors scooped up its offerings on Wall Street, usually sizable issues of bonds convertible into common stock.

The rise of Digital Equipment along with Wang and Data General began to erode IBM's once solid footing in the computer field. IBM stumbled and fell to one knee because it didn't come to grips with the growing importance of minicomputers, one of several factors that led to the near-collapse of Big Blue in the early 1990s.

Ken Olsen was hailed as a genius, and Digital's rise appeared unstoppable. Olsen thought he had mastered the game. Then his world crumbled. Yes, Olsen believed, you have to keep improving what you do by fine-tuning the basics, and his minicomputers were the nemesis of IBM. But what he didn't see coming was the personal computer. Instead of responding to a growing threat by changing his strategy and operations, he stuck to tinkering with his beloved minis.

In the late 1970s and early 1980s, Apple Computer, founded by Steve Jobs and Steve Wozniak, burst on the scene. The new Apple personal computers were to mainframes and minicomputers what fractional horsepower engines had been to the mammoth turbines of the industrial era. New companies, such as Osborne, Commodore, and Atari, jumped into the business, as did older, more established ones such as Texas Instruments.

Skeptics, including Olsen, kept asking, What exactly do you use these PC things for? PCs were certainly more efficient than typewriters, and they could be handy for spreadsheets. They might even help you keep track of music on your vinyl phonograph records (this was before DVDs and iTunes) or your favorite recipes. But were they serious office equipment? Critics declared there was no chance they would succeed, except perhaps in the publishing industry.

In the mid-1980s, the PC bubble burst, Atari and Commodore crashed, and Texas Instruments exited the business. Olsen declared that PCs were but a passing fad, mere playthings for hobbyists. This observation turned out to be as prophetic and farsighted as the remark of a prominent Englishman in the 1880s that the new telephone could never replace messenger boys delivering telegrams. In fact, the computing power of PCs grew exponentially once people got the hang of them and figured out how to network them so they no longer had to function in isolation.

PC sales soared as networking made them easier to use than either minicomputers or mainframes. Workstations—souped-up versions of the PC that were networked for businesses—proliferated in corporate America as minicomputers were consigned to the high-tech junkyards. As a result, Digital's decline in the markets was breathtaking. The value of its stock plunged. In 1998 Digital was sold to rising PC maker Compaq Computer, at less than half of its 1988 price—and that buyout price, it quickly became apparent, was overly generous. Demand for its products continued to shrink. It was an ignominious end for a company that once looked as though it would be a permanent part of the corporate landscape. But Digital wasn't alone in its fall, as competitors Wang and Data General also disappeared from the scene.

IT'S NOT BRAWN BUT BRAINS THAT COUNT

The countryside to the east of Babylon was under the control of one of Nebuchadnezzar's best generals and most competent administrators. Frustrated with the corrupt administration of the king and his son, he went over to Cyrus. But not all the administrators and their cities in Mesopotamia willingly joined Cyrus, and those who resisted found he could be as unmerciful as any conqueror. When the inhabitants of one city on the Tigris River refused to surrender after repeated requests, Cyrus ordered them burned to death as an example to others who might resist him.

For Cyrus this type of response was the exception, not the rule. It was customary in the ancient world for a conqueror to level cities he conquered and enslave the residents. What made Cyrus unique is that, in general, he replaced destruction with construction and slavery with freedom. Overall he showed respect for the cultures of those he conquered.

To take Babylon, Cyrus used engineering and psychology, not force. The Euphrates River flowed through the city, so Cyrus had his engineers divert the river several miles upstream. This lowered the level of the water flowing beneath the walls and allowed elements of Cyrus's army to slip under at night. When Cyrus took Babylon, there was no wide-scale looting or burning. Supporters of the Babylonian king were beheaded to mark the end of one era and the beginning of a new one, but in general the transition seems to have been peaceful and orderly. Business continued as usual, and the change of regime actually boosted commercial activity as confidence soared with the prospect of new opportunities.

* * *

Procter & Gamble uses its brains when making acquisitions by keeping the heads of key people in acquired companies on their shoulders and working for P&G. Throughout its history, P&G has expanded by means of internal development of new consumer products. But it has never hesitated to buy companies and move into bigger, potentially more lucrative markets. Back in 1965 it acquired Folgers Coffee Company and made its coffee product one of the top brands in the United States. P&G sold Folgers to the J.M. Smucker Company in 2008 for an impressive $3 billion. In 2005, P&G acquired Gillette for $57 billion, and CEO A. G. Lafley pulled off one of the most difficult tasks in the corporate world—a major merger in which one company is absorbed into another with minimal disruptions.

The people at Gillette cooperated in making a smooth transition because they knew that P&G was not going to resort to wholesale firings and slashes in R&D spending to boost short-term results. Lafley, like Cyrus, had a reputation for decisiveness and a light touch when it came to control. Profitably integrating acquired companies like Gillette, not looting them, was Lafley's approach. As a result, P&G is today one of very few companies that is both large and nimble.

LEADING FIRMLY BUT LIGHTLY

Once Babylon was secured, Cyrus made a triumphal entry into the city through the famous Ishtar Gate. Its massive bronze doors were opened to receive him, and palm branches were spread before his feet to soften his steps. In his first speech to the people, Cyrus proclaimed peace, prosperity, and stability. He blamed the chaotic conditions on the prior rulers who had turned their backs on the gods of their ancestors and lost touch with the commercial pulse of the city. Then, in a symbolic but highly effective gesture, he reopened the temples of the traditional god Marduk and worshipped at the main temple. This astute political move ensured the support of the conservative priests, who proclaimed Cyrus the rightful ruler of Babylon and bestowed on him their blessings.

With Babylon as part of his empire, Cyrus could boast he was "king of the world," and he pledged that all his subjects would be free to practice whatever religion they chose. This promise was particularly significant for the Jews who had been enslaved when Nebuchadnezzar's armies had taken Jerusalem, the principal city of Judaea, in 586 BC. Jewish prophets hailed Cyrus as the anointed one of the Lord, the messiah who would free them, and he made their dream come true in 537 BC when he decreed that all the races and tribes brought to Babylon as slaves were free to return to their homes.

Once Cyrus had taken Babylon, he rested his hand lightly but firmly on the city. He left the prosaic details of administration to his satrap, as he did in most of the conquered territories. As a result, Babylon prospered and became the most important city in the empire, and the satrapy of Babylonia—encompassing southern Iraq, Arabia, Syria, Phoenicia, and Judaea—became the most prosperous of the provinces.

Having conquered his last obstacle, Cyrus returned to southwestern Iran to build a capital for his new empire. He chose a remote valley lying on the great north-south road of the high Iranian plateau, which stretches from the mountains in the north all the way to the Persian Gulf in the south, and named his capital Pasargadae, after his tribe.

Cyrus's architects incorporated design ideas from across his empire and created a city that reflected the king's appreciation for diversity.

For the remaining years of his rule, Cyrus focused on building the infrastructure for his empire. He ordered the construction of highways to link the empire from east to west and north to south. This network of royal roads allowed the quick flow of information from the most remote parts of the empire to its center. Racing camels were used to carry important mail, and strategically placed way stations permitted riders to change mounts and cover great distances in 24-hour intervals—a system that would be utilized two thousand years later in the American west. The U.S. Postal Service would even adopt as its motto a Greek description of the Persian riders—"Nothing stops these couriers . . . not snow, rain, heat, or darkness"—and inscribed it over the main post office entrance in New York City.

In 530 BC, a problem arose on the far northeastern frontiers of Cyrus's empire. The nomadic Massagetae, led by Tomyris, a particularly aggressive warrior-queen, began marauding in the region between the Caspian and Aral seas. Because the tribe was interfering with the flow of commerce along the trade routes, Cyrus decided to subdue it and planned what was to be his last campaign.

The Cyrus who set out against the Massagetae in 530 BC was not the same leader who had built the empire years before. Success had made him arrogant and deceived him into thinking he was invincible. He was overconfident and believed that the good fortune he had enjoyed nearly all his life would continue forever.

When Cyrus reached the borders of the Massagetae, he first attempted a political solution to his problem by sending emissaries to the queen with a proposal for a royal union. The queen had been recently widowed, and Cyrus thought marriage might be a less expensive alternative than war while allowing him to expand his empire at minimal cost. But war, not matrimony, was on the queen's mind. She proposed that if Cyrus wanted to fight she would come to him in Persia, or he could come to her. In either case she promised to give him his "fill of blood."

Cyrus turned to his advisers, who agreed that the better strategy would be to let the Massagetae come into Persian territory. But Croesus disagreed and urged Cyrus to be the aggressor, warning that it would not seem proper to see the ruler of Persia retreat at the command of a barbarian, and a woman at that. Furthermore, Croesus pointed out, if Cyrus lost the battle, the Massagetae would have the advantage of being deeper into Persian territory, but if Cyrus won he would be deeper in their territory and able to follow up his victory.

Croesus urged the king to cross the Oxus River (the present-day Amu Darya, which forms the boundary between Uzbekistan and Afghanistan) and push into the territory of the Massagetae. But remembering his own fate as king of Lydia, Croesus also cautioned Cyrus to be careful, for the lives of all men are regulated by a wheel of fortune and the movement of that wheel never allows a man to be lucky all the time.

Cyrus decided to press forward and ordered his heir, the crown prince Cambyses, to remain safely on the Persian side of the Oxus River. The first night in enemy territory, Cyrus had a dream in which the son of one of his satraps, wearing a purple robe and standing arrogantly astride the world, grew an enormous pair of wings. Summoned to interpret the dream, the Magi warned there was a plot to overthrow him, but they missed the real significance: Cyrus was about to die in battle, and while his son Cambyses would succeed him for a short time, it was young Darius, a distant relative, who would become Persia's next great king.

By the second day, the Persian army was well into enemy territory, and Cyrus detected something in the Massagetae he was sure could be exploited to his advantage: their gluttony. The army made camp, and Cyrus ordered a feast prepared with copious quantities of wine. When the banquet was laid out, Cyrus withdrew his main force under cover of night, leaving behind a contingent of his most unreliable soldiers as guards.

Before long, a detachment of Massagetae, led by the son of the queen, attacked the camp, easily overcoming the defenders. Elated by their victory, the Massagetae feasted with no thought to their security. After allowing the effects of the food and wine to set in, Cyrus attacked just as dawn broke. The son of the queen was captured and, disgraced at having been deceived by such a simple trick, took his own life.

Flushed with success, Cyrus became less cautious as the queen drew him farther into the steppes through a series of light skirmishes, which she allowed him to win. Then at the right moment she unleashed all her forces and massacred the Persians. The Massagetae cut off Cyrus's head, and the queen immersed it in a goat skin filled with human blood—keeping her promise to give Cyrus his "fill of blood."

The death of Cyrus in 530 BC was unexpected. He had ruled Persia successfully for nearly thirty years, but in the end fell victim to his own vain belief that he was protected by the gods and destined to rule forever. The wheel of fortune had turned, and his number came up unlucky. Cambyses ransomed his father's head and body from the Massagetae and took them to Pasargadae for burial. The corpse was exposed on a high rock ledge to be picked clean by vultures, and the bleached bones and skull were then laid in a sarcophagus of gold and placed within the simple tomb Cyrus had ordered constructed years earlier. Inside was a table filled with modest offerings: a sword, a necklace of gold inlaid with precious stones, and robes dyed in the royal purple.

Even today the tomb is striking in its simplicity. Located in the valley southwest of the palace complex, it rests atop a stepped platform that is approximately 49 feet by 56 feet at the base and ascends to a height of nearly 10 feet. Constructed of massive limestone blocks, it is a remarkably simple monument to a great leader. A weathered inscription over the entrance reads, "I am Cyrus who built an empire for the Persians; do not begrudge me my simple resting place." Two hundred years later, when Alexander the Great came to pay his respects, the tomb had fallen into a state of disrepair. Impressed by its simplicity and by Cyrus's accomplishments, Alexander provided money to restore and maintain it.

THE LEGACY OF CYRUS

More important than the territory Cyrus conquered were his policies of tolerance and inclusion. With minor exceptions his policies were followed by his successors for nearly two hundred years after his death. Cyrus recognized individual differences and appreciated what diversity could bring to his empire. He tried to win over his enemies through trust and inclusion—an approach that must have seemed amazing at a time when the usual tools of conquest were destruction, massacre, and enslavement. What made Cyrus successful was not only his ability as a warrior but also his belief that conquered peoples need not be enslaved or exterminated but could be brought into the empire as productive members.

He treated his subjects mercifully and appears to have accepted the institutions or customs of those he conquered. But even though Cyrus tended to bring into partnership those he conquered, he remained the "king of kings." His philosophy of ruling others may be summarized in this way: Subjects who paid their taxes, offered homage, remained loyal subjects of the empire, and in some cases engaged in military service were permitted to follow their own customs and to a considerable extent retain their own forms of government and laws.

●   ●   ●

Another thing we learn from Cyrus that can be applied to the world of business is that gaining acquisitions in a buoyant economy is fairly easy, but integrating them seamlessly into the corporate whole is quite another matter. Today, too often, the value of corporate empires put together in the euphoria of a roaring economy becomes less than the total value of their component parts. When this happens, investment bankers then collect large fees for taking apart what they previously had helped ambitious CEOs put together. A textbook example of the "buy it and then sell it" approach is provided by Harold Geneen, whose career is examined in more detail in a later chapter on Alexander the Great. As CEO of ITT Corporation from 1959 until 1977, Geneen made some 300 acquisitions. But his successor, Rand Araskog, sold off some 250 of them, netting the investment bankers who handled the transactions millions in fees.

When it comes to modern parallels with Cyrus, none is stronger than Jack Welch. Welch became CEO of General Electric in 1981, and like Cyrus, he was growth focused and systematic in building his empire. He insisted that every GE enterprise had to be first or second in its field, and if it was not and growth prospects were limited, the enterprise was sold or closed. Welch would never have allowed GE to acquire, say, a bread company, even if its financials were enticing, because the bread industry lacked growth potential. Cost-cutting measures might bring a temporary boost in profits, but in the long term there was no future in bread.

After a few years, under Welch, GE had bought over 300 businesses and product lines and sold more than 200 others. Acquisitions and divestitures were never made for short-term gains. Welch had a well-thought-out strategy to acquire rapid top-line dynamic growth businesses. High sales growth and productivity made for a healthy bottom line at GE. Managers had the leeway to run their businesses, just as Cyrus allowed his satraps to oversee their provinces. But they had to produce for GE, just as the Persian provinces had to generate income for the empire. The genius behind GE's operations is that the company always moves up the food chain, generating higher profits as it goes.

While Cyrus's prize catch was Babylon, Welch's was the credit industry. He recognized that the money-lending business could generate huge returns if it was carefully and scientifically managed. By the time Welch retired in 2001, over half of GE's earnings were coming from GE Credit Corporation, an entity involved in everything from insurance to the leasing and financing of heavy industrial goods, inventories, and real estate. GE literally feasted on financial services and then aggressively moved into health care equipment, which also has positive long-term prospects.

Jeffrey Immelt, Welch's successor, has continued the strategy of acquisition and divestiture, selling off some of GE's financial assets. Immelt even tried to divest GE of its lightbulb business until the financial crisis made such a sale impossible. With an eye to the future, Immelt is pushing this lithe behemoth into "green" businesses and products. A fundamental test of his leadership will be the continued health of GE's financial businesses, which have been the source of much of its growth.

The credit crisis that reached such tsunami-like proportions in 2008–2009 hit the stocks of all financial companies, even General Electric. To reassure the markets and rating agencies, Immelt raised $12 billion in new equity and then negotiated an investment in preferred stock of $3 billion from the ultimate rating agency—Warren Buffett. GE's management style and disciplined approach recall the genius that Cyrus brought to the creation and management of his own empire, but the times ahead will be tough for GE, and whether Immelt can keep it on track remains to be seen. The odds are good, however, that disciplined GE will recover from the battering it has taken and continue, as it has always done, to prosper.

*   *   *

It was near the end of his life that Cyrus lost his sense of direction as a CEO, just like many leaders today who let their ambitions blind them to what they really need to do and where they need to go. Bill Paley, for example, created CBS, which for many years was the dominant television network. But Paley believed his success in radio and television could extend to other areas and his management skills to other businesses, including pianos, toys, publishing, and sports. In the early 1960s, he purchased the New York Yankees just as the team went into a decline, and only after a syndicate led by George Steinbrenner bought the team in 1973 did the Yankees start winning again. Steinbrenner, by the way, paid $10 million, $3.2 million less than the price CBS had paid a decade earlier. Today the Yankees are worth more than a billion dollars.

Even leaders who think they are doing everything right can fail to achieve success. One grim example is Angelo Mozilo, founder of Countrywide Financial, once the darling of the mortgage industry and now the poster child of the financial meltdown that began in 2007. Mozilo founded Countrywide forty years ago and developed it into the largest mortgage bank in the United States. He was routinely included on the Forbes 400 list of richest Americans and admired as a great leader.

In 2005, Mozilo recognized that the mortgage industry's lending standards were going downhill, and he was appalled to see big loans being made to anyone who could walk through the door and sign his name. But even though he knew that what was going on was bad lending practice, he couldn't resist the pressure to make money in a booming market. So Countrywide became a boiler room for making questionable loans. As volume became paramount, the quality of the mortgages being underwritten rapidly deteriorated. When the chickens came home to roost in August 2007, Countrywide was overwhelmed with write-downs and sold to Bank of America for barely one-tenth of what it had been worth only three years earlier.

Mozilo lost his job but walked away with $56 million in compensation, in addition to the hundreds of millions of dollars he reaped by selling his shares just prior to Countrywide's collapse. But the way things are looking, he may not be able to walk too far, since he probably will be spending much of his fortune battling lawsuits and dodging criminal indictments.

part ▌▌

3

CLASSICAL GREECE

Do Thinkers Make Good Leaders?

As the Persians were ruling the eastern half of the ancient Mediterranean world, a unique development was taking place in the western part: the rise of the Greeks. Even though Cyrus regarded the Greeks as a "dishonest and depraved people" who cheated one another in their markets, they stood apart in the ancient world. At a time when individuals counted for very little, the Greeks recognized the right of each of their citizens to have a voice in how the affairs of state were conducted. They believed that man was a political animal and that his fulfillment came through membership in a society in which his voice could be heard. The foundation of that society was consent, and that consent manifested itself through discussion and debate by citizens in public forums. The Greeks showed the world that government has a higher purpose than just benefiting those who rule. It exists to try to make a just and comfortable place for its citizens in a world that is often unfair, unforgiving, and brutal.

The Greeks were not perfect. They talked about democracy, but they were not always as democratic as historians and popular misconceptions have made them out to be. Their history stretches well over a thousand years, from the earliest Minoan and Mycenaean civilizations (1800–1200 BC) when they were ruled by kings to the brief, but democratic, Classical Age (500–400 BC). The Greeks had their contradictions

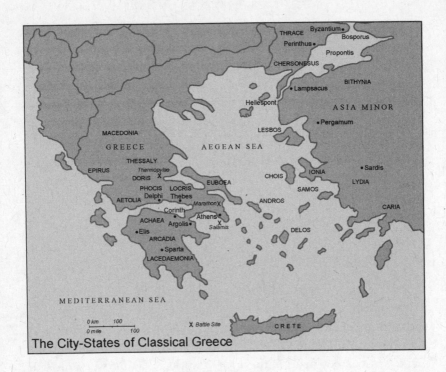

The City-States of Classical Greece

and dark sides. While they guaranteed and protected the liberty of their own, they made slaves of others. Their philosophers taught them that nature had divided humanity into two types: Greeks and barbarians. Considered intellectually and culturally inferior, barbarians were deemed suitable only for enslavement or extermination.

The Greeks could be harsh toward their own as well. A basic distinction was drawn between male citizens and everyone else—women, children, slaves, and foreigners. It was the Greek males who dominated their society and in essence constituted the *polis*, or "state." The rights of women and children were severely restricted, and in some Greek states, like Sparta, weaker infants were exposed to the elements and left to die in order to build a stronger society.

Yet in spite of their shortcomings and contradictions, the Greeks are a people to be admired. Given how harsh life was in the ancient world, the concept of individual freedom has to be considered a remarkable development. The Greeks conceived it, nurtured it, refined it, protected it, and then passed it on to the Western world. That accomplishment stands out as no less than a miracle given that practices such as political discussion and debate, elections by majority vote, and trials by jury all ran counter to the monolithic absolutism that characterized the ancient world and continues to characterize a great deal of our world today.

The earliest Greeks were ruled by kings, but by the end of the sixth century BC, they were rapidly moving away from monarchical systems. The democratic city-states for which Greece would become famous were emerging. The philosopher Aristotle wrote in the fourth century BC that the Greeks were the best governed of all people because they lived in small, independent cities and had no national or central government to destroy their individuality or drain their resources. At the height of their civilization in the fifth century BC, they were organized into a coalition of independent city-states that was unique to their time. Historians estimate that there were hundreds of small cities and towns that were independent of any central authority and managed their own affairs with considerable participation by their citizens. Five among them stand out: Athens, Sparta, Thebes, Argos, and Corinth. They became the defining entities of the period in Greek history that we know as the Classical Age.

The city-state was a political arrangement unique to the Greeks. A metropolitan center like Athens or Sparta and its surrounding countryside constituted a miniature sovereign state ruled by its male citizens. City-states ranged in size from a few hundred people in the most rural areas of Greece to as many as several hundred thousand in Athens. Each city-state maintained its own citizen army, retained its unique customs, and formulated its laws through its own governing bodies.

All city-states did not have the same form of government. Some were oligarchies ruled by landed aristocrats; others were ruled by tyrants. But in all of them, councils or assemblies of male citizens made the laws. As the *demos*, or "common people," in Greece gained more of a political voice over the decades, these broadly representative forms of government began to dominate the political process.

At Athens the last king was replaced with an elected magistrate toward the end of the seventh century BC, and within a few decades the government of that city was directed by nine elected *archons*, or "magistrates." One of the first was Draco, who dealt with a rising crime rate by imposing the death penalty for every offense. The crime rate plummeted, but the Athenians eventually replaced him after deciding they would rather live with crime than under such a severe code. In 594 BC, they elected a particularly astute and far-thinking archon named Solon (638–558 BC) and entrusted him with the development of a new law code. Solon retained the homicide laws of Draco because under them the responsibility for punishing murder had been removed from the hands of the victims' family or clan and given to the state. It was an effective way to curtail the blood feuds, which plagued many of the Greek city-states, and at the same time laid the foundation for the development of criminal law in the West. Perhaps Solon's greatest accomplishment was to organize the Athenians into groups based on their wealth. Political participation became based on holdings and income levels rather than on hereditary titles of nobility, a development that was a significant advancement toward democracy.

Solon was followed by Peisistratus (reigned 560–527 BC), a tyrant who ruled Athens with an iron hand. Today we associate the word *tyrant* with cruel dictators, but for the ancient Greeks it had a different connotation. A tyrant was a representative of the common people who seized power outside the accepted legal channels when the aristocracy monopolized the government and ruled in their own interests instead of the comman good.

Peisistratus drew his support from the poor, and his first move was a redistribution of land, which made him immensely popular with the common people and hated by the aristocrats. Under his rule, Athens flourished. Archons continued to administer the city, and the popular assemblies met to decide the course of government; but Peisistratus was the boss. As long as things went as he thought they should, a form of paternalistic "guided democracy" prevailed in Athens.

The ancient Greeks were never able to unite into one nation, but they saw themselves as one people. Each citizen took pride in belonging to his own city-state but at the same time enjoyed a sense of ethnic identity that set him apart from the rest of the world. The Greeks spoke a common language, believed in a common philosophy, and developed a strong sense of ethnic identity that came to be called *Pan-Hellenism*. They worshipped the same gods at sanctuaries like Delphi and Olympia, and celebrated periodic festivals and games, like the Olympics, to which all the city-states sent contestants. Their societies were similar in their routines of daily living and in their political institutions. Although each city-state generally seemed to go its own way, when the Greek way of life was threatened by invaders, Greeks set aside their differences and came together to defend their freedom.

Mainland Greece is a small and impoverished country. The rocky soil that allowed philosophy to take root and nurtured democracy has never been able to feed the people who live on it. It is a land of mountains with little good soil and too many hungry people. Unable to live off the land, the ancient Greeks turned to the seas that surrounded them to make a living and to distant lands to make their fortunes. They became successful traders and by 750 BC had established prosperous colonies along the coast of Asia Minor (western Turkey) and on the nearby islands. By 600 BC, Greeks were living around the shores of the Black Sea and along the coast of southern Russia. In time there were Greek trading posts along the coasts of Syria, Egypt, and Libya, and as far west as southern Italy, Sicily, and the southern coasts of France and Spain.

These colonies and trading posts developed into prosperous cities that retained strong ethnic ties with mainland Greece. Some of the cities along the coast of Asia Minor, as well as those in southern Italy and Sicily, advanced to such an extent that they rivaled those of mainland Greece and often exceeded them in wealth. The colonies along the fringes of the Persian Empire became a source of contention between the mainland Greeks and the Persians.

As the Greeks watched the Persian Empire expand westward, they feared that in time their cities might be drained of their wealth and come under the domination of the king who ruled in Persepolis. Serious problems developed at the beginning of the fifth century BC when Darius I attempted to bring the Greek colonies in Asia Minor under his control. They revolted and with Athenian encouragement burned the city of Sardis, an important Persian administrative center. Darius responded by burning Miletus, a Greek coastal city. Revolts continued to break out along the coast of Asia Minor followed by periods of Persian repression. By 492 BC, Darius had become so fed up with the colonists and their supporters on the Greek mainland that he sent an army to bring the western borders of Asia Minor under Persian control.

Flushed with his initial success, Darius demanded the surrender of all Greece. He sent envoys to Athens and Sparta, the most powerful city-states, to demand earth and water as symbols of their submission. According to the Greek historian Herodotus, when the Persian ambassadors approached the Athenians with the king's demand for earth, they were thrown into a pit and told to dig for it. And when the ambassadors approached the Spartans with the king's demand for water, they were thrown into a well and told to drink their fill.

In response Darius sent an army across the Aegean Sea. His forces landed in Euboea and destroyed the city of Eretria, killing all the men and taking the women and children as slaves. An Athenian citizen army blocked the Persian advance northeast of Athens on the plains of Marathon. The heavily outnumbered Greeks defeated Darius's army through superior tactics, and when the battle ended, a soldier ran 26 miles to Athens to announce the victory. Darius's defeated army returned to Asia Minor, and ten years would pass before another Persian king invaded Greece.

In 480 BC, Xerxes, Darius's son and successor, led an army from Asia Minor into northern Greece to avenge his father's defeat at Marathon. The Persians crossed the Hellespont, a narrow strait separating Asia Minor and northern Greece, by means of what might have been history's first pontoon bridge. Once the army was safely on land, it moved quickly south into central Greece. The Persian advance came to a stop at Thermopylae, a defile between the mountains and the sea. Three hundred Spartan soldiers controlled the pass and held Xerxes' army at bay until a Greek traitor betrayed them and led a large Persian contingent over the mountains to attack them from the rear.

Facing overwhelming numbers and having no avenue for escape, Leonidas, the Spartan leader, prepared his men for the impending massacre. After reminding them of their duty to the laws of Sparta and their allegiance to Greece, he advised them to eat a hearty breakfast, for that night they would all be dining in hell. The Spartans were massacred, but the war was far from over.

While the Persian army marched south toward Athens, the king's fleet entered the narrows between the Greek mainland and the island of Salamis. The Athenian navy was lying in wait. When the battle was over, the sea was "strewn with wrecks and slaughtered Persians." The Greek victory at Salamis was followed in 479 BC by spectacular land victories at Plataea and Mycale. The Greek city-states, led by Sparta, drove Xerxes and his army back to Asia Minor.

Elated, the Greek colonies in Asia Minor revolted once more against Persian authority. In 478–472 BC, they moved under the protective umbrella of a newly formed alliance of Greek city-states organized by Athens called the Delian League. Members of the League met on the island of Delos with the avowed purpose of "ravaging the lands of the Persian king" and defending Greece. The Athenians, however, had their own agenda, and it involved more than just ravaging the lands of the Persian king and defending Greece. Over the next several decades, they used the League to build their own empire around the shores of the Aegean Sea and the southern Mediterranean.

The members of the League were required to support it through yearly contributions, and by 454 BC, the treasury at Delos had become so full that, at Athenian suggestion, the gold was moved into a more "secure environment," the temple of Athena at Athens. After the transfer of the treasury, the Athenians undertook the most massive and expensive building campaign in their history. They built the Parthenon and made improvements to the Acropolis, transforming their city into one of the most beautiful in the ancient world.

Athens entered the period of intellectual, cultural, and artistic development now known as the Classical Age. Generations continue to marvel at "the glory that was Greece," and an unparalleled era in human history. From the end of the Persian Wars in 479 BC until the beginning of the Peloponnesian Wars in 431 BC, not only Athens but mainland Greece as a whole developed into one of the most fertile areas ever found in humankind's intellectual and artistic garden.

Athens became the center of learning in Greece and under the leadership of the liberal statesman Pericles boasted a concentration of artistic, political, scientific, and philosophical genius such as the world had never seen. In addition to great philosophers such as Socrates (469–399 BC), there were historians, mathematicians, playwrights, satirists, and artists. Aeschylus (525–456 BC) and Sophocles (496–406 BC) wrote plays about the weaknesses of human nature. Aristophanes (444–380 BC) wrote political satire that continues to resonate with audiences today, while Herodotus (484–420 BC) and Thucydides (471–401 BC) refined the scope and writing of history. Hippocrates (460–357 BC) established the foundations of medicine. The Athenians excelled in architecture, as is reflected in the beauty and grace of their temples, and in sculpture they brought the human form to a state of perfection.

By this point in history, all the major Greek cities except Sparta had adopted some form of democratic government. The Spartans proved to be the most reactionary of all the Greek societies as they stubbornly held on to the ways of their forefathers. Life was based on a status quo that had been in place for nearly six hundred years and had given the society a degree of social and political stability that other Greek city-states admired in theory but avoided in practice. In Sparta, every person knew what was expected of him or her. The Spartan system seems to have made no allowances for individuality and thus stifled all creativity and intellectual endeavor by requiring each member to play his or her precisely assigned role for the good of the whole.

Spartan government was an unusual combination of dual kingship and popular political participation. The city was governed by two kings, an advisory council of elders, elected magistrates called *ephors* (similar to the Athenian archons), and a popular assembly of all male citizens, a system set up by the legendary Spartan lawgiver Lycurgus sometime in the seventh century BC.

The Spartans were firm believers in the concept of survival of the strongest. Infants were inspected to determine which were likely to be good soldiers or healthy mothers when they matured, and those who were weak or deformed were left in the wilderness to die or hurled from a cliff.

Sparta was a society oriented toward war. Males from the age of seven until the age of sixty spent their lives in the military and had little private or family time. During their prime, Spartan males lived together in barracks and ate a bland gruel at communal meals. Conversation was kept to a minimum because Spartan society valued a man who said little and accomplished much. Young Spartan women were required to train alongside the men in order to bear healthy children for the state. In theory, all Spartans were equal, for there was no monetary system or concept of private property. Land was communal and distributed in equal lots to each male citizen along with an allotment of state-owned slaves to work it. The system provided each Spartan with a guaranteed minimum to live on and equal status before the law.

The Spartan system, though harsh, was effective because of its consistency and rigidity. By the fifth century BC, the Spartans had become the most feared and accomplished ground soldiers in the ancient world. They gained that reputation because their strict discipline and precise organization gave them an advantage over other armies, even those many times their size. First and foremost they were raised not to fear death, and they lived in accordance with a code that allowed them only two ways to return from war, either carrying their shields in victory or being carried on their shields in death.

When Athens became the dominant power in fifth century mainland Greece, the other city-states looked to Sparta as a counterbalance. Athens and Sparta along with their allies engaged in a particularly devastating series of civil wars that lasted from 431 BC until 404 BC (Peloponnesian Wars) and spelled the end of the Classical period and democracy in Greece.

In spite of their cultural superiority and military prowess, the Greeks were never able to set aside their differences long enough to bring the ancient world under their control as the Persians did or the Romans would. Sparta and Athens fought off and on for years without a clear advantage going to either side. As the financial costs of the conflict increased, both sides turned to the Persian king Darius II for help. Darius recognized a relatively cheap and effective way to increase his influence on the western fringe of his empire by becoming a power broker. As long as Greeks fought among themselves, he would have a free hand in Asia Minor. So Darius provided money and offered troops to both sides, but ultimately his help proved unnecessary because the Athenians managed to lose the war on their own in a single disastrous afternoon.

The Athenians depended on their fleet to keep them supplied with grain. Their ships made regular runs through the Hellespont to the grain-rich Crimea in southern Russia and back to Athens. In 405 BC the fleet was left unguarded on an Aegean beach just outside the entrance to the Hellespont when the Spartan navy came upon them unexpectedly and destroyed them. Without a fleet of supply ships and surrounded by the Spartans, the Athenians faced starvation. Realizing the hopelessness of their situation, they surrendered, and the long war finally ended.

The city-states of Corinth and Thebes urged the Spartans to destroy Athens, but the Spartans could not bring themselves to burn the city whose people had sacrificed to save Greece on the plains of Marathon and in the straits of Salamis. The Spartans demanded that the walls of the city be destroyed and Athenian government be placed in the hands of thirty aristocratic families with strong ties to Sparta.

Many of those families had been exiled and their property confiscated during the period when the advocates of democracy had control of Athens, and now they returned with the support of the Spartan armies and undertook a bloody purge of their political opponents. Athenians endured the rule of "The Thirty" for nearly a year before democracy was restored.

Athens was not the same city it had been before the Peloponnesian Wars and would never recover its primacy among the Greek
city-states. Long years of fighting had depleted the city's resources
and manpower, its navy had been destroyed, and plague had taken a
heavy toll. The Spartans were the new masters of Greece, and in city-
states throughout the mainland, they imposed oligarchies favorable
to their policies.

After the Peloponnesian Wars, mainland Greece became an unsettled place. Thousands of men, released from military service and unemployed, roamed the countryside. They had sacked and looted
cities and had no desire to return to the impoverishment and tedium
of the life they had known before. Soldiering for them was a way of
life and even a profession. As they looked for ways to fill their pockets,
they formed large, well-organized groups that began to menace some
of the smaller Greek city-states.

Traditionally the citizen army of each Greek city-state constituted
only a small proportion of the total adult male population. The backbone of the army were the heavily armed infantrymen, or *hoplites,* recruited from among property-owning citizens. The richest men served
in the less militarily effective but more socially prestigious cavalry.
During the Peloponnesian Wars, the role of the lower orders of Greek
society in combat increased, as the poor were called on to serve an
auxiliary role as lightly armed fighters called *peltasts.* Over time, they
became a match for the slow-moving, heavily armed hoplites, much as
infantrymen in the late Middle Ages would become more effective
than the heavily armored knights. War ceased to be a part-time occu-
pation for poorly trained citizen conscripts and entered a new stage
of lethal refinement. By the end of the fifth century BC, Greek soldiers and methods of warfare were the best in the ancient world.

Greek society did not know what to do with them. After so many years
of war, the economy was fragile, and there was little work in the already
overcrowded cities. They could not be resettled in the countryside because of the shortage of good land. A large and impoverished population of drifting ex-soldiers became the most unsettling demographic
feature of mainland Greece as the fifth century BC came to a close.

One strategy for dealing with the bands of roving ex-soldiers was to hire them as mercenaries. Not only in Greece but elsewhere in the ancient world, mercenaries began to displace citizen armies. The reason for this change was economic expediency. A Greek city-state or a foreign despot could hire professional soldiers in time of need, who would usually give excellent service as long as the money and the opportunities for plunder lasted. When the need for their services ended, they could be sent on their way with no further obligation on the part of the hiring authority—an ancient form of military outsourcing.

Another solution to the problem lay across the Aegean Sea in Asia Minor. The Greeks had always entertained exaggerated notions of the wealth of the Persian Empire. For the leaders of the city-states, there was an appealing logic to the argument that a war against Persia under Spartan leadership could be an effective way of allowing the Greeks to unite and focus their energies against a common enemy. The conquest of Persia could mean a new standard of living for the impoverished Greeks and a solution to the problem of the unemployed ex-soldiers roaming the countryside. The dream of a war against Persia, followed by Greek resettlement of the conquered lands, caught hold as the turbulent fifth century BC was coming to a close. In the winter of 402–401 BC, an opportunity presented itself and is the subject of the next chapter.

From 400 BC to 380 BC, there were a number of Greek incursions into Persian territory, all of them led by Spartans and confined mostly to western Asia Minor. When the conquests did not pan out and returns were meager, the Greeks reverted to their usual pattern of fighting among themselves. Another round of civil wars broke out, and a Persian king once again became a power broker. Using his gold, Artaxerxes played Athenians off against Spartans, Corinthians, and Thebans and generally kept the Greeks busy fighting each other. Not until the middle of the fourth century BC did the Greeks stop fighting, unify themselves, and present another threat to Persia—this time, under a Macedonian king, Alexander the Great.

Greek history in the fourth century BC is dominated by Alexander. Democracy was out for the Greeks; monarchy was in. Athens and the other Greek city-states retained the facade of democracy well into the Roman period, but the reality was that the dominant political force in Greece was the Macedonian monarchy. Alexander's father, Philip, united the Greeks and Alexander led them into Persia. But Alexander's rule was short, and after his death his generals took control of Greece and his eastern empire, initiating a period known as the Hellenistic Age. They cast themselves in Alexander's mold and fought among themselves, further depleting Greece of manpower and resources. The Greek city-states were too weak to rebel against the Hellenistic monarchies and became little more than pawns in the larger power struggle going on around them. The ancient world would not be united again until the rise of the Romans in the first century BC.

4

XENOPHON

Building Consensus and Finding Direction

*"In life a man must resign himself to expect anything,
and never count on anyone but himself."*
—XENOPHON

The Athenian philosopher Socrates was once asked by his pupils who makes the best leader. He replied without hesitation: the man who steps forward in a time of need—motivated not by ego or financial gain but by a sense of duty to benefit the society to which he belongs—then, when the task is completed, returns to his former life, no wealthier than when he began.

How many people today would come forward in a time of crisis to serve their company or nation and then, when the job is done, leave no materially richer than when they began? The public-spirited dollar-a-year people who served in Franklin Delano Roosevelt's administration to help get the country through World War II are all too rare in our society.

Xenophon, a young scholar in his twenties and a student of Socrates, was that kind of selfless leader. He came forward in a time of crisis to take command of a despondent army of Greek mercenaries trapped in the middle of a hostile Persian Empire and resigned to dying. With only limited experience in command, he stands as a classic example of how great leaders sometimes emerge from the most unexpected circumstances to turn a desperate, seemingly hopeless situation around.

Effective leadership of course takes more than the altruistic desire to help advocated by Socrates. Good leaders have a feel for the ebb and flow of moving things forward. Xenophon brought these and other skills to the table, including his ability to inspire those he led to confront, bluff, and escape from an enemy many times their size and strength. He also had to instill and maintain the confidence and morale necessary for his army to find its way through more than 1,500 miles of deserts and mountains before reaching safety. In addition to fighting nature and the enemies in front of and behind him, Xenophon had to contend with divisive factions within his own command and, later, adverse political developments in his homeland that threatened not only his leadership but his life.

After more than twenty-five hundred years, his story still resonates with lessons and insights about leadership. This ancient leader shows us the value of decisive action when initial objectives fail. He stands out as a leader who turns a bad situation around by working with what he has rather than complaining about what he lacks. Some might call him the ancient equivalent of today's turnaround artists, although that label doesn't do justice to the magnitude of Xenophon's accomplishment.

In every organization, leaders struggle not only against their known enemies—the competition—but also against divisive, sometimes hidden factions within the very culture they are trying to lead. Internal resistance can come straight at you from the rank and file or sneak up behind your back from the highest echelons of management. It can result from disagreements over compensation and working conditions, controversial corporate philosophy and marketing decisions, or simply the way things get done.

Leaders constantly face challenges from division managers or product managers who are so focused on their own narrow concerns that they undermine or obstruct the broader corporate objectives. The trick for a good leader, as Xenophon will show us, is to get everybody calmed down, seated in the boat, and rowing together in the same direction.

The Western Part of the
Persian Empire
The Route of Xenophon

Xenophon was born into an aristocratic Athenian family during the Peloponnesian Wars, and by virtue of his background and education, we would classify him today as a political conservative. Although he believed that enlightened monarchy was the best system of government and discipline the most effective tool of command, he lived during a time when the forces of democracy were rapidly gaining strength throughout Greece. The soldiers Xenophon led valued discussion and the right of everyone in the army, from private to general, to express his views in a public forum and have a vote in matters that affected him. As their elected leader Xenophon had to accommodate these forces and work with what he had.

Accepting the mantle of leadership today practically requires you to channel your "inner Xenophon" even if you secretly pine for the good old days when CEOs ruled like kings. There is really no choice other than substantively and creatively working with your constituencies up and down the chain of command, from the shop floor to the board room. Like the Greeks in Xenophon's army, everybody seems to have an opinion nowadays on how things should be done, and sometimes even the rank and file of an organization can have a significant influence in determining whether a leader stays or goes. Xenophon excelled because he was able to work with these forces and channel them in a way that accomplished what he thought best for the group.

HOW LEADERS DEVELOP CONSENSUS TO SET NEW DIRECTIONS

An effective leader must value and evaluate input from those he leads, even when reshaping an environment or culture that, in his opinion, is doing more harm than good. A classic case of a leader taking over an unresponsive or potentially hostile culture is Lou Gerstner's accession to IBM's corporate throne in 1993. IBM had been one of the most profitable and dominant corporations in the world, and its grip on the mainframe market seemed unshakable. Almost all of its competitors had abandoned the field, with huge losses to boot. At year end 1968, IBM's outsized market share had prompted the federal government to file a sweeping antitrust suit against the company (which was subsequently dropped in 1982).

The man who made IBM such a fearsome foe, Thomas Watson Sr., instilled in the company what would today be described as a paternalistic culture. For years, employees routinely sang hymns at company meetings extolling the glories of IBM and Tom Watson. Big Blue's culture had become notoriously and dangerously insular. Watson's son and successor, Tom Jr., ended the singing, but IBM's distinct culture remained largely intact.

The world changed faster than IBM. The company was blindsided first by the rise of minicomputers and then by networked personal computers. The mainframe was no longer the be-all and end-all of high technology, and by the beginning of the 1990s, IBM faced not only a financial crisis but the prospect of going out of business. In 1993, to salvage the situation, Lou Gerstner, the head of RJR Nabisco and the former CEO of American Express Travel Related Services, was brought in by a desperate IBM board of directors.

When Gerstner arrived for work his first day, he was astonished at how oblivious everyone seemed to the fact that the company already had one foot in the corporate graveyard. Nevertheless, although the culture resisted Gerstner's presence and his far-reaching reforms, the direness of the situation helped him succeed in fundamentally reshaping—and saving—IBM.

IBM had lost $10 billion over the three previous years. Its finances were in distress, yet Gerstner found a culture that in its day-to-day activities couldn't recognize what was happening on the outside. There was too much internal turf fighting; IBM executives and managers didn't hesitate to block each other's initiatives. So Gerstner brought an end to the autonomy of the division managers and country managers. As a result, if you thwarted a rival's initiative, you did so knowing that you might be reducing your own compensation as well. Compensation depended on how well the company did as a whole, not just your piece of it. Everyone had to be part of the team and rowing the big blue boat in the same direction.

Even small things mattered. IBM's infamous dress code—everyone was required to wear a white shirt and tie to work—was a vestige of an earlier, more formal era. In the 1990s, IBM's customers were likely to be wearing blue jeans when IBM reps arrived to call on them. Times were changing, but IBM was not changing with them. At his first meeting with his managers, Gerstner entered the room wearing a colored shirt. At the next meeting, everyone was wearing a colored shirt, and the old dress code went out the window as Gerstner moved the company in a new direction.

IBM had been dominant for so long that it had practically dictated to the market. In the 1990s, things changed as buyers insisted that IBM pay attention to what they wanted and needed. Growing numbers of competitors were eager to work with these clients if IBM wouldn't. Under Gerstner's prodding, IBM became less of a computer manufacturing company and more of a service and consulting business to corporations that didn't want to set up or run their own computer operations. In other words, IBM began to listen to its customers and offer comprehensive solutions for their computing problems.

When Gerstner took over, he fired sixty thousand workers even though nearly a hundred thousand had already been laid off from a culture that had fostered the expectation of lifelong employment. The layoffs were necessary to cut costs and avert bankruptcy. With Gerstner's new direction IBM became a dynamic, growing company again. Nine years later, when Gerstner retired, IBM had sixty-five thousand more employees than there had been when he first arrived.

Compare Gerstner's accomplishment in revitalizing IBM's stagnant culture with Carly Fiorina's impact at Hewlett-Packard. HP had been one of the icons of Silicon Valley and the epitome of innovation and market versatility. But in the late 1990s the company lost its edge. The very culture that had once made HP so formidable was seen as an obstacle to responding to a fast-changing environment. *Insular* was the word outsiders used to describe HP. In 1999 a concerned board of directors brought in Fiorina from Lucent, an AT&T spin-off, to restructure HP.

Unlike Gerstner, Fiorina did not achieve a Xenophon-like success. While Gerstner was shaking things up at IBM, he was careful to show respect for the company's past even as he emphasized the need to adapt to a radically changing environment. Fiorina also shook things up, but she showed disdain for HP's past and for the traditional "HP way" of doing things. Bill Hewlett and Dave Packard, the founders of HP, were revered figures, yet Fiorina replaced their portraits at corporate headquarters with her own. Fiorina dealt with her key executives in a brusque manner. They were unaccustomed to being treated like that, and when her quarterly projections were not met, she blamed and fired many of them.

When Fiorina proposed that HP acquire Compaq, a competitor in the PC business, the antipathy of the old guard intensified. Skeptics predicted that merging two also-rans would be a disaster. A fierce fight erupted within the company and spread to the board of directors. Critics declared that Fiorina was destroying the company and trampling on HP's culture. They complained she was concerned more with publicizing herself and socializing with entertainers and high-fashion figures than with promoting HP and running the business. There were even rumors that she was positioning herself to run for political office.

Nevertheless, the merger with Compaq was accomplished, although her triumph was short-lived. But because HP wasn't in the dire straits that IBM had been in when Gerstner took the helm, and because Fiorina's lack of tactfulness alienated many allies she might have had, the board of directors ousted her in 2005 when she failed to meet quarterly projections.

Mark Hurd, the new CEO, seems more comfortable with the "HP way," and the company has finally begun to turn around. It is a more nimble competitor in the PC market as well as in its other key businesses like printers and desktops. In Fiorina's defense, there are those in the industry who argue that the turnaround proves that her basic strategy was the right one, and they insist that she wasn't allowed the time to reap what she had sown. Gerstner clearly had more running room than Fiorina to bring about change, because IBM was on the verge of going under and HP, though stagnant, was still profitable. Fiorina came into a situation that was not as desperate as that of IBM's—or of the Spartan army's in Persia—and her high-handed attempts at transformation were resisted and led to her ouster. Both Gerstner and Fiorina are examples of leaders coming in to take charge of strong, suspicious, and entrenched organizational cultures, as Xenophon did more than two thousand years ago. But Gerstner's success resulted from his superior ability to size up a desperate situation, decide how to proceed, and convince others to follow his lead.

EXITING A DESPERATE SITUATION

The Greeks Xenophon led were mercenaries hired to tip the scales in a war between two brothers over the throne of the Persian Empire. This was a minor conflict, as wars in the ancient world go, but it set in motion a chain of events that led to the end of the Persian Empire, the rise of Alexander the Great, and the dawn of a new age.

Darius II was one of Persia's longest-ruling kings (reigned 421–404 BC). He had two sons, Artaxerxes and Cyrus. Encouraged by his mother, Cyrus expected to become king when his father died. He was his mother's favorite, and his father had named him after the founder of the empire, Cyrus the Great. Though he was the younger son, he based his claim to the throne on having been "born into the purple"— an expression Persian legal scholars used to denote the first son born to a man *after* he became king. Artaxerxes, born *before* Darius became king, based his claim to the throne on the legal concept of primogeniture: the exclusive right of the eldest to inherit.

Before Darius died, he designated Artaxerxes to succeed him, and the friction between the brothers became more than just their differences over Persian legalities. Cyrus decided to raise an army and take the throne by force. As satrap of Sardis in western Asia Minor, the young prince had frequent contact with the Greeks whose colonies lined the Aegean coast. Greek soldiers were the best-trained and best-equipped infantry in the ancient world, and Cyrus believed they could give him the advantage on the battlefield against his brother.

Finding soldiers to hire was not a problem. Plenty of veterans with few prospects were roaming the countryside of mainland Greece, and Cyrus recruited them with promises of lavish rewards and the chance for a new start in Asia. Nearly fourteen thousand answered his call and converged on Sardis. History has dubbed these Greeks "the ten thousand" because of the presence of a formidable phalanx of ten thousand Spartan infantrymen among them. Xenophon joined the expedition as a member of the cavalry, against the advice of his teacher Socrates.

When Cyrus assembled his army, he had close to forty thousand men under arms—not only Greek mercenaries but members of local tribes and Persians discontent with the new king. The massive force moved east nearly 1,500 miles into the center of the Persian Empire and in September of 401 BC engaged the army of Artaxerxes at Cunaxa, a dusty plain along the Euphrates River a few miles west of modern Baghdad.

The Greeks took up a position on Cyrus's right flank, and as was typical in ancient warfare, Cyrus commanded from behind the center, much as a quarterback directs plays from behind his linemen. Artaxerxes' army, however, was so large, several hundred thousand, that when it deployed for battle the front line stretched from the Euphrates River well beyond Cyrus's left flank. As the armies engaged, the Spartan phalanx, supported by cavalry, drove into the opposing Persian infantry, which collapsed in panic and disarray.

But on the far side of the vast battlefield, a different scenario was unfolding. The night before the battle, the Greek commanders had advised Cyrus to stay behind his center and well away from the fighting. Yet once the battle began, the young prince, eager to demonstrate his bravery and daring, led an impetuous charge directly into the Persian line and was killed. The massive right flank of Artaxerxes' army then slowly but methodically wheeled around to envelop Cyrus's confused and demoralized soldiers, who quickly surrendered in return for their lives. By the time the Greeks learned what happened, not only the battle but the war was over.

At the end of the day the exhausted Greeks returned to their camp and found it looted and burned, their women and slaves killed or carried off, and few supplies left. The most senior Spartan commander, a menacing bear of a man named Clearchus, ordered the Greeks to regroup on a nearby hill while he assessed the situation and pondered their options. Surrounded and vastly outnumbered, the Greeks were down to the last of their food and water.

Days passed as the Greeks scanned the horizon waiting for the first signs of a Persian assault. But nothing happened. Artaxerxes had chosen to wait and allow the relentless desert sun, heat, thirst, hunger, and despair to weaken the Greeks. In spite of the size of his army, he was hesitant to risk a direct assault. The Greeks, especially the Spartans, had a fearsome reputation among the Persians, and given their easy success against his soldiers in battle, he decided to avoid an assault for the moment. Then one morning, he sent heralds to the Greeks to discuss a truce. Before allowing the Persians to enter the camp, Clearchus ordered his soldiers into full parade formation. In spite of having had little to eat or drink for days, the Greeks remained a formidable and intimidating looking group.

The Persian emissaries reminded the Greeks that they were surrounded by the largest and most powerful army in the world and urged them to surrender their weapons to the "king of kings." Clearchus replied that if the "king of kings" wanted their weapons he should come and take them. The Persians suggested a truce, and Clearchus replied that there would be no truce because his soldiers had nothing for breakfast and there is "no man on the face of this earth who will dare talk to Greeks about a truce until they have first had their breakfast."

When the Persians reported to Artaxerxes that the Greeks would not even discuss a truce unless they first had breakfast, the king was impressed and sent wagon-loads of provisions to them and an invitation for the senior Greek commanders to dine with him. When the Greeks arrived in the Persian camp protected by what they thought was a universal respect for the laws of hospitality, they were set upon, and those not immediately killed, including Clearchus, were sent to Babylon to be beheaded.

One of the Greek officers wounded in the carnage managed to return to the Greek camp. When the soldiers heard what had happened, most resigned themselves to dying, and a malaise descended on the army as they anticipated each dawn would be their last. Days passed and nothing happened. Then one night, unable to sleep, Xenophon asked himself, "Why am I lying here just waiting to die? Nobody is doing anything to defend the camp so why should I just wait to see if someone comes forward? Am I too young to take command myself? I will never get any older if I do nothing."

STEPPING FORWARD

Xenophon recognized a leadership void that needed to be filled quickly if the Greeks were to survive. He began by urging the men around

him to lift themselves out of their despondency and join him in finding a way home. As support for his idea spread, Xenophon called for
a general assembly so he could address the army. He was straightforward
about the seriousness of their predicament, as he explained his plan to
pull them together and march out of Persia.

Xenophon's words began to lift the morale of the soldiers and rekindle their sense of unity. He told them they were free men who fought
because they chose to, not because they were driven by the whips of
masters. As he recounted how their forefathers had defeated larger
Persian armies at the famous battles of Marathon (490 BC) and Thermopylae (480 BC), nearly a century before, a soldier suddenly sneezed.
The assembly became silent, and the superstitious Greeks fell to their
knees at what they believed was a favorable sign from Zeus, king of the
gods.

In spite of Xenophon's persuasive words and the divine sneeze,
there were Greeks who rose to oppose his plan and offer alterna-
tives. Some spoke in favor of begging clemency from the king, while
others suggested offering their services as mercenaries. A few
diehards pledged to take a stand on the hilltop and fight to the last
man. Xenophon warned against trusting the king who had murdered
their officers. If they were fated to die, he argued, why not die trying
to get home rather than waiting to be massacred? He urged his fellow
Greeks to remain a well-disciplined force and presented his plan as
more than just a chance for survival: It was an opportunity to confirm
to the world the superiority of Greeks over barbarians.

Xenophon came to the fore with no leadership experience, especially not the kind to help him with the tough job of commanding mercenaries. Yet he masked whatever insecurity and self-doubts he might
have harbored and presented a clear plan and realistic assessment of
the obstacles that lay ahead. The Greeks would have to escape the Persian king and then live off what was sure to be a barren land. They
could not return home by the most direct route, through the deserts of
Syria and on through central Turkey to the coast of Asia Minor. On the
way in with Cyrus, they had stripped the land of everything, and the flat
desert terrain would give the king's cavalry and chariots a lethal ad-

vantage over them. The only route open was north along the Tigris River, then over the mountains of Armenia to the southern coast of the Black Sea and the safety of the Greek cities that lay there. That route was no cakewalk then, nor is it today. It is still dangerous and unsettled territory where Kurdish rebels, Iranian operatives, Turkish army units, drug smugglers, and bandits all vie for control.

Xenophon believed that securing provisions would not be a problem, because there were sure to be villages and towns along the way where they could take what they needed. His hope was that Artaxerxes would return to Babylon with the bulk of his army rather than pursue them. The Greeks would, however, be vulnerable to attack by elements of the king's army that would be sure to shadow them until they reached the mountains. Once in the mountains, Xenophon warned, their biggest problems would be crossing the peaks and warding off attacks by the local tribes. It was already mid-September, and some of the highest passes might be blocked by snow by the time they got there. In spite of the risks, the soldiers voted their support.

Xenophon recognized that the army had to fill the positions of the murdered senior officers as quickly as possible, so he offered himself as a candidate. At the same time, he made it clear that he was willing to follow as a common soldier. Elections were held, and Xenophon was given command of the rear guard.

What made Xenophon effective as a leader was his ability to communicate. From the start he was able to present a clear plan of action, and later, when things became difficult, he was able to motivate his army to stay the course. Xenophon—an Athenian among Spartans, a philosopher among soldiers—entered a potentially hostile culture, won it over, brought it together, and made it work again.

•   •   •

Earlier we identified Lou Gerstner as an example of a leader who led a beleaguered company out of the financial wilderness. Another interesting example is Finbarr O'Neill, a former auto industry executive who was appointed president of J. D. Power and Associates in January 2009. O'Neill's biggest career challenge probably came when he took the top job at Hyundai Motor America in the late 1990s. Like Xenophon and his Greeks, Hyundai had lost its direction and was surrounded by larger hostile competitors threatening to devour it.

There was a leadership void at Hyundai. The board of directors, desperate to keep the company alive, appointed O'Neill the interim leader while they searched for a new CEO. He no more fit the profile of an automotive CEO than the scholarly Xenophon did of a military commander. O'Neill had been Hyundai's corporate counsel and, unlike most automotive chief executives, lacked both know-how and experience in automotive design, engineering, marketing, or sales. But like Xenophon, O'Neill had an innate leadership ability and stepped up to the plate when no one else could.

At a 1998 company meeting in Monterey, California, Hyundai dealers from around the country clamored for direction. O'Neill rose to speak and began by asking the dealers what direction they thought the company should be going in. They started yelling out advice, and O'Neill called for a time-out while he found an easel. Then he started writing down the problems they identified and their suggestions for solutions. Momentarily overwhelmed but confident and in control, he turned to the group and said, "I can't work on all of these at once, so let's pick the top ten and that's where I'll start." Hyundai's Xenophon moment occurred when O'Neill took charge and gave the corporation a dose of inspiration and a sense of direction.

Like Xenophon, O'Neill came forward in a time of crisis. He was confident, articulate, and modest. He listened to his people about what needed to be done, then devised a plan and followed it. O'Neill was so persuasive that Hyundai could succeed that he won over the skeptical dealers and went on to lead one of the most unexpected and successful turnarounds in the automotive industry.

For both Xenophon and O'Neill, articulating a cause and formulating a strategy were only the first steps in resolving a crisis. A leader must be able to sustain enthusiasm and commitment when the going gets tough and the casualties mount. Both Xenophon and O'Neill accomplished this by being honest about the situation and the challenges that lay ahead. They had realistic expectations so there was no spin, no sugarcoating, and no pie in the sky. Great leaders can succeed in motivating others to stay the course because they are able to convince them that, as dark as things appear at a particular moment, a better future lies ahead.

LEADING BY EXAMPLE

After the elections, Xenophon took aside the new officers in his command to give them some practical advice about leadership. First he advised them to set an example: "The men you command will look to you . . . If you are a coward, they will be cowards. You must excel, not only in bravery but in every facet of command." Then he concluded by telling them that leadership is not only about reaping rewards when times are good. It is also about inspiration and effectiveness when times get tough.

As the Greeks prepared to move out, Artaxerxes sent word that he had decided to grant them safe passage along the northern route and would provide them with guides and a military escort. What was the king thinking? He had decided to avoid a battle, anticipating that the mountains would do much of the killing for him. To finish off any Greeks who survived, he dispatched a large force due west, by the inland route, to reach the coast of Asia Minor and lay in wait for them. Then, content with his preparations, the king returned to Babylon to celebrate his victory over Cyrus.

The Persian guides, accompanied by elements of the king's army, led the Greeks north along the Tigris River to the mountains. There was tension, because the Greeks mistrusted the Persians and expected an attack at any time. But weeks passed, and as the column moved slowly along the river, no attack came. When the Greeks finally reached the mountains, the Persians turned back, leaving them to find their own way through.

When the Greeks passed through the lower elevations, they looted villages for supplies and forced tribal elders to guide them. Ambushes by the mountain tribes were frequent. Hunger, exhaustion, and disease took away their weak and sick. The higher they climbed, the deeper the snow and the colder it became. There was a shortage of warm clothing, and boots wore out. Frostbite crippled and gangrene killed. The bright reflection of the sun on the snow blinded many, but Xenophon kept the column moving, driving the weary men forward and upward—week after week and month after month. This proved to be the most difficult part of the long journey, but it also was the high point of his command, as the Greeks came together as a cohesive, well-disciplined unit.

Early one spring day, while the column was making its way over a particularly high mountain pass, soldiers in the vanguard caught their first view of the Black Sea. A cry was raised—"the sea, the sea"—and the soldiers built an altar of rocks at that point, as an offering to Zeus for what they mistakenly believed was the end of their ordeal.

The first city the mercenaries encountered when they came down from the mountains was Trapezus (the modern Turkish city of Trabzon), where they were welcomed as fellow Greeks. Games were held in the Olympic style to celebrate their safe passage, and during the festivities the mercenaries honored Xenophon for his leadership. From Trapezus the commanders decided to lead the army west along the Black Sea coast to the Spartan-controlled city of Byzantium (Istanbul), where they were confident they would find ships to sail back to Greece. Everyone anticipated this would be the easiest part of the journey, for they would come under the protection of the Greek cities that lined the coast and the marching would not be difficult. But what should have been easy turned out to be difficult and fraught with danger.

The route from Trabzon to Istanbul is about 600 miles, through a desolate and impoverished region that John Prevas traversed a few years ago when he traced Xenophon's route. The eastern part of the Turkish coast along the Black Sea is a polluted, economically depressed area lined with empty, half-finished concrete hotels built in anticipation of vacationing Russians who never came.

It took nearly six months for Xenophon and the mercenaries to complete this part of the journey. In the absence of threats from nature, the Persian army, or mountain tribes to keep them united, old cultural and political rivalries among the Greeks began to resurface. There were conflicts with local Greeks along the coast as well, and Xenophon found himself facing challenges to his leadership that were completely different from what he had encountered in bringing the army through the mountains.

The unity that sustained the army in the mountains dissipated as conditions along the coast improved. Discipline began to break down as soldiers vented their discontent with their officers and questioned orders. Units left the main body without permission and pillaged and burned inland villages and towns. When they found the pickings slim, rogue elements began looking for larger and richer prey, even menacing a few small Greek towns.

Outside the walls of Cotyora, a small Greek city, a tense standoff developed when the mercenaries threatened to storm the locked city gates. The standoff ended when a delegation from Sinope, a larger Greek city along the coast, arrived and warned the mercenaries that if they took Cotyora by force they would be branded outlaws and denied help by other Greeks along their route.

Xenophon explained that they had sick and wounded among them and were short on provisions. He pledged that his soldiers would pay for what they needed as long as the local people set up a market for them at fair prices. But, Xenophon warned, his men would do what was necessary to survive—even against fellow Greeks if they had to. The threat proved effective, and the gates were opened. The mercenaries remained at Cotyora for several days without incident before they moved on to Sinope. At Sinope the few who had money were able to buy their way home aboard merchant ships that plied the coast. The remaining mercenaries were now more interested in finding money and taking slaves than in remaining a well-disciplined military unit. Most had left Greece to escape poverty and planned to return wealthy; others had intended to settle in Asia with Cyrus to begin a new life. Now it looked as though they would all be returning home poorer than when they left.

SUBSTANCE AND STYLE

Xenophon's problem in trying to restrain the mercenaries from loot-ing and keeping them focused on returning home confirms what mod-ern research has found: Managers at the top often have difficulty in getting people to do what they want; what is accomplished often has more to do with how subordinates carry out directives. In other words, a leader's best efforts can be neutralized by events and circumstances beyond his or her control.

Robert Nardelli, who took over as CEO of Home Depot in 2000, is an example of a leader whose downfall stemmed from a management style that was the exact opposite of what the business he was hired to direct felt it needed. Home Depot was a growing, highly successful enterprise when its founders, Bernard Marcus and Arthur Blank, decided the company needed a new CEO. They were looking for someone who could bring a more disciplined focus to management and enable the company to grow rapidly and profitably in the future. Nardelli had a successful career at General Electric, where he had been president of its power system business. He was so well respected that he was one of three finalists in the running to succeed the legendary Jack Welch. When Nardelli was passed over at GE, Home Depot was delighted to hire him.

As CEO, Nardelli instituted new reporting procedures in an effort to help his managers get a handle on how all parts of the company were doing, which stores and products were succeeding, and which were not. He imposed cost-cutting measures and didn't hesitate to challenge the conventional wisdom or sacred cows of Wall Street, such as the importance analysts placed on comparing same-store sales from one year to the next. Nardelli felt that was a meaningless measure, es-pecially since Home Depot was opening new facilities and a new store might take business away from an existing one. What mattered most, Nardelli insisted, was the combined sales from all stores. During his reign, Home Depot's overall sales and earnings-per-share more than doubled.

But in spite of the favorable numbers, Nardelli encountered resistance from the start. Employees and managers at Home Depot were outraged when he fired many full-time employees and replaced them with part-timers. While he saved money for the company, critics felt that service at Home Depot suffered, giving rival Lowe's an advantage. Nardelli liked the idea of going into new businesses and not focusing only on Home Depot's traditional core strengths. So he pushed hard for the company to build Home Depot Supply—an offshoot to provide services to professional contractors—and invested $7.6 billion in the project.

The chorus of complaints against Nardelli increased as Home Depot's stock price first stagnated and then fell. At one annual meeting he arrived without the board of directors and took only 30 minutes of questions from shareholders. This gave Nardelli's enemies even more ammunition to use against him. Critics complained that his pay and benefits package was too generous, and even after he made a concession, giving up an annual $3 million bonus, that still wasn't enough for the increasingly restive board and unhappy shareholders.

At the beginning of 2007, Nardelli and Home Depot parted ways. His severance package of $210 million was greeted with howls of protest from employees and shareholders. But the protestors overlooked the fact that almost the entire amount was what Nardelli would have received had he stayed at GE and that the Home Depot board had agreed to pay it in order to hire him away. Nonetheless, critics made Nardelli a poster child for outrageous golden parachutes and excessive executive compensation.

Why was Nardelli forced out? It was not because he was incompetent as a CEO, but because his leadership style, which had worked so well at GE, clashed with the more relaxed entrepreneurial style of Home Depot.

Nardelli was not a free agent for long. His services were still in demand, and within months, the private equity fund Cerberus Capital made him a lavish offer to fix a broken Chrysler Corporation. As the new president of Chrysler his timing was terrible. The collapsing auto market in 2008–2009 is threatening the company's survival, and like the CEOs of GM and Ford, Nardelli made the mistake of flying in a corporate jet to Washington to plead for a federal bailout. He later drove to Washington for a subsequent session. While Washington provided some immediate life-saving cash, Chrysler's future in the industry remains problematic at best.

Richard Ferris, a former hotel executive, was an outsider like Xenophon when he first joined United Airlines as head of food services in 1971. When Ferris became CEO in 1979, he went out of his way to win over the company's pilots and cultivate goodwill, even learning how to fly. When the industry was deregulated, Ferris confidently predicted that deregulation would do for the airlines what the jet engine had done for air travel.

The industry did change, but not in the way Ferris thought it would. Deregulation resulted in fare wars that put United under tremendous financial pressure. Formerly content pilots became angry labor activists, demanding that management address their concerns and provide positive direction for the company. Ferris responded by cutting costs and making acquisitions. In an attempt to create what he believed would be a stronger and more diversified company, he began piecing together a travel conglomerate that included Hilton hotels and Hertz rental car operations. He called his new creation Allegis, a name critics contended sounded like a drug for some middle-aged malady. While his acquisitions turned out to be profitable, Ferris lost his direction as an airline CEO, and the result was a bitter and divisive strike.

As conditions deteriorated, Ferris dug in his heels and refused to reach an accommodation with the pilots, something he regarded as "caving in." The pilots responded by going on strike and then trying to buy United out from under him for $4.5 billion. The strike created hostilities that hampered the company's progress, and Ferris was ultimately forced out. He had not learned one of Xenophon's basic lessons: A leader cannot afford to adopt a rigid position when confronted with dissension in the ranks. Communication, not confrontation, is the key to winning people over to your ideas and goals.

United's current CEO, Glenn Tilton, is facing a similar management crisis. United continues to be in big financial trouble, and the pilots union recently called for Tilton's replacement because of his "inability to lead," his "incompetence as a manager," and, most damaging, his failure to invest in and maximize the "goodwill" of the employees, who have lost their faith in United.

In contrast to Ferris and Tilton, Michael Volkema, the CEO of furniture-maker Herman Miller from 1995–2004 and now chairman of its board, is a leader with an understanding of his corporate culture and a straightforward approach to meeting challenges. Herman Miller's sales plunged from $2.2 billion in fiscal year 2001 to $1.3 billion twenty-four months later. Volkema was candid with his people. He told his executive team and then the rank and file that hard times lay ahead. He admitted he did not see a quick turnaround in the cards and warned it was likely that deep cutbacks were coming. Sure enough, the company was forced to lay off more than a third of its workforce.

Unlike many CEOs, Volkema didn't send out pink slips on a Friday afternoon. Instead, he went before his workers to tell them why he was laying many of them off. He resisted the temptation to promise that better times were just around the corner, and he told those he retained in the workforce, as well as management, what it would take to survive the crisis and get the company moving once more.

Facing not only a bad business environment but also foreign competition, particularly from China, Volkema concluded that Herman Miller had to take major risks to survive. He poured tens of millions of dollars into research and development to try to achieve genuine breakthroughs, instead of merely tweaking existing product lines. On the marketing and sales side, he established Web sites to encourage large corporate customers to order furniture at discount prices, as well as to hook suppliers into the company's accounting and order systems via the Internet to speed delivery and reduce costs. The money invested in new products paid off. A modular electrical system, for example, "allows users to easily move around data ports, phone lines, and lighting, and program them with a simple handheld device, making reconfiguring office space 'idiot-simple,'" as noted in an admiring article in *Fast Company* magazine.

Volkema's candor, coupled with a clear recovery plan and a focused direction, gave employees the confidence to follow him through an uncertain and turbulent period. Herman Miller regained its place as one of the most successful commercial furniture lines in the world, and *Smart Money* magazine in 2008 rated it as a top place to work when it comes to employee satisfaction.

LEADERS AND FACTIONS

At Sinope, the commanders assembled the soldiers to discuss the remaining leg of the route to Byzantium. There were two options: travel overland to Byzantium through potentially hostile territory or find the money to sail there on ships. As the mercenaries debated, Xenophon made a startling proposal: Stay and build a city. The area was thick with forests, so they could prosper by trading in timber and find wives among the local people. Some of the soldiers immediately rejected the idea of "living among barbarians." They wanted to return to Greece and accused Xenophon of wanting to found a city so he could become its king.

Xenophon told his critics that he was motivated by his feelings for them, not by any desire to be their king. They had shared the hardships of a long march together, and in the face of so much adversity, he had come to view them as his brothers, not his subjects.

Then, a faction of malcontents diverted the assembly by accusing some of the senior officers of incompetence. They demanded the assembly impanel juries to investigate their accusations and hold trials. The first charges were leveled against Xenophon by soldiers who alleged that he had beaten them months before in the mountains. A jury was seated to hear the case, and the penalty upon conviction was set at death by stoning.

Xenophon chose to defend himself and began by admitting he had struck men on the march. After a skirmish between his rear guard and some of the local tribes, he had ordered the cart drivers to transport the severely wounded. When some of them refused to unload what they had looted from villages, Xenophon beat them into compliance with a whip. Then a little farther along the route he discovered that those same drivers had unloaded the wounded and buried them in the snow to die. Outraged, he beat them a second time and had the wounded placed back on the carts.

Another charge brought against Xenophon was beating stragglers. Once more he admitted that he had struck men who had fallen out of the line because they claimed they were too sick or too tired to continue. Should he have left them behind to be captured and killed by the local tribesmen? he asked the jury. As their commander, he had done what he thought was best by forcing them back into the column. Soldiers came forward and testified that they had survived the mountains because Xenophon used a combination of discipline and encouragement to rekindle their morale and give them the strength to continue.

At the conclusion of his trial Xenophon told the jury that if they believed he had abused the responsibility of his command then he was prepared to accept execution. Impressed by his sincerity and motives, the assembly, in one voice, demanded his acquittal and the jury readily complied. After the last of the trials was concluded, the soldiers voted to end the use of assemblies. Democracy and its responsibilities had become burdensome; they claimed they were tired of the endless discussions and wanted quick action by one commander. A list of candidates was drawn for the position, and Xenophon's name was first. Many soldiers had developed a deep affection and respect for him and often referred to him, in spite of his youth, as "father."

Though flattered, Xenophon refused the nomination. His experiences as a leader had confirmed Socrates' warning that democracy could be a dangerous form of government. People can be irrational at times and capable of turning on their leaders with a vengeance if things do not go as they expect. Xenophon suggested that the soldiers elect a Spartan as their supreme commander because they were close to Byzantium, a city under Spartan control. A Spartan at the

head of their army might result in a warmer welcome. So Cheirisophus, a Spartan and one of the original co-commanders, was elected.

Not accepting the position when it was offered to him may have
been a shrewd move on Xenophon's part. By rejecting supreme leadership of the army, he may have preserved, possibly even enhanced,
both his influence with and his authority over the soldiers. In addition to warning about the pitfalls of democracy, Socrates also had advised Xenophon that, when it comes time to select a leader, men
naturally look to the person who is most reluctant, not to the one who
is most aggressively vying for the position. It was certainly flattering for
Xenophon to think of himself at the head of the parade, triumphantly
leading the army to Byzantium and perhaps even back to Greece. But
declining the offer was probably a wise decision and may even have
later saved his life.

As its last act, the assembly voted to follow the inland route to Byzantium instead of taking to the sea. The sea route would be easier and
safer, but there was not enough money to transport the entire army
and Xenophon did not want to leave anyone behind. The inland route
was shorter; but the mercenaries would have to contend with hostile
tribes and risk encountering sizable elements of the Persian army.
Many of the soldiers favored the inland route because there were villages along the way that could be looted, and this was their last opportunity to return home with at least some money.

Before moving inland, the mercenaries stopped at a small Greek
coastal city called Heracleia. They were within 100 miles of Byzantium,
probably less than a week's march, but supplies were low. Ignoring their
earlier decision to forgo assemblies and rely on the decisions of one
commander, the soldiers called for an assembly. Over the objections of
Cheirisophus and Xenophon, they voted to send a delegation to extort
money and provisions from the inhabitants by threatening to loot and
burn their city.

City officials received the delegation and agreed to consider their demands. But once they had been escorted out of the city, the gates were
locked and guards were posted on the walls. Angered, the mercenaries
called for an assembly, and the mood turned hostile as they sought

to place blame. Some of the soldiers turned once again on Xenophon even though the Spartan, Cheirisophus, was their sole commander. Some soldiers shouted that it was shameful for Spartans to be influenced by an Athenian with so little military experience; others praised Xenophon's leadership. The arguments swung back and forth with no basis in reason or fact as the soldiers used the assembly as a forum in which to vent their frustration with their situation.

When the assembly concluded, the army separated into three antagonistic factions. Each group elected its own officers and chose its own route home. Xenophon was distraught, but there was little he could do. Cheirisophus, who had never been able to effectively command the army, became ill and died from the efforts of his doctor to cure him. The army now numbered only seven thousand, and by dividing, they dangerously weakened themselves further.

The first group set off for Byzantium by the direct overland route. The second contingent of mercenaries, under the command of Xenophon, followed by a day or two, while the third set out for Byzantium along the coastline.

Along the way, soldiers in the first group began to plunder the countryside, but they were no longer a formidable military force and suffered heavy casualties fighting the local tribes. Eventually they found themselves surrounded and for the first time had to ask for a truce just to bury their dead. Complicating an already bad situation, advance cavalry elements of the Persian army began to appear. As long as the mercenaries had remained along the coast, the Persians were content to leave them alone. But once they ventured inland, the satrap in command began to deploy his forces in a more aggressive manner.

When Xenophon's scouts told him what was happening ahead, he prevailed on the soldiers under his command to set aside their differences and rescue their fellow Greeks. To disguise their small numbers, Xenophon's soldiers spread out and burned everything in their path. The rising smoke gave the impression that their force was larger than it was, and the local tribes released their hold on the trapped Greeks.

The two groups were able to unite and then make their way north to the safety of Calpe, a small harbor along the coast. There they found the third contingent, and the soldiers voted to return to their old command structure of elected officers and continue on to Byzantium as one unit.

The Spartan governor at Byzantium had heard about the mercenaries heading toward his city and their exploits along the coast. When they arrived, he tried to bar them from entering, but they forced their way in. The governor fled to warships anchored offshore while his garrison barricaded itself in the citadel. The angry mercenaries were on the verge of burning and looting when Xenophon and some of the other officers brought them to order in a large plaza. Xenophon acknowledged that they had been dealt with unfairly, but he warned that burning Byzantium would outrage the Greek world. They would be declared renegades and find themselves at war not only with the Spartans but with all of Greece. Nor could Xenophon watch a Greek city pillaged and its people murdered by fellow Greeks.

Byzantium was spared, and Xenophon was able to reach an accommodation with the governor, allowing the mercenaries to camp outside the city walls for a few weeks. Soldiers were permitted to buy provisions in the marketplace, but they had to return to their camp each night. Meanwhile, the governor sent to Sparta for directions on what to do with them. The mercenaries were dangerous and reports had reached mainland Greece of how they had menaced cities along the Black Sea coast. The leaders of the mainland city-states worried that, finding few economic opportunities at home, the mercenaries would threaten some of the smaller mainland Greek cities if they returned. Something had to be done with them, but that something did not include bringing them home.

Weeks passed as the governor at Byzantium waited for word from Sparta. Conditions in the camp outside the city deteriorated quickly. Most of the soldiers were idle and destitute. Discipline broke down and eventually vanished. Few had money left to buy provisions, and many were dying from disease. Others were sold into slavery as punishment for infractions. Desertions increased as men simply disappeared into the countryside never to be heard from again. The weeks outside Byzantium marked Xenophon's lowest point as a leader.

Just as the army was on the verge of coming apart, a Thracian warlord sent word that he wanted to hire them. Thrace was a large mountainous area extending from northern Greece to Bulgaria and the western shores of the Black Sea. With the blessing of the Spartan governor, Xenophon led the army south along the western coast of the Sea of Marmara to the city of Perinthus. There the warlord, Seuthes, met the Greeks and explained why he needed them. His father had been king of Thrace some years before but had been driven out by his subjects and died in exile. Seuthes wanted the throne back and needed the mercenaries to supplement his small army. He promised to pay generously for their services and offered land along with wives and slaves as bonuses to any Greeks who wished to remain in Thrace as his vassals.

The mercenaries were skeptical. They had heard this kind of talk less than two years before from Cyrus. But Xenophon reminded them that winter was upon them and they had missed the period of calm weather and prevailing winds necessary to sail home. Nor did they have any money. It might be better to join Seuthes and wait until the spring of the following year to return to Greece. The assembly voted in favor of joining Seuthes, and Xenophon was sent to negotiate the final terms.

All that winter the mercenaries conquered towns and burned villages; they drove men from their homes and forced them to join Seuthes' army. But when it was time to collect their pay each month, the Thracian always had excuses for making only partial payments. By spring, the Greeks had suppressed all resistance and Seuthes was king, but he owed them a sizable amount of gold.

One day, two Spartan envoys arrived with an offer of employment for the mercenaries in a new war against Persia. The pay was low, and the soldiers vented their anger in assembly. Xenophon was accused of having led them on a worthless expedition in Thrace. They complained that after suffering through a cold winter they had nothing to show for their service but Xenophon had profited. Then one of the soldiers proposed that as settlement of their back pay Xenophon should be stoned to death.

Once again Xenophon was facing a death penalty and was compelled to defend his actions before those he led. He began his defense by lamenting that in life a man must resign himself to expect anything and can never count on anyone but himself. He reminded the soldiers that they had voted to follow Seuthes and that he had not forced the decision on them. He admitted he had misjudged Seuthes' character and mistakenly accepted him as a friend. But that friendship was over, and Xenophon had not taken one piece of gold that was owed the Greeks.

The soldiers believed Xenophon, and the proposal for his execution was withdrawn. They voted to accept the Spartan offer, and Seuthes was delighted at the prospect of being rid of them. He took Xenophon aside and urged him to remain in Thrace with a small contingent of his mercenaries, but Xenophon refused. As the mercenaries prepared to leave, they began looting Thracian towns and villages for provisions, taking slaves and any valuables they could find. Seuthes sent envoys to demand they stop, and the army sent Xenophon to demand their back pay.

As they negotiated, Seuthes continued to make excuses about why he could not pay. But Xenophon warned him that when the mercenaries finished their service with the Spartans they would return to Thrace and collect their debt from him. He reminded the new king that his people had not become his subjects willingly and might join with the mercenaries to overthrow him. It would be cheaper in the long run, Xenophon advised, to give the Greeks their back pay and settle the matter.

Seuthes tried again to bribe Xenophon, this time by offering his daughter in marriage and a city on the coast. Again Xenophon refused. Then Seuthes offered to settle his debt to the Greeks with a combination of slaves, cattle, and sheep. Xenophon insisted on gold. After nearly two days of negotiating, Seuthes finally paid what he owed, and Xenophon accompanied the wagons back to the camp.

As arrangements were undertaken to distribute the gold, arguing broke out over who should get what. Greed, desperation, and poverty begat chaos. The Spartan envoys tried to bring order to the mayhem by establishing paymasters, but they eventually gave up. Disheartened by what he was witnessing, a despondent Xenophon retired to his tent and let matters settle themselves.

The Spartans sent ships to transport the mercenaries across the Sea of Marmara to Asia Minor, and even though Xenophon was eager to return to Athens, his sense of responsibility and affection for those he led compelled him to remain with them a little longer. By the time they reached Asia Minor, Xenophon was destitute and had to sell his horse and weapons to book passage on a merchant ship home. As word spread that he was leaving, many of the mercenaries came to his tent and implored him to remain until they entered the service of their new Spartan commanders. Then, to show how much his leadership meant to them, they took up a collection and bought back his horse and armor for him.

Once more Xenophon was compelled by his sense of duty to put aside his personal feelings. He led the mercenaries from the coast of Asia Minor inland toward the city of Pergamus, where a large Spartan army was being assembled for the new war against Artaxerxes. At Pergamum he learned that he had been banished from Athens by the new democratic government and that his family estate had been confiscated. He also learned that Socrates had been executed (399 BC) for his conservative political views. With no home to return to, Xenophon had no choice but to enter the service of the Spartans, by whom he was appointed a general.

During the long months finding their way out of Persia and the winter campaign in Thrace, the mercenaries had forgotten what disciplined soldiering entailed. The Spartan commanders at Pergamum regarded them as little more than an undisciplined band of thugs, so they were assigned to new units under strict officers.

The days of electing officers and debating options were over. The mercenaries were required to drill incessantly and follow orders without question or suffer harsh punishment. At Pergamum they found themselves less than 100 miles from where they had begun with Cyrus two years earlier. They had come nearly full circle and were more impoverished than when they had started. Only six thousand were left.

The Spartan wars in Asia Minor ended inconclusively a few years later, and Artaxerxes became one of the longest-ruling kings in Persian history. Xenophon finally returned to Greece, where the Spartans found a place for him in the western Peloponnesus. He married a local woman and spent the remaining years of his life in modest circumstances—farming, raising two sons, and writing philosophy and history.

Among his surviving works are a recounting of the years when he led the mercenaries out of Persia (401–399 BC) and his views on leadership. When it came to leaders, Xenophon was impressed by two: first being young Cyrus, who had hired the Greeks, because he was "most like a king and deserving of an empire" and always kept his word to his subjects. In addition he was modest, thoughtful, and generous. As an example, Xenophon relates that when Cyrus sampled a good wine, he would send the remaining container to his friends with a simple message: "Cyrus has not for a long time come across a better wine than this; so he has sent some to you to finish with those whom you love best."

The second was Clearchus, the Spartan who led the mercenaries into Persia and perished at the hands of the king. Clearchus was a disciplined, tough, and effective leader—in Xenophon's words, "a man born to war." At the time of the expedition, he was in his fifties, with an intimidating presence and a harsh voice. Clearchus believed that maintaining discipline was the only way to command effectively and that a soldier ought to be more frightened of his own commander than of the enemy. Therefore punishment of both officers and enlisted men could be severe, and there were occasions, Xenophon tells us, when Clearchus regretted his impulsive and harsh actions.

Another thing about Clearchus that impressed Xenophon was that he would not ask anything of his men that he himself would not do. He would slog through mud to help his men push a cart, and he ate the same food as his soldiers and slept on the same hard ground. The money he received for his services he used to buy equipment for the army, and he never took anything for himself. In combat he was always at the forefront. But Clearchus had no family and soldiering was the only life he knew. His end came at Babylon, where he was beheaded. The Persian queen-mother won his body and head in a dice game and later had him buried in a simple grave lined with palm trees.

Xenophon's style was very different from the leaders he admired, such as Cyrus and Clearchus. He was neither a prince nor a general, and his effectiveness lay in his ability to build consensus and confidence among those he led and to keep morale high when times got tough. As a leader he saw an important correlation between the level of morale in his men—difficult conditions aside—and the way they thought. Xenophon believed that if morale were kept high and the soldiers remained focused on their mission, they would be more inclined to think about what they had to accomplish rather than dwell on what might happen to them if they failed.

All of Xenophon's experiences have valuable implications for understanding the essentials of leadership, but the episodes from his trials and the breakup of the mercenary army into factions are particularly valuable. They show us that leaders whose actions reflect the values of their organizations are likely to be accorded more leeway when they attempt to bring about significant change or impose discipline.

During the second phase of the journey Xenophon was constantly trying to restrain the mercenaries from looting, pillaging, and alienating the Greek coastal cities, whose support was crucial to their safe return. He was not always successful. Setbacks are a normal part of command; sometimes, no matter how hard a leader tries to influence the course of events, circumstances dictate the outcome. A good leader has to accommodate and make whatever changes are necessary in management style to remain focused on the objective yet keep the support of those who follow.

What is very clear from Xenophon's story is that ego was not what motivated him to step forward and lead the Greeks. He took command out of a sense of duty; leadership was a means to getting home, not an end. A number of characteristics were integral to his success as a leader: personal integrity (he never enriched himself at the expense of those he led); honesty (he told the soldiers exactly what they faced); loyalty (he remained with them when he could have left); and a genuine desire to help.

In spite of his aristocratic background and his belief that enlightened monarchy was the best form of government, Xenophon was motivated by a genuine desire to do what was best for those he led. But some of his most admirable characteristics caused him to be too trusting of those who were least deserving of his confidence and friendship, such as the warlord Seuthes. Response to a crisis entails more than just giving orders. An effective management structure is crucial to the implementation of a successful plan, and this is something Xenophon realized from the outset. His first move when he took command was to fill the void left by the murders of the senior Greek officers, because he understood that a leadership infrastructure is essential to a successful turnaround.

•   •   •

In the early 1990s, Dow Corning was facing a large number of lawsuits for alleged defects in its silicone breast implant products, and the company's future looked dim. Gary Andersen, then CEO, responded to the crisis by seeking out key people within the organization who could provide stability through a difficult time and plan for the future. Just as Xenophon filled the positions of the murdered senior officers to provide the infrastructure the army lacked, Andersen established a young leaders program. "We at the top knew where we wanted to go and some of the challenges we faced," he said. "But we had them help us develop the strategy to get there." The move raised morale and promoted a feeling among employees that they had a stake in the company and its success. It also built a cadre of new managers who, under Andersen's direction, stayed the course and led the company out of a difficult time.

A skillful blend of optimism and realism enables leaders like Xenophon and Andersen to establish a level of credibility in a time of crisis. That credibility in turn becomes the foundation from which their success emerges. William G. Crutchfield Jr., founder and CEO of Crutchfield Corp., the consumer electronics retailer, calls that process of credibility leading to success *alignment*. He believes that leaders must possess the right set of core values and be able to align those who work for them with those values. In that regard a leader needs to embody the values and philosophy his organization stands for.

When Southwest Airlines founder Herbert Kelleher and company president Colleen Barrett (who retired in 2008) faced serious challenges for market share from giant competitors such as Continental Airlines, they excelled at instilling a sense of mission in their employees. Kelleher inspired his people to view their mission in terms of winning or losing against the competition and as an opportunity to build an airline that would be unique in the industry, an airline where service mattered. Kelleher and Barrett's positioning of the struggle to have Southwest succeed in a hostile and competitive industry as an "us-versus-them fight" brings to mind the way Xenophon presented the dilemma facing the Greeks in Persia. In the end, Kelleher's ability to articulate his cause and inspire his people enabled him to extract longer workdays for less money from the unions, avoid the labor disputes crippling the rest of the industry, and run the business at a profit.

Joe Scarlett, the former CEO of Tennessee-based Tractor Supply Company, a large farm and ranch retailing outfit, and now its nonexecutive chairman of the board, is another leader who believes that his people need to understand the mission if the company is to succeed. "We have built a team where people understand the mission, the value structure, and the market so that we can empower them with the confidence and trust that they will make the right decisions," he once told *Chief Executive* magazine. Scarlett visits at least 150 stores a year and talks to literally thousands of his people. This way, he believes, employees are empowered with the confidence and responsibility to make the right decisions and move the company forward.

This approach can have the opposite effect of the one intended if a leader does not instill a sense of vision beyond that which simply benefits him or her. Former Lucent CEO Rich McGinn, for example, struggled to increase his company's revenues during a difficult period, and in a vain attempt to inspire his sales force pleaded, "If you guys don't do it for me this quarter, I'm out of a job." Well, the guys didn't do it, and McGinn was out of a job in 2000. Is it any wonder? The obvious defect in his style was an inability to create a sense of urgency beyond his own immediate need to keep his job. As one observer recounted to a CNET reporter, "McGinn would announce a decision, and all the executives would nod in agreement. But then those who didn't like the decision would just pocket it and not take action."

Like Xenophon, Judy George, former chair and CEO of national furniture retailer Domain Inc., recognizes the correlation between strength and limitations: "In the first few years as CEO I was blinded by the passion of my ideas and by being an entrepreneur. I thought I could conquer any odds single-handedly. I put together teams so similar to my own style of managing a business that critical technologies and operations didn't really get addressed. Luckily, I learned from my mistakes. I learned that my greatest strength—the ability to motivate, build a brand, and sell my ideas—was also my greatest weakness. So I flipped things around. I hired people who were *not* intrigued by my great salesmanship, who would *not* be enamored with my style or were even turned off by it. If I mesmerized them in the interview, they were not a candidate. Then I stopped playing the role of saleswoman, sat, and listened. I let people say no to me and I accepted it."

"Her business strategy was very compelling," said Mitt Romney during an interview with the *Boston Globe*. The former governor of Massachusetts and presidential contender, who cofounded Bain Capital, also commented on her flair: "Everything indicated she was a leader who could make things happen." Like Xenophon, Judy George clearly had a flair for inspiration, but sadly she ultimately did not have his ability to build a team of capable, trustworthy lieutenants to operate her business. After a disastrous sellout to another company, she and two others bought back the damaged company. She put an investor who did not have the ability to do the job in charge of day-to-day operations, and her troubles mounted. The housing collapse forced Judy George to make what had to have been one of the most difficult decisions of her life and file for bankruptcy.

Anne Mulcahy, chair and chief executive of Xerox, believes that great business leaders have a "paradoxical blend of personal humility and professional will." She points to former eBay CEO Meg Whitman as an example of a leader who fits this description. Like Xenophon, Whitman understands limitations. Even as her business grew at one of the fastest rates in history, the company she directed was characterized as "radically democratic."

Like the soldiers in Xenophon's army, eBay's rank and file often have a say in how things are done. In a 2005 interview, Whitman observed that management today is no longer simply command and control. It is a collaborative approach that requires an understanding of limits. Hers was a highly fragmented and participatory business model in which the collective intelligence and enthusiasm of customers determined and drove the daily actions of the employees.

This type of management requires a special breed of corporate leader, someone who keeps a light but firm and steady hand on the reins of power—much like Xenophon—not someone who jerks at them. Whitman listened and then formulated questions for her team of managers so they could come up with the right answers. She steered and influenced relationships instead of trying to control them, building consensus and trust through discussion, transparency, and accessibility. Like Xenophon, Whitman was dealing with an unusual situation. She had to create a business in which she would appeal to both buyers and sellers, none of whom had to show up for work each day.

A collaborative management style does not require a leader to relinquish control. Nobody who ever worked for Whitman mistakes her sensitivity and receptiveness for weakness. In fact, she is a strong believer that principles take precedence over profits in the marketplace. That is why she banned the sale of weapons on eBay. "Meg is a hybrid," one observer said, "and that's the model for the future." She is a combination of "decision manager" and "open-minded influencer."

More than once, Whitman changed the pricing structure for eBay's so-called storefronts and raised howls of protests among eBay retailers. She faced severe criticism when she bought PayPal, the online payment system. Critics and many shareholders contend that she grossly overpaid, but events quickly confirmed that Whitman understood her business better than the skeptics: PayPal is a huge success.

Like Xenophon, Whitman didn't always get it right. In 2005 she paid too much ($2.6 billion) for Skype, a global Internet communications company with expertise in Internet voice communications. At the time, Whitman was sure that "communications would be the heart of e-commerce and community." She was committed to the idea that combining the leaders in Internet voice communications with eBay would create an extraordinarily powerful environment for business on the net. The acquisition did not pan out, and the lesson is that leaders must not be afraid of occasionally doing things wrong. Management paralysis is a sure-fire formula for failure.

Meg Whitman made eBay the successful enterprise it is today. She stepped down voluntarily in 2008 and is positioning herself for a new career in politics as she prepares to run for governor of California.

●   ●   ●

Xenophon's story is replete with valuable lessons about leadership, and one of the most important is that retreat, done correctly, does not always mean failure. Through effective communication Xenophon was able to transform despair into hope and failure into success. His example proves that an effectively led and strongly motivated group, even when surrounded by an adversary many times its size and strength, can accomplish amazing things.

Xenophon and his small group of Greek mercenaries did not

conquer any empires or radically change the course of world history. What they did do was put a big crack in the Persian Empire by showing the world that it was not the monolith everyone feared it to be, and seventy years later, Alexander the Great drove a wedge into that crack and split the empire into pieces. How he did it is the subject of the next chapter.

5

ALEXANDER THE GREAT

The Price of Arrogance

"I set no limits to what a man of ability can accomplish."
—ALEXANDER THE GREAT

Few figures in history are as venerated as Alexander the Great, the young Macedonian king who believed that ability, focus, and determination in a leader would enable him to conquer the world. The Romans were the first to append the moniker "the Great" to his name, and history and popular perception have kept his legend intact for centuries.

In literature and film Alexander is portrayed as the young man who conquered the ancient world before he was thirty years old and brought Greek learning and culture to the "barbarians" of the East. American audiences have a special affinity for him as the personification of rebellious youth. His short life and glorious career stand as affirmation of the uniquely American perspective that youth, unfettered by the conventional restraints of its elders and free to pursue its own dreams, knows no limits to what it might accomplish. And certainly Alexander's career bears that out. Born into the ruling family of Macedonia in the fourth century BC, he was given his first command at age sixteen and his first taste of battle at eighteen. By age twenty he was king of Macedonia and by twenty-six master of the entire eastern half of the ancient world. But he was dead just a few days before his thirty-third birthday, and with his death everything quickly came to an end.

As a CEO, Alexander would have been effective, successful, and comfortable in today's multinational business world. He would have been sure to make headlines in business journals, dazzle Wall Street with his hostile takeovers, and instill a combination of admiration and fear in the hearts of his investors, managers, allies, and adversaries with his tolerance for risk and in-your-face management style.

There is no question that, whether in the corporate or in the political realm, Alexander would be the boss, setting the direction and the pace. Initially investors or voters would love him. But inevitably, overextending himself with too much debt and too many expensive acquisitions, driven by an ego that compelled him to conquer everything in sight, and engaging in an excessive lifestyle of partying hard and drinking too much, he would become an expensive embarrassment and have to be pushed out of the corporate jet with a multi-million-dollar parachute to soften his landing. Our corporate Alexander would probably enter rehab for a month or two and on discharge get hired by an equity fund to start all over again.

Alexander's leadership style reflected his conviction that a man of ability and determination could inspire and direct others to accomplish anything he set his mind to. For Alexander it was all about conquest—"acquisitions" in today's corporate world. He was willing to pay whatever price was necessary to achieve his goal of nothing short of conquering the world. In the early years of his career, Alexander was pragmatic enough to recognize that success does not come without cost: The path is difficult and requires great personal sacrifice. Alexander was able to connect with those he led because he exuded determination, projected confidence and ability, and generated excitement and passion for what he was doing.

As the CEO of his enterprise, Conquest Inc., he was intensely involved in operations at every level; he believed in leadership by example. While he drove his officers and soldiers—sometimes mercilessly—through jungles and deserts and over mountains, he also inspired them with his personal courage and rewarded them generously for their efforts. His willingness to remain at the forefront of every operation, never asking more from those he led than he himself was willing to give, is what enabled him to keep his army behind him for so long.

SELF-DISCIPLINE AND THE COST OF LOSING IT

At this point it might be interesting to digress for a moment and examine an old adage regarding power and success. The ugly stepsister of success is often a loss of discipline. The same drive to win that propels an Alexander to unimaginable heights of power and wealth can just as easily result in out-of-control behavior with disastrous consequences. Hard-driving corporate leader Linda Wachner is an example of what happens when lack of self-discipline and arrogance converge in a leader. Rising quickly from department store buyer to be CEO of clothing manufacturer Warnaco, she led a leveraged buyout of the company in 1986. Like Alexander she proved she could put together an empire but couldn't make it last.

Through acquisitions and strong marketing, Wachner quadrupled the company's size. Warnaco luxury brands such as Chaps by Ralph Lauren, Calvin Klein jeans, Speedo swimwear, and Olga bras were sold worldwide in more than 50,000 outlets. The lingerie-cum-jean company had $1.95 billion in revenue by 1998.

But Wachner's intense hunger for money, combined with an abrasive and abusive style of management by ego, resulted in her undoing. Her blunt manner began driving away key management talent. In her heyday, Wachner was often depicted by the media as a hard-charging, swearing boss, an Alexander in heels, who won praise from investors by cutting deals and building a stable of brand names that brought in billions in sales revenues. Customers and stockholders loved her, and competitors feared her. She became one of the highest-paid executives in her time, pocketing more than $158 million in salary, bonuses, dividends, and special stock deals between 1993 and 1999.

Wachner was so confident that the key to success was boosting revenue that she ignored the advice of subordinates and unloaded her line of prestigious brands on discount retail outlets, often at very low prices. The result was a cheapening of the brands in the eyes of consumers, a decline in sales, and a lawsuit filed against Warnaco by Calvin Klein for selling licensed products to unlicensed retailers.

Like Alexander, Wachner won the battle. The suit was settled, and Warnaco Group retained rights to Calvin Klein until 2044, but the situation had become so acrimonious that Klein himself considered Wachner his "personal enemy." Even though Wachner insisted to employees and investors alike that all was well in the corporate realm, real earnings vanished by the end of 2000 as debts from acquisitions and licensing agreements mounted.

No matter how aggressive Wachner became, she couldn't staunch the flow of red ink or stave off the inevitable. The company lost $334 million in 2000 and filed for Chapter 11 protection. Eventually it emerged from bankruptcy in February 2003. Wachner was dismissed but she wasn't finished. She owned 22 percent of the company stock and demanded $25 million in severance. Facing accusations from the SEC of defrauding investors, she compromised, giving up her demand for $25 million and accepting $3.5 million in new Warnaco stock and $200,000 in cash. Two years later, having adopted a low profile, Wachner and two other Warnaco executives agreed to pay $12.85 million to settle the SEC charges.

Wachner could be autocratically cold-blooded and driven when it came to achieving her goals, and the only people who seemed to survive in her corporate jungle were those who either played her game or became desensitized to her scathing criticism. Her ego, coupled with a seemingly insatiable appetite for power and Olympian-sized pay packages, placed a fatal strain on her company and brought her down. The CEO who managed others through intimidation ended her career dismissed for nonperformance and without the customary golden parachute. In summing up her tenure at Warnaco, one of her former subordinates commented to the *New York Times* that "She was the main reason it (the company) fell apart. There is some genius there, but she could not run a $2 billion corporation by herself."

ALEXANDER: THE GOOD, THE BAD, AND THE UGLY

An idealized or romantic view of Alexander's conquests often overshadows some of the negative aspects of his leadership style, especially in the latter stages of his career. Though idolized in the West, he is not always viewed in the East as an enlightened leader guiding the barbarians toward the light of Greek learning and culture. He is sometimes demonized as the Hellenic version of Genghis Khan, sweeping across central Asia in 330 BC and bringing suffering, enslavement, and death to millions. Some of the countries that Alexander subjugated nearly twenty-four hundred years ago—Iran, Afghanistan, and Pakistan—make up today's "terrorist belt," areas in which anti-Western sentiment is at its most virulent. There, Alexander, or Iskander as he is called, is often portrayed as an early example of Western cultural arrogance and exploitation.

The real story of Alexander is a tragic case of what happens when too much power is concentrated in hands not strong enough to use it constructively or wisely. Each successive conquest and the power and wealth that came with it bred arrogance in Alexander instead of caution, moderation, and reflection. He not only destroyed himself but carried with him an entire civilization that believed his success was confirmation of its cultural superiority over the rest of humanity. Ancient philosophers termed such arrogance *hubris*.

Alexander is a cautionary example for today's leaders. Success not only in the corporate world but in politics, entertainment, and professional sports can frequently end in personal tragedy and failure. It can undermine the best achievements of the most brilliant leaders if they lack self-control and the discipline to remain focused on what is important and keep their success in perspective. Relatively few entrepreneurs and CEOs today seem capable of managing lofty levels of success while maintaining a sane perspective. The dramatic downturn in the current economy is providing a humbling lesson for many at the top as they see their fortunes radically devalued and they become the focus of federal and state investigations for financial irregularities.

Leaders like Alexander often have an inclination to rely on their instincts and abilities instead of on objective information and analysis to conduct business. Seduced by their success and the constant praise of those who surround them, they come to believe that they alone know what is best. They stop seeking, listening, and learning. They become rigid, authoritative, and no longer receptive to feedback from subordinates in their own organizations or the markets. When this happens, a corporate version of hardening of the arteries sets in, the flow of fresh ideas to the top is slowed, and the end is usually close.

POWER CORRUPTS . . . BUT ABSOLUTE POWER CAN BE DELIGHTFUL—AT LEAST FOR A WHILE

Another interesting parallel to Alexander is Dennis Kozlowski, the former CEO of Tyco, who is serving 8 to 25 years in prison for taking millions of dollars in unauthorized bonuses, and other corporate crimes. At his peak, Kozlowski was acquiring companies for Tyco as fast as Alexander conquered countries—some two hundred from 1993 to 2001. The total cost of his conquests came to $64 billion. For a while his success was phenomenal, and Tyco's stock price soared. Kozlowski was featured on magazine covers, and the media dubbed him the world's most aggressive CEO. Flushed with success, he bragged to associates and competitors alike that he would go down in history as the world's greatest business leader.

But for Kozlowski, like Alexander, it was more about the game and personal glory than about the company and its investors. Success at the top transformed him from the disciplined manager he had once been into an autocratic, increasingly erratic emperor. Power and success corrupted him. The more he was paid for Tyco's soaring stock prices, the more he believed he was invincible and even above the law.

Kozlowski started diverting corporate funds to pay for an extravagant lifestyle including everything from elegant homes and large yachts to expensive art. He plundered Tyco to siphon off cash for himself, losing his moral compass and violating his fiduciary responsibility to shareholders. While living extravagantly at corporate expense, he set earnings goals for Tyco's operating divisions that forced managers to pinch pennies. To boost his immediate cash flow, he shrank companies he had acquired. He pushed the envelope too far when he hosted an extravagant birthday party for his wife on the Mediterranean island of Sardinia, complete with a statue of David urinating Stolichnaya vodka, and then expensed more than $1 million to the company. Eventually Kozlowski was indicted for fraud and then convicted of grand larceny, conspiracy, securities fraud, and eight counts of falsifying business records. In 2005, he was sentenced to New York state prison.

How did such a promising and seemingly effective leader go so wrong? For help with that answer we need to turn to Bill George, former CEO of Medtronic. George described how the CEO of a multibillion-dollar corporation can be easily corrupted by success and power. "The rules of the game are simple," he wrote. "Report quarterly earnings that rise and then treat yourself as a god for managing them. When anybody suggests that you made a blunder, bury the mistake in divestiture and a series of restructuring charges. Mastering the game can make you feel like a master of the universe, but one day you wake up and realize the game has mastered you. Ambition, ego, call it what you will—it is a demon I have struggled with throughout my entire career."

ALEXANDER: THE INNOCENT YEARS

Alexander's career began in the court of his father, Philip II, king of Macedonia. Philip had a number of wives over the years, and Alexander was his second son. An older half-brother would have been Philip's heir, but the boy suffered from seizures and this illness positioned Alexander to take the throne.

The Macedonians were a rustic people who occupied northern Greece, and the question of how Greek they were is a bone of contention even today. Many historians point out that the Macedonians and Greeks spoke different dialects and that the Macedonians clearly lacked the cultural and political sophistication of their Athenian, Corinthian, and Theban cousins to the south. In a relatively short period of time, however, Philip transformed them into the strongest military power on the mainland and managed to attach a thin veneer of Greek civilization to their primitive exterior. Regardless of what historians might believe, modern Greeks passionately claim Alexander as their national hero and were even willing to go to war a few years ago when one of the former Yugoslav republics took the name Macedonia and tried to claim Alexander as its indigenous hero. When the new republic received U.S. recognition as Macedonia, diplomatic relations between Greece and the United States cooled. Even Greek Americans and the Orthodox Church rallied to the cause, lobbying President George W. Bush not to recognize the former Yugoslav republic under its new name.

Philip believed in education and retained Aristotle, the Athenian philosopher and the most respected teacher in Greece, to tutor Alexander. Aristotle spent three years with Alexander, schooling him in everything from geography and science to philosophy and politics. Among the lessons he tried to impress upon his young pupil were several regarding leadership. The most important, a lesson that still resonates today, is that self-control is the foundation of success and a leader who conquers himself is to be respected more than one who conquers others. Aristotle also taught Alexander that each age produces a natural leader, one so superior in ability that he can be deemed "a god among men." That man, Aristotle believed, answers to no law but his own, a dangerous and potentially self-destructive concept concerning leadership. But Aristotle also taught Alexander that such a leader has a duty to ensure the "harmonious functioning of the society." If the day ever comes when he violates his sacred trust, he will be a tyrant, liable to assassination in the interests of preserving the good of the state.

While Aristotle was teaching young Alexander philosophy, Philip was teaching him to command an army in the field. By age sixteen, as previously mentioned, Alexander was commanding a cavalry unit. At home, his mother, the domineering and aggressive Olympias, was teaching him the ins and outs of court intrigues and political manipulation. Initiation into the sometimes brutal world of politics came in 336 BC with the murder of Philip.

Historians have long speculated that Alexander and his mother were directly involved in Philip's murder. The king was a notorious philanderer and had recently divorced Olympias to marry a younger woman. Olympias was not Macedonian but from the neighboring kingdom of Epirus. The new bride made Olympias fearful that an heir to the throne, pure Macedonian, might displace Alexander. When, at Philip's wedding, the young bride's uncle proposed a toast expressing the hope that the new marriage would produce a "legitimate" heir to the throne of Macedonia, Alexander reacted violently. An inebriated Philip, rising to intercede between the two quarreling men, tripped over his couch and fell to the floor. An angry Alexander straddled his drunken father and mockingly proclaimed to the guests that the king who had boasted he would one day cross the Hellespont to conquer Asia could not even cross over his own drinking couch.

Philip banished Alexander and his mother but recalled them a year later when some of his nobles reconciled father and son. Shortly after, Philip was murdered during a ceremony in full view of his subjects. Alexander, who had been serving as his father's bodyguard, killed the assassin before he could be interrogated and was immediately proclaimed king of Macedonia by the friends who surrounded him. There was a tense moment as Alexander, the crown upon his head and the blood of the assassin still fresh on his tunic, looked toward the leaders of the Macedonian army for their approval.

The two most powerful men in Macedonia next to Philip were his military commander, Parmenio, and his senior adviser for political affairs, Antipater. They confirmed Alexander as king, clearing the way for the young ruler and his mother to consolidate their power. Alexander ordered the executions of anyone he considered a rival. He spared his older half brother, but many members of the Macedonian aristocracy were put to death, including Philip's new wife and infant son, who were roasted alive over hot coals.

Antipater and Parmenio would play important roles in Alexander's career. Both men were in their sixties when Alexander became king, and either one could have changed the course of history by withholding his support. In the years to come, Antipater would rule Macedonia and Greece for Alexander as his regent, and Parmenio and his sons would accompany the young conqueror to Asia as commanders of his infantry and cavalry.

The plan to conquer the ancient world was not entirely Alexander's. It began with his father's idea to unite the continually feuding Greeks and lead them against a common enemy: Persia. As we saw in Chapter 4, Xenophon and his small group of Greek mercenaries had already shown the world how vulnerable Persia could be. To the Greeks the wealth of the Persian Empire was the stuff of dreams. They felt justified in taking whatever they could because they considered the Persians to be barbarians suited only for slavery or extermination. A war against Persia would benefit Philip, too, for it had long been his dream to build Macedonia into a regional power to be ruled by his heirs. But Philip does not appear to have thought much beyond that. It was Alexander who conceived of building an empire that encompassed the entire ancient world and stretched from the Pillars of Heracles (the Strait of Gibraltar) in the west to the Indus River in the east.

Like the Greeks, the Macedonians were a superstitious people, and Alexander's generals demanded that he consult the oracle at Delphi before they would follow him to Asia. The shrine was the most sacred religious site in Greece, and people from all parts of the ancient world came to have their questions about the future answered by the priestess of Apollo. When Alexander arrived, the oracle indicated that she was not inclined to make prophecies that day so Alexander would have to wait until she was ready. Impatient, Alexander seized the young girl by her hair and dragged her across the marble floor to the altar. Before he could even pose his question, she exclaimed, "You are invincible," and Alexander replied that was all the prophecy he needed.

Alexander's first move was to establish his authority over the city-states of Greece. At the battle of Chaeronea in 338 BC, Philip had defeated the Athenians and Thebans and loosely united all the city-states except Sparta, but when word of his murder spread, they revolted.

Thebes had been the first to revolt, so Alexander attacked the city, slaughtering all its defenders and selling the surviving women and children—some thirty thousand—into slavery. Anxious to avoid the same fate, Athens and other city-states, but not Sparta, returned to the fold.

Two problems had always prevented the Greeks from becoming the dominant power in the Mediterranean world, and Alexander exploited both to his own ends. One problem was poverty. The rocky soil of Greece was too poor to sustain its people. There was little arable land, and the small amount that existed was firmly in the hands of the aristocracy. Most of the population was impoverished and disgruntled. The second problem was that the Greeks continually fought each other. They spent most of the fifth century BC and a good portion of the fourth in a series of civil conflicts. By offering the wealth of Persia to alleviate their poverty and a common enemy to stop their quarreling, Alexander unified the Greeks.

All wars need a pretext, and Alexander found his in an offense against the Greeks that had occurred some 150 years earlier. In 490 BC, the Persians, under Darius I, invaded Greece but were foiled on the plains of Marathon by the Athenians. In 480 BC, under Xerxes, Darius's son and successor, the Persians tried a second time. Once again they were foiled, this time by the delaying actions of a small band of Spartans in a narrow pass called Thermopylae and later by the Athenian navy at Salamis.

During the second war, the Persians occupied Athens and looted the temple of Athena. For the Greeks, the looting of their temple was a sacrilege, and it became Alexander's rallying cry in his crusade for a war of revenge against the "barbarians" of the east. What Alexander sold to the Greeks was the idea of a war of national pride, one which would end their internal squabbling and at the same time be immensely profitable. He was elected *strategos*, or "supreme commander," of the Greeks and now had his chance to show the world that he could surpass his father. Philip had transformed Macedonia from a country of sheep-herders and farmers into the dominant military power on the Greek mainland, but Alexander intended to transform the entire ancient world into his personal empire. Persia would be only the beginning.

ALEXANDER IN ASIA

When Alexander landed on the northwestern shores of Asia Minor in 334 BC, he was twenty-two years old and leading a combined force of Greek and Macedonian soldiers numbering about thirty thousand. He had used all the gold in his treasury, as well as whatever he could squeeze out of the Greek city-states, to finance the expedition but was perilously close to bankruptcy. With barely enough to pay his soldiers' wages for the first month and with the loyalty and dependability of his Greek allies always suspect, he was anxious to begin looting Persian cities to generate income.

Alexander fought three battles in Persia that are often cited as examples of his tactical genius and leadership. Each of these battles also offers valuable insights into some of his shortcomings as a leader. The first battle took place in 334 BC on the banks of the river Granicus, a few miles east of the ruins of Troy. The Persian king, Darius III, was not present, but several of his satraps (governors) and a competent Greek mercenary general named Memnon commanded his army. At the center of the Persian battle line was a contingent of twenty thousand Greek mercenaries, many of whom had fled Greece when Alexander brought the city-states under his control. In fact, over the next few years, more Greeks would face Alexander as adversaries in Persia than were likely with him as allies in his army.

While Alexander was ultimately victorious at the Granicus, he was nearly killed because of his poor judgment and impetuous nature. Only the intervention of a close friend saved his life, and the skillful and steady hand of his senior commander, Parmenio, turned a tactical blunder into victory.

When Alexander and his army approached the river at the end of a long and tiring march, the Persians were already in place on the opposite bank. Parmenio did not like what he saw and advised Alexander to rest the army, formulate a plan, and wait until the next day to engage.

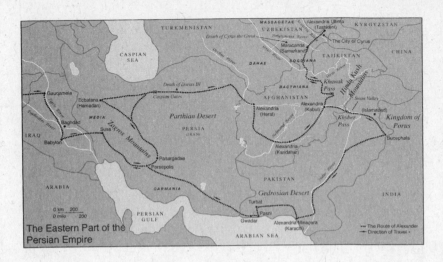

The Eastern Part of the Persian Empire

But an excited Alexander responded that he had come to Asia to fight, not rest. And with that he impulsively led a contingent of his cavalry, known as the "companions," into the cold and swiftly flowing river against the Persian positions. The charge was motivated by his enthusiasm to engage the enemy and his desire to duplicate a legendary feat of the Homeric hero Achilles.

No other work of literature had influenced Alexander more than Homer's *Iliad*, and throughout his life, he carried an annotated copy of the epic poem about the Trojan War with him as an inspiration and leadership manual. According to Homer, in one day of fighting at the Scamander River the hero Achilles slew so many Trojans that their corpses dammed the water's flow and the river-god rose up and begged him to cease the slaughter. This was one of Alexander's favorite stories. But this was not the Trojan War, and Alexander was not Achilles.

Everything was against Alexander that day: His men were tired and hungry after their long march. The river was deep, and the Persians, with their Greek mercenaries at the center, held the high ground. To launch an attack under those conditions, with no prior planning and without taking the elements into consideration, was simply poor leadership, and Alexander paid the price. The Macedonian cavalry suffered heavy casualties, and after several unsuccessful attempts to take the opposite bank, they were forced to withdraw to the taunts and jeers of the Persians and the Greek mercenaries.

Early the next morning Parmenio sent Alexander with the cavalry to cross farther upriver and come down behind the Persian camp while he coordinated the main infantry in a direct assault against the Persian line. The plan worked. Focused on repelling the infantry assault coming at them across the river, the Persians panicked when Alexander and his horsemen appeared unexpectedly behind their lines. During the fighting Alexander fell from his horse and was about to be killed by a Persian satrap when a friend, Cleitus the Black, intervened to save his life. This was one of those moments when the course of history could have been changed by the simplest of actions. If Alexander had died at the Granicus, his career would have ended, and he might have entered the pages of history as no more than an insignificant footnote.

But the battle ended in victory and the Persians fled. The mercenaries held their position and asked for quarter. But the proud young commander refused and personally led the assault against the Greeks who had inflicted the greatest casualties on his cavalry the day before. The young king buried the memory of that defeat with their bodies.

From the Granicus, Alexander moved his forces south along the Turkish coast into what today constitutes Syria and Lebanon. During the march, the army came to a particularly difficult stretch of coastline where steep cliffs and the sea came together, but an unusually low tide allowed the army to move over the seafloor instead of scaling the precipitous cliffs. As they marched over the exposed seafloor, Cleisthenes, a nephew of Aristotle and Alexander's hand-picked historian, proclaimed in jest that the sea had recognized Alexander as its new master and receded in obeisance. Alexander and his companions laughed at what was initially a joke but proved to be the beginning of something that later would grow to monstrous proportions and cost many Greeks and Macedonians their lives.

In the course of the next two years Alexander systematically conquered all of western Asia Minor and the coastal areas of present-day Syria and Lebanon. The second major battle with the Persians occurred in 332 BC, along the Syrian coast at Issus. Darius had personally taken control of a vastly reinforced Persian army after the defeat at the Granicus, and he chose his battlefield carefully. He caught Alexander by surprise, wedging his army into a narrow strip of land between the mountains and the sea.

Alexander was once again facing a numerically superior foe with a strong contingent of Greek mercenaries at its center. Again the opposing armies faced each other across a river, but this time Alexander exhibited the military forethought and judgment for which he has become famous. In a brilliant and daring tactical maneuver, he led his cavalry through a shallow part of the river and around the left flank of the Persians. At the same time Parmenio directed the Greek and Macedonian infantry directly against the center and the right flank of the Persian line.

When Darius saw Alexander and his cavalry bearing down on his collapsing left flank, he lost his nerve and fled. The Persian army, disheartened by the desertion of its commander, surrendered practically en masse. The Greek mercenaries, having heard what happened to their brothers at the Granicus, didn't even bother to discuss terms but escaped to the island of Cyprus.

When Alexander took the Persian camp, he found Darius's mother, wife, two daughters, young son, and a large portion of the royal treasury. He also discovered a Persian noblewoman, Barsine, who according to the ancient sources first introduced him to the pleasures of heterosexual love. Barsine was considerably older than Alexander, became a surrogate wife to him, and eventually bore him a son, Heracles. She remained with him until the day he died.

Among the captives, Alexander's men found Athenian and Spartan ambassadors, whose presence has long fueled speculation that Alexander may not have been the beloved national leader and hero that contemporary Greeks portray him to be. It was evident that the ambassadors were there negotiating with the Persian king behind Alexander's back.

That night as Alexander reclined in the warm, scented waters of the luxurious bathtub that Darius had left behind, he commented,

"At last I know what it is to be a king." After his bath, Alexander turned his attention to the family of Darius. He would keep them as hostages over the years, eventually becoming a son to Darius's mother, a lover to his wife, and a husband to his daughters.

After the victory at Issus, Alexander moved his army farther south to the city of Gaza, which in Persian means "king's treasure." There the defeated governor was tied by his ankles behind Alexander's chariot and dragged to his death around the walls of the city. Once more Alexander was playing out another fantasy from the Trojan War. Achilles had defeated Hector, the eldest son of King Priam, in combat and then dragged him around the walls of Troy in triumph. The difference was that Hector was already dead when Achilles dragged his body behind his chariot—the Persian satrap was alive!

From Gaza, Alexander moved into Egypt, where he was welcomed as a liberator from Persian oppression and proclaimed pharaoh. The Egyptians revered their kings as divinities, and Alexander got his first taste of what it is like to be worshipped. The Egyptian high priests proclaimed him the son of Zeus, king of the gods, and at the same time Alexander received letters from his mother in which she told him that Zeus had impregnated her on the night before her wedding to Philip.

Now it all came together for Alexander. His success as a conqueror, coupled with his mother's revelations of her divine encounter, caused the impressionable young king to become convinced he was descended from the Olympian gods. In celebration of his divinity, he laid out the boundaries of a magnificent new city to be built along the Mediterranean coast of Egypt and named Alexandria. That city eventually became a center of Hellenistic learning with the greatest library in the ancient world and a lighthouse at the entrance to its port that became one of the seven wonders of antiquity.

With Egypt secured on his southern flank, Alexander led his army east through the deserts of Syria to the banks of the Euphrates River, intent on conquering all of Persia. A distraught Darius sent letters to Alexander pleading for an end to hostilities and the safe return of his family. As an inducement he offered Alexander the entire western half of his empire, from Asia Minor to Babylon, a vast amount of treasure, and his eldest daughter in marriage.

Parmenio advised Alexander to accept the offer, scale down the scope of his conquests, and focus on building an empire for the Macedonians and Greeks. But Alexander rejected the advice and the king's offer. He remarked that perhaps an "old man" like Parmenio might find such an offer tempting, but why should Alexander, "a young man," accept what he already had? What Alexander wanted was all of it and even beyond in the unknown Indian kingdoms.

Alexander and Darius met a second time, in October of 331 BC at Gaugamela, a site along the eastern banks of the Tigris River and a few miles north of modern-day Baghdad. When Alexander arrived with his army on the western bank of the river a few days before the battle, what he saw unfolding worried him. The massive Persian army moving into position was much larger than the forces he had encountered at the Granicus and Issus. Organized waves of infantrymen from all regions of the Persian Empire were followed by thousands of cavalrymen and hundreds of chariots. They stretched across the horizon, and the reflections from their glistening shields and flashing spears seemed to light the sky above them. According to some exaggerated ancient sources, their numbers exceeded a million.

At the sight of the advancing Persian army, panic verging on mutiny spread among Alexander's soldiers. They complained openly to their officers that Alexander had led them into the center of the Persian Empire to be slaughtered for nothing more than his vanity. For the first time, the young hero questioned his own ability and doubted his chances for victory. That night he sacrificed to the gods to suppress his fear, and only in the early morning hours did he finally fall into a deep sleep. The next morning, Parmenio had to rouse him, and the usually brash and fearless young commander donned his heaviest protective armor. There was no going into battle this time without a helmet, as he had done at Issus and the Granicus.

Darius had the advantage once more. His army outnumbered Alexander's, and he had prepared the site carefully so he could utilize his "scythe-bearing" chariots to their most destructive effect. He intended to roll over the Macedonians and Greeks, but luck again favored Alexander. Parmenio once again directed the infantry against the Persian center while Alexander led the cavalry in a coordinated attack on the flanks. Alexander and his cavalry penetrated an opening in the Persian battle line, and Darius panicked. He fled the battlefield before the outcome had been decided and headed east toward the safety of his mountain fortress at Ecbatana (the modern Iranian city of Hamadan). But this time the Persian army did not give up and continued to fight under a number of competent commanders. Alexander set out after Darius with a small detachment of cavalry but broke off the pursuit when Parmenio called him back to relieve the pressure on the Macedonian infantry.

After his victory at Gaugamela, Alexander moved to Babylon, the commercial center of the Persian Empire. The inhabitants of Babylon had a reputation for living life on the edge, and they entertained Alexander and his army in the lascivious style for which they were infamous.

Traditionally Greeks and Macedonians began the serious drinking after the meal, at what was called the *symposium*. It was a time of conversation among male guests and their host about philosophy and politics. The ancient sources tell us that in his youth this was Alexander's favorite part of any banquet, not because of the wine but for the conversation. At the beginning of his career, Alexander was a moderate drinker, but at Babylon, he developed a taste for "unmixed" wine and began a steady descent into the heavy drinking that would contribute to his demise. The ancient Greeks diluted their wine with water to reduce its potency and considered the drinking of unmixed wine to be a barbarian practice. He began to sponsor contests in which the winners were awarded gold in return for how much wine they could consume. One Macedonian officer drank three gallons in one sitting, accepted his prize, and dropped dead.

WHAT A TRILLION-DOLLAR WAR CHEST
WILL BUY: MORE EGO

After a month at Babylon, Alexander moved his army east into the Zagros Mountains of Iran. He was heading for Persepolis, the repository of the empire's wealth, and for the moment, Alexander gave it priority over Darius. Less than 100 miles from the city, he fell into a devastating ambush. Anxious to secure the treasury at Persepolis, Alexander had divided his forces, sending the main column under Parmenio along a relatively secure but longer route to the south while he took a detachment of faster-moving light infantry and cavalry units into the mountains searching for a shorter route.

Entering a deep gorge known as the "Persian Gates," Alexander and his force were ambushed by elements of the king's army under the command of the satrap of Persepolis. The Greeks and Macedonians took heavy casualties as they tried to extricate themselves, and their wounded and dead had to be left behind—something many of Alexander's soldiers never forgave him for. The Persian resistance was overcome only after Alexander led an elite and highly mobile force over the mountains to come down behind the satrap's army.

Persepolis surrendered without a fight in January of 330 BC. The inhabitants opened their gates to welcome Alexander as a hero, and he found more gold and silver in its treasury than he had ever imagined: 120,000 talents, bars or bricks of gold or silver, each one weighing close to 60 pounds. Persepolis contained the largest depository of gold and silver anywhere in the ancient world. This was a staggering amount of treasure, and although there is no reference indicating exactly how much was gold and how much silver, the value of Alexander's take could well have exceeded a trillion dollars today.

From the outset, it was clear that the treasure belonged to Alexander and would not be shared. The building was secured by an elite element of his guards and placed off-limits to the rest of the army. As the young conqueror stood on the terraces of the magnificent palaces of the Persian kings, he was now the richest and most powerful man in the world—at the age of twenty-six. The wealth of Persepolis, however, changed him and not for the better. He was no longer dependent on Macedonia or the Greek city-states to finance his campaigns, and was free to reformulate his objectives in terms of what he wanted, not what they expected. Wealth and success allowed him to open a new chapter in his life, one that would be defined by his desire to rule the world and become a living god.

Alexander did two things at Persepolis that scholars have long tried to understand. After taking a city that willingly surrendered, he turned his soldiers loose on its defenseless population. For a night and a day the Greeks and Macedonians raped, looted, and murdered. There was no forewarning to the people, and Alexander justified the action by telling his soldiers that no city was more hateful to them than Persepolis. In this city, he claimed, orders to make "godless war" on Greece had been issued the previous century by Darius and his son Xerxes. Nothing could have been further from the truth. Most Greeks and Macedonians had never even heard of Persepolis because it was so remote and overshadowed by Babylon. It was a pretext that revealed just how thin was the veneer of Greek civilization.

Parmenio advised against looting and burning the city, but Alexander refused to listen. So the people suffered because they were a symbol, not because of anything they had done. According to the ancient sources, what had been one of the richest and most beautiful cities now "exceeded all others in misery."

As if the slaughter were not enough, four months later, on the eve of his departure, Alexander committed another outrage. During a banquet at which he and his companions were drinking heavily, an Athenian harlot, Thais, challenged Alexander to let her set fire to the palaces of the Persian kings so that it might be recorded that the women of Greece inflicted more punishment on barbarians than did the men.

Alexander agreed and led the procession of drunks and harlots into the magnificent palace of Xerxes, where they set the first of the many fires that would consume the city. Seeing the fires, Alexander's soldiers ran to assist in putting them out. When they saw it was their king who was burning the palace, they joined him in burning the rest of the city, thinking that his actions signified the end of the war and his decision to return home. Nearly two days later, when Alexander awoke from his drunken stupor and saw the destruction, he is said to have regretted what he had done.

After the burning of Persepolis, most of the Greeks and Macedonians expected to go home. But Alexander had no intention of returning to Macedonia and Greece for the foreseeable future. He had decided to capture Darius and then conquer the lands that lay beyond the great Salt Desert of Iran: present-day Afghanistan, Uzbekistan, and the kingdoms of India. Alexander wanted to find the great ocean that Aristotle had told him lay at the very edge of the earth, and now he had the money and power to do it.

Parmenio led the main part of the army north to the fortress city of Ecbatana, carrying the treasure from Persepolis. Twenty thousand mules were needed to pull the wagons and three thousand camels to transport the entire treasure. Alexander ordered Parmenio to establish a large base at Ecbatana from which to support him and his troops as they advanced into the far eastern reaches of the Persian Empire.

Darius had fled Ecbatana and was moving east across the desert toward his provinces in Afghanistan. With a highly mobile detachment of infantry and cavalry, Alexander pursued him relentlessly. When he was within a day of reaching the rear elements of the Persian column, Alexander left his infantry behind and pressed ahead with the best of his cavalry. He caught the Persians just before dawn and charged into their midst with as few as sixty horsemen following him. The Persians were so terrified of Alexander that rather than stand and fight, most of them—including four thousand Greek mercenaries—surrendered or fled into the surrounding mountains. Had the Persian cavalry, or even just the Greek mercenaries, turned on Alexander and his small force, the history of the ancient world would have been written differently.

When Alexander found Darius, he had been chained to a wagon and murdered by his senior officers. Greek ambassadors among the prisoners confirmed again that the Greeks continued to negotiate with the Persian king behind Alexander's back right up to the end. When Alexander's infantry caught up to him several days later and learned Darius was dead, they demanded to be paid and sent home. Reluctantly Alexander complied. New recruits from Greece and Macedonia joined him as mercenaries for a daily rate and a share of future spoils. Significant numbers of Persians joined his army as well, looking for opportunities in the administration of a new empire. Many—including Darius's brother—had been officers and administrators in the Persian Empire, and their inclusion was a clear sign that Alexander was recruiting those who could help him rule the new world he was intent on building.

The restructuring of the army produced a new generation of officers—Greek, Macedonian, Persian—who were tied to Alexander largely by self-interest. A small cadre, mostly Alexander's childhood friends, remained because they were devoted to him, but promotions were now made on the basis of personal loyalty to Alexander and bravery in battle, not on family standing and political connections in Macedonia and Greece as had been the case previously.

Alexander's ego, his success, and his enormous wealth compelled those around him to tell him what they thought he wanted to hear, not what he needed to know in order to rule his empire and maintain a proper perspective on himself. In return, Alexander was very generous, especially when it came to dispensing other people's money. Obedience was rewarded handsomely, not only with money but with grants of land and governorships in the new empire.

Alexander caught and executed the men who had murdered Darius. Then he crossed the Hindu Kush Mountains into Uzbekistan and moved through the Khyber Pass to the Indus River. He traveled with an ever-growing entourage of bodyguards, cooks, slaves, and entertainers, as well as the harem, eunuchs, and catamites taken from Darius. He took to wearing the royal robes and tiara of the Persian kings and slept each night in an elaborate tent. Most of all, Alexander enjoyed being courted by his subjects and entertained in what the Greeks termed the "barbarian manner."

THE LEADER UNHINGED:
EGO, THE GREAT DESTROYER

The Persians who surrounded Alexander worshipped him as a god and took to prostrating themselves in his presence, lowering their chins to the floor. This Eastern ritual, known as *proskynesis*, was the customary way in which they acknowledged their king as a living god. To the Greeks and Macedonians, it was a disgusting, barbarian gesture of subservience, and a disgruntled faction of officers began to form in reaction to it.

Most of Alexander's officers came from a conservative Macedonian background, and they disapproved of their leader's new lifestyle and the presence of Persians in his inner circle. They believed it was one thing to obey a monarch who ruled by their consent, but something else to worship him as a god. Yet for the time being they contained their discontent to their own inner circle.

As Alexander moved east, he seemed to be conquering only for the sake of conquest. The interplay of the personal demons that drove him forward and his material success transformed him. He slaughtered anyone who stood in his way and conducted purges among those around him who disagreed with him or refused to acknowledge his divinity. Both Macedonians and Greeks were arrested for treason—defined as disloyalty to Alexander—and tortured to extract customized confessions. Among the condemned were some of Alexander's boyhood friends, including Philotas, Parmenio's oldest son.

As the scope of the purges widened, it reached the top echelons of command. Alexander sent an assassin by racing camel more than 1,000 miles across the vast Iranian desert to murder Parmenio, then continued his search for disloyalty, extending the purges even into the rank and file. Soldiers were encouraged to write home to their families, and Alexander offered to send their letters by special couriers. But once the letters were submitted, censors read them and anyone who had written anything critical was arrested and tried for treason.

The army continued through Afghanistan and crossed the Oxus River (the modern Amu Darya, which forms the current boundary between Afghanistan, Uzbekistan, and Tajikistan). There Alexander was surprised to find a prosperous city inhabited by a Greek-speaking people called the Branchidae. They were descendants of Greeks who had migrated from the western coast of Asia Minor in the century before, and they welcomed Alexander and his soldiers as countrymen.

In the course of his stay among the Branchidae, Alexander discovered from one of his Greek officers that the ancestors of these people had assisted the Persians in looting a shrine sacred to the god Apollo on the coast of Asia Minor nearly a hundred and fifty years before. There had been so much outrage in the Greek world at the time that Xerxes resettled the Branchidae in the most remote outpost of his empire to protect them. In retaliation for the heresy of their ancestors, Alexander massacred the Branchidae. Like his earlier actions at Thebes, Gaza, and Persepolis, this was another indication of how impulsive and violent he could be at the slightest pretext.

As the army moved north onto the steppes of central Asia, Alexander's soldiers encountered considerable resistance—not traditional battles but rather something similar to what coalition forces encounter today in Iraq and Afghanistan. It took Alexander nearly two years to pacify the area, and he employed some ruthless yet highly effective tactics, methods that today would probably bring him before an international tribunal on charges of genocide and waging war against humanity.

Alexander's first controversial tactic was to deny the insurgents a base of supply by burning villages and towns. As a result, when winter set in, hundreds of thousands starved or died from exposure. When that policy did not prove effective enough to break the insurgency, Alexander ordered the execution of every male over the age of ten, to deny the insurgents recruits. This tactic coupled with a policy of cash rewards for information about resistance leaders finally broke the back of the insurgency. Alexander was able to purchase the head of the resistance leader, Spitamenes, who is revered in Uzbekistan as the country's first national hero.

The farther east Alexander pushed, the more fantasy replaced reason and the harder he drove his army. His mind became filled with romantic notions of the legendary accomplishments of superhuman heroes like Heracles and gods like Dionysus. He promoted cultural integration between his soldiers and the local people, and he envisioned himself fathering a new race of men who would one day rule the world. To set the example, Alexander married a local Bactrian princess, Roxanne. Later, when he returned to Babylon, he married Darius's eldest daughter, followed by a third marriage, to the granddaughter of the Persian king Artaxerxes III.

Many of the senior Greek and Macedonian officers now openly criticized Alexander's autocratic style and his attraction to Persian culture. They held to their traditional values, such as the right of every citizen to be heard in assembly, the right to a trial before one's peers if accused of a crime, and the belief that a king rules by the consent of those around him, not because he thinks himself to be a god. They watched Alexander living in a state of self-indulgent Oriental debauchery, and many of them began to hate him because of it.

Just before the army moved into India, Alexander hosted another of his infamous symposiums, which by then were exclusively opportunities for drinking, not for discussions of philosophy and politics. As entertainment, he had commissioned his poets to mock some Macedonian officers who had recently been killed in combat. The implication of the entertainment was that they had been cowards and caused their own deaths. When the poets finished, they began to praise Alexander, telling the audience that he had exceeded not only the accomplishments of Philip his father but even those of the legendary hero Heracles. They suggested that all were in the presence of a living god and that not just Persians but Greeks and Macedonians as well should worship him.

This was too much for some of the Macedonians present. Cleitus the Black, who had saved Alexander's life at the battle of the Granicus, shouted back that the king owed his success to Philip, his true father, and to luck. Both men had been drinking heavily, and the argument got out of hand. When Cleitus called Alexander a tyrant, the king drove a spear through him.

After Cleitus's death, Alexander lapsed into a severe depression.

For three days and nights, he refused to eat or drink and lay in his bed sobbing. Those around him feared he might even take his own life and began a suicide watch. Finally, the court philosophers convinced Alexander that the killing was excused because he was a god and a god by definition could do no wrong. He accepted the explanation, and the army was convened to exonerate him by acclamation.

Eventually Alexander made his way out of Afghanistan, through the Khyber Pass, and into what is today Pakistan. Along the route his army burned and looted while Alexander continued his policy of cultural integration by founding new cities of brick and mud, which he populated with soldiers who were too sick to go on, malcontents, and any he suspected of disloyalty. Against their will, Greeks and Macedonians were forced to remain behind as masters over the local people, with orders to stay until Alexander relieved them.

The army crossed the Indus River to fight the Indian king Porus. The battle occurred during a violent storm, and lightning strikes killed almost as many men as the combat. After defeating Porus, Alexander and his army continued east through snake- and mosquito-infested jungles until they came to the banks of what the ancient sources called the Hyphasis, probably the Beas River, which flows through eastern Pakistan. The army refused to go any farther. Many of the soldiers were sick from malaria or worn out from the incessant monsoon rains that had inundated them day and night for two months. All they could imagine before them were more of Alexander's enemies to fight, more jungles to hack through, and a river to cross that was even wider and more treacherous than the Hyphasis: the crocodile-infested Ganges.

The soldiers no longer shared Alexander's vision of finding the ends of the earth, nor did they believe in his invincibility. They could see no end to his wars and no reason to continue for the sake of his glory. They did not want to populate his cities and live with his barbarians. All they wanted was an end to their misery other than a shallow, nameless grave in some jungle. They wanted to go home.

Alexander tried to divert their attention from their misery and discontent by turning them loose to rape and pillage the countryside around the river for a few days. But the return on that tactic was short-lived. Then he tried bribing them with gifts and promises of generous pensions, but money no longer mattered. Alexander tried motivation by telling them they were on the verge of accomplishing something great. But when he ordered them to move forward with him and conquer the kingdoms of India, they refused. When he ordered them to follow him and find the ocean that marked the very boundaries of the earth, they shouted back that he should go and look for it with his father, Zeus. When Alexander threatened to go on without them, alone if need be, they laughed at him.

Then Coenus, one of Alexander's most loyal senior commanders and a childhood friend, came forward to speak on behalf of the army. He begged Alexander to put an end to his conquests and turn back for home. Alexander refused and replied that he set no limits to what he could accomplish. Coenus told him that what made a great leader was not continual conquest but an understanding and acceptance of limits. This was a dangerous thing for anyone to say to Alexander. Angry, the "Lord of Asia" retired to his tent and sulked for three days and nights while hundreds of soldiers surrounded his tent, wailing incessantly for him to lead them home.

EMPIRES NEED TO BE MANAGED, NOT JUST EXPANDED

The very characteristics that make leaders successful and effective— particularly intense ambition and boundless energy—can be the very qualities that lead to their ruin. Some people don't know when to stop or leave well enough alone. Look at Time Warner as an example. According to a theory developed in the late 1980s and early 1990s, the communications industry would consolidate in a pattern similar to what happened in the auto industry and other sectors of manufacturing. Before 1920, there had been over three hundred auto manufacturers in the United States. Just a few years later, after consolidation kicked in, only a handful were left.

A strong believer in this theory of industrywide consolidation was Steve Ross, who started out in the funeral business, then branched out into parking lots, and finally amassed an empire consisting of

Warner Bros. and some publishing companies. Ross eventually got rid of the parking lots and funeral homes and focused on making one of the biggest acquisitions of the era happen: buying Time Inc.

Business bluebloods expressed astonishment that Ross even considered making a play for a venerable institution like Time. But Ross knew how to charm, and eventually Time management bought into the idea of media synergies and accepted his offer. The merger occurred in 1990, and Ross took home a record $78.2 million pay package. Time Warner, the new entity, was hailed as the prototype of the modern communications conglomerate and at first seemed to have it all—movie studios, broadcasting networks, cable television, books, and, of course, magazines.

Ross succumbed to cancer at the end of 1992. His successor, Gerald Levin, became the CEO of Time Warner in January 1993, and he continued Ross's Alexander-type conquests, including Turner Broadcasting, home of CNN in 1996. Beguiled by the stock market boom in high technology, Levin in 1999 was convinced by Steve Case, the chairman and CEO of AOL, a successful Internet access company, that a merger was the way to guarantee that Time Warner would dominate the new web age. Time Warner stock rose as investors were carried away by the euphoria of the merger, ignoring the enormous amount of debt burdening the company's balance sheets.

Like Alexander and so many other leaders, Levin was better at expanding his empire than at managing it. It soon became apparent that the hype about synergies between the disparate parts of Time Warner was only that—hype. The various entities and subentities rarely cooperated, and in fact there was more hostility than camaraderie. Instead of being a spearhead of the new media age, Time Warner quickly became a lumbering, inefficient giant. After Levin was ousted, his successor, Richard Parsons, spent most of his time reducing Levin's debt and dismantling the ramshackle empire.

Other interesting examples of the inability to set limits are Fannie Mae and Freddie Mac, known as government-sponsored enterprises (GSEs), which were at the center of the 2008–2009 economic collapse. Fannie Mae was created during the Great Depression as a government agency to help provide liquidity to the housing market by buying mortgages from the banking industry. In the 1960s, Fannie was semiprivatized when shares were sold to the public. This arrangement gave Fannie a direct line of credit to the U.S. Treasury and implicit backing for its bonds by the federal government. The president of the United States appointed several directors, while the majority were elected by shareholders. Freddie Mac was launched in 1970 with essentially the same mission as Fannie.

At first, the two entities held a small portion of home mortgages. Their task was to buy mortgages from banks, package them together, and sell the packages as bonds to institutional investors such as pension funds and insurance companies. But instead of providing helpful liquidity to the housing industry, Fannie and Freddie soon were elbowing out the private sector and in effect came to dominate the mortgage industry.

Today over half of the mortgages in the United States are either owned by Fannie and Freddie or guaranteed by them. The two GSEs soon contracted a bad bout of empire building in the style of Alexander. They expanded and practically became money machines, borrowing at almost Treasury-like rates, buying mortgages with high yields, and then selling them at a profit. But then they became really greedy and decided not to sell all the mortgages but to keep some for themselves. The spread between what they paid for the money and what they effectively lent it out for was very lucrative.

Fannie and Freddie kept hundreds of billions of these instruments on their own balance sheets, and because of Uncle Sam's implicit guarantee for their bonds, the two could borrow amounts that no private company would dare to risk. Their debt-to-equity ratios would have been untenable without the confidence that Washington and the U.S. Treasury would back their bonds 100 percent if they got into financial trouble.

Why did Congress let these two corporations reach such a monstrous size and engage in accounting procedures that would have been flat-out illegal in the private sector? Because the people running them understood the political environment in Washington and how to work it to their advantage. Fannie and Freddie became the two most effective lobbies in the nation's capital and even formed charities that employed relatives and friends of influential members of Congress. The Cato Institute, a prestigious libertarian think tank in Washington, received a $100,000 grant from a Fannie Mae foundation, but realizing the money was intended to gain their political support, the institute directors wisely sent it back.

So influential did these two GSEs become that they even informed local banks when a politician was hostile toward them. Often very influential in their communities, the local banks could galvanize public support for or against a member of Congress. Washington politicos and their staffers quickly learned that it was in their best interests to cooperate with Fannie and Freddie by sponsoring and voting for favorable legislation. When the Republicans took over Congress in 1994, Fannie and Freddie spread the largesse around to both parties. Legislators on both sides of the aisle reaped rewards such as campaign contributions when they needed them and lucrative jobs for their staffers after they left the Hill that made private-sector positions pale in comparison. Pay packages at the two companies were obscenely high.

Inevitably the day of reckoning arrived. Fannie Mae executives had played games for years with the numbers to ensure their targets were met, thereby generating millions of dollars in bonuses for themselves. Enron executives went to jail for similar behavior, but all Fannie's and Freddie's top people got were mild congressional and government reprimands.

In 2008, the financial markets finally realized how precarious these GSEs were, and their stock collapsed. But instead of reforming Fannie and Freddie, the government made an implicit guarantee explicit, and made it clear that no real reforms would take place. The need to calm financial markets may have necessitated overt guarantees, but there was no reason why the Bush administration could not have put radical reform on the table as a condition for the help.

One suggested reform would be to recapitalize Fannie and Freddie, break them up into ten or twelve companies that have no ties to the government, and force them to compete with each other in the free market. But that will never happen. Instead, the status quo is likely to prevail. Fannie and Freddie will once again be spun off from the government after superficial reforms and probably collapse again just as Alexander's empire did after he died. The only question is when and at what cost to taxpayers.

CELEBRATING YOUR OWN SUCCESS

Alexander finally emerged from his seclusion and ordered sacrifices to determine the will of the gods. He examined the entrails of the victims and announced that the gods indicated the army should return home. The soldiers were jubilant, and for the first time in his career Alexander the Great was forced to submit to a will stronger than his own.

To mark the limits of his conquest, and to assuage his bruised ego, Alexander ordered his engineers to erect massive statues of the Olympian gods along the riverbank. The statues were followed by the construction of oversized barracks and stables to give the impression to the Indian kings across the river that Alexander and his soldiers were a race of giants.

•   •   •

Excessive celebration of personal success and self-proclaimed genius did not begin and end with Alexander the Great. Remember Dennis Kozlowski's over-the-top party for his wife in Sardinia? Consider the similar behavior of Saul Steinberg, who began building an empire in the late 1960s and became a feared figure in American board rooms. Steinberg began his career by undercutting the price IBM charged for leasing its mainframes to customers. His company—then called Leasco—would buy mainframes outright and then lease them at rates lower than IBM charged.

IBM traditionally kept its retail prices very high, but Steinberg knew that IBM could wreck his company, or any company that depended on IBM products, simply by dropping prices, driving the rival out of business, and then raising prices again. To protect against that scenario, Steinberg went on an acquisition spree, following the old stock portfolio adage that diversification offers the best protection against market fluctuations. He used Leasco stock to trap his prey. His big catch was Reliance Insurance, then a major property and casualty entity. Insurance companies such as Reliance were coveted as virtual piggy banks. Those companies took in premiums and kept a large amount of money set aside in reserves to cover future losses. "Conglomerators" like Steinberg saw that if they were clever enough they could use much of that money for their own ends before it had to be paid out in claims to policyholders.

Steinberg helped enrich himself by making forays against Disney, the *New York Times,* and other companies. In most cases, fearful incumbent executives bought the stock back at a premium to get him to go away. Before he was thirty, Steinberg made an unsuccessful bid for a real blue-blood commercial bank, Chemical (which subsequently, after a number of its own acquisitions, transformed itself into JPMorgan Chase).

By the late 1980s, Steinberg was one of the richest men in America, and to mark his fiftieth birthday, his wife threw him a party that allegedly cost over a million dollars. Steinberg collected the art of the "old masters," and among the highlights of the party were tableaus of paintings he owned performed by live models. When his daughter married into the powerful and prestigious Tisch family (whose corporate flagship is Loews Corp), the event was held at the Metropolitan Museum of Art and had the air of a royal wedding.

But storm clouds were gathering over Steinberg and his empire. Reliance was being run into the ground in the 1990s in an effort to generate cash: Policies were being sold at very low prices. The board at Reliance was dominated by Steinberg and voted him $48 million in salary and bonuses along with dividends of another $100 million based on his 31 percent share of the company's stock. When the inevitable downturn came and the impact of the losses was felt, Steinberg's empire came apart. In 2001 Reliance went into bankruptcy, and before the ordeal was over Steinberg suffered a debilitating stroke.

ALEXANDER'S LONG MARCH HOME

When the giant statues, stables, and barracks had been completed and his ego satisfied, Alexander led the army back to the shores of the Indus River, where they built a fleet of barges and sailed south to what is today the port city of Karachi. There, Alexander divided his army, sending a small group to Babylon by sea, and a second, larger group overland by way of Kandahar, in southern Afghanistan. Alexander took command of the third and largest group, some fifty thousand soldiers, along with their women, children, and slaves, and led them due west into one of the most desolate and inhospitable places on earth: the scorching and arid Gedrosian Desert. The desert lies along the shores of the Indian Ocean between southwestern Pakistan and Iran. It is known today as Baluchistan, a troubled tribal area where the trade in slaves, drugs, and weapons continues to prevent its development into anything even approaching a civilized corner of the world.

Alexander could have chosen an easier route, but overconfidence and vindictiveness drove him to cross Gedrosia. The ancient sources offer no better explanations than that he was determined to do what legend said had been done before only by the god Dionysus, and to punish those in the army who had defied his will. It took two months to cross the desert. The relentless heat, dehydration, starvation, and disease took nearly half the force, and then one night a raging flash flood swept through the camp carrying nearly all the women, children, and slaves to their deaths.

The crossing of Gedrosia was Alexander's greatest defeat. He lost more soldiers than in any battles with the Persian or Indian kings. As rumors surfaced that he had perished in the desert, revolts broke out all over his empire. Those who had been forced to colonize his cities in Afghanistan, Uzbekistan, and India returned home. One of his most trusted friends looted the treasury at Ecbatana and fled to Athens. Alexander's mother, Olympias, and his regent, Antipater, began fighting over control of Greece and Macedonia.

When Alexander finally emerged from the desert, he found his empire in turmoil. To reestablish his authority, he punished those he deemed corrupt and disloyal. Satraps and officers from all over the eastern part of the empire were summoned to Persepolis and were executed in large numbers in the fields outside the city. Even Alexander's eunuch served as a prosecutor, designating for torture and death any who had incurred his displeasure.

From Persepolis Alexander and his army moved to Ecbatana, where Alexander's lover and closest friend, Hephaestion, died of gluttony and alcohol poisoning. As a result the king went into a deep and vindictive depression. The doctors who attended Hephaestion were crucified, and Alexander waged war against the nearby villages to vent his grief.

When Alexander recovered, he returned to Babylon to plan the conquest of Arabia, Africa, and the western Mediterranean. But the Greeks and Macedonians in his army continued pressuring him to go home. More mutinies broke out, and in response Alexander ordered more executions. He moved closer to the Persians in his entourage, giving them more important positions in his new administration, as well as in the hierarchy of his military forces.

This policy drove the wedge between Alexander and his countrymen deeper. They resented taking orders from Persians and being forced by Alexander to follow Persian customs. In an attempt to develop more cultural integration, Alexander sponsored a mass marriage between thousands of local women and his Greek and Macedonian soldiers. The Persian women were provided with generous dowries to make the marriages more appealing, and the debts of every soldier who married were paid from Alexander's personal treasury. But when these "bought" husbands were eventually discharged from military service, most of them chose to return home, deserting their Persian wives and children.

Thousands of male children orphaned by Alexander's conquests or deserted by their Greek and Macedonian fathers were placed in special schools to be educated in Greek and trained in Macedonian battle tactics. As they matured, Alexander intended to transform them into a new army devoted to him—the only father figure any of them would ever know.

The new "Lord of Asia," as Alexander now styled himself, spent most of his time sequestered in his magnificent palace at Babylon, planning new conquests, making sacrifices to the gods, and drinking. Alexander became easily agitated and impatient with those around him. The more he was agitated, the more he drank, and the more he drank, the more bizarre his behavior. He saw omens and manifestations of the divine in everything, and he surrounded himself with seers, priests, mystics, purifiers, and diviners—all experts in the occult and most of them Persians. He often became deranged from his drinking, imagining treason and disloyalty among his family, slaves, and soldiers. Throughout Greece concern mounted about what would happen when Alexander finally returned home. Greeks and Macedonians were not about to live under a tyrant.

Antipater, denounced by Olympias because of their personal animosity toward each other, was summoned to Babylon—an indication that he was under suspicion of disloyalty. Remembering what had happened to Parmenio, Antipater was cautious and sent his eldest son, Cassander, to discover what the king was up to. When Cassander arrived at court and saw the Persians prostrating themselves before Alexander in the audience hall, he laughed uncontrollably. In a fury, Alexander sprang from his throne and nearly beat him to death. Years later, even when Cassander had become king of the Macedonians, the memory of the incident still caused him to tremble.

In the end, Alexander had to be eliminated. An assassin was sent from Macedonia with poison, and one night during a drinking party, Alexander downed a huge container of wine and immediately fell ill with severe abdominal pain. Standing nearby was his cupbearer, Iolas, Antipater's youngest son. Aristotle had sent the poison to destroy the tyrant he had helped create.

It took nearly eleven days for Alexander to die. Each day, his condition worsened, and he became weaker. The Macedonians in attendance at his bedside maneuvered to succeed him and shortly before he died asked to whom he left his empire. Alexander responded weakly, "I leave it to the one strong enough to hold it." His dying words plunged the eastern half of the ancient world into civil war that lasted for decades.

The empire Alexander had built by the force of his will quickly broke apart. There was no sound management infrastructure in place and no clearly defined line of succession. Alexander always had been interested more in conquest than in consolidation and administration. He had become caught up in his own cult of personality and never thought the day would come when the world would go on without him.

COMING APART AT THE SEAMS

Large corporations often come apart for the same reasons as Alexander's empire—that is, leaders don't create structures and cultures that keep them functioning profitably when the founder or creator leaves the scene or is carried out. Alexander's empire disintegrated as soon as he died. In the corporate world, big companies can founder on the rocks and break apart even with their leader still at the helm. One recent example was Vivendi, a multinational company based in France.

Originally named CGE, the company was created in 1853 to supply water to Lyon and Paris. In the mid-1970s, it began to build its empire in a series of takeovers that extended its interests into waste management, construction, real estate, energy, and transport services. In the early 1980s, CGE helped to start Canal Plus, the first pay-TV channel in France. In 1994, thirty-nine-year-old Jean-Marie Messier, the French Alexander, took over.

Though young, Messier seemed the epitome of the French establishment. He had studied at the prestigious Ecole Polytechnique and and Ecole Nationale Administration. He held posts at the French ministry of finance and then went to work at Lazard Frères. In 1994 he joined CGE as CEO.

When it comes to egos, Messier was the equal of Alexander. He wanted CGE to become the dominant player worldwide in environmental services, media, and communications. In 1998, he changed the company name to Vivendi and promptly sold off its seemingly unglamorous property and construction divisions. Eventually he got bored with environmental services and spun the company's water, waste, and transport service businesses into a new company named Veolia Environment in 2003.

Messier felt the real glamour could be found in media and entertainment. In 2000, he began a head-turning buying spree that would have impressed even Alexander. He plunked down $3 billion for the French theater chain Pathé and its stake in Britain's BSkyB satellite service. Then came his biggest conquest—buying Universal Pictures via its parent company, Seagrams, and then scooping up the remaining shares he didn't own of Canal Plus. Voilà! There was another name change: Vivendi Universal.

More conquests followed. Messier bought U.S.-based publisher Houghton Mifflin and Internet music service provider mp3.com. He also engineered the $10 billion purchase of USA Network, which gave him a 10 percent stake in EchoStar, the second-largest satellite TV operator in the United States.

Vivendi Universal reached sales of nearly $50 billion and net income of $2.1 billion. Then almost as quickly as it had been created, it fell apart. The company was drowning in debt. In 2001 economic recessions in the United States and Europe played havoc with Messier's finances. Losses mounted as assets were written down. In July 2002 Messier was out of a job. Unlike Alexander, who was killed by his unhappy associates, Messier moved to New York City and became a consultant. In the end, Vivendi Universal collapsed because top management had given little thought to the creation of an infrastructure to tie the acquisitions together, coordinate the disparate parts, and keep the organization moving forward with a purpose other than conquest.

Even the strongest, ablest, and most energetic leader learns the hard way that no one can control all the circumstances in which he operates. India's monsoons broke the morale of Alexander's army. In the corporate world, outside factors such as politics can upset the most carefully laid plans of hard-driving CEOs. A classic case is Harold Geneen of ITT. In the early 1970s, the press portrayed him as one of the most powerful and malevolent multinational corporate monsters in the world. He was vilified as a man who bought politicians and fomented coups. Yet in the 1960s, Geneen had been hailed as one of the giants of business history, the man who had turned a sleepy international version of AT&T into a powerhouse that rivaled General Electric. Geneen was unconventional in his work habits and even unpredictable in his politics, for example backing Robert Kennedy for president in 1968.

Geneen's parents brought him to the United States from England when he was a youngster. He became a CPA and eventually went to work at ITT, which at the time was called International Telephone and Telegraph Company. Geneen's intelligence and tirelessness propelled him to the top. He was named CEO in 1959, but he was not content to preside over a collection of sluggish telephone companies. Geneen put the company on an expansion path that Alexander would have approved. Unlike Alexander, though, this corporate king was obsessed with details. Every entity of ITT had to submit reams of financial data for Geneen to evaluate every month. His desire for information was on par with Alexander's for wealth.

Like Alexander's officers ITT executives had to resign themselves to the fact that working for Geneen meant no life outside the corporation. They were on call 24 hours a day, and the key people met with him to go over results every month in Brussels. No jet lag was acknowledged. Woe to the man who did not know his business inside out and could not explain every number. Although reporting requirements were intense, Geneen, again like Alexander, gave his best subordinates considerable leeway and discretion in their areas of responsibility. He made it a point to give young executives more and more authority, and he paid them well when they performed. He became something of a creator of executive talent for other businesses, because when his people could no longer stand the heat in his kitchen they went elsewhere.

By 1970 Geneen was the highest-paid corporate executive in the United States, with an annual pay package of $767,000 (even adjusted for inflation, that is not much by today's corporate standards). ITT had acquired some two hundred companies since Geneen ascended the corporate throne and had revenues approaching $8 billion and profits of over $350 million. It was one of the largest companies in the world. With Alexander-like confidence, Geneen predicted that ITT would double sales within five years with profits to match. That was not to be.

Geneen ran afoul of the federal government's antitrusters. In those days, Washington took a dim view of conglomerators acquiring insurance companies, many of which were being used to finance the acquisition of corporate empires. Geneen wanted to buy the giant Hartford Fire Insurance Company. Despite the red flags that were raised in the regulatory halls of Washington's bureaucracies he found a way to take control of the company. Geneen ultimately reached an agreement with the government to buy Hartford in return for divesting several other companies, including Avis Rent A Car.

Then the infamous Dita Beard memo surfaced. Beard, an ITT lobbyist, wrote a memo linking the Nixon administration's settlement of an antitrust case against ITT with a generous contribution from ITT to help underwrite the 1972 Republican National Convention. Columnist Jack Anderson obtained the memo, and the matter became public knowledge and the subject of a Senate hearing. The site of the convention, originally set for San Diego, was shifted to Miami, which wound up that summer hosting both the Democrats and the Republicans as they chose their presidential candidates.

The Dita Beard memo was followed in 1973 with the Chilean fiasco. Geneen was livid when the quasi-communist pro-Castro government of Chile threatened to nationalize ITT's operations there and pay the company pennies on the dollar for its assets. Geneen pressured his political contacts in Washington to stop the takeover. Salvadore Allende, president of Chile, could have survived Geneen's opposition, but his radical leftist policies aroused intense resistance in his own army. Allende's government was overthrown on September 11, 1973, in a military coup led by pro-American General Augusto Pinochet. Leftist mythology, though, credited Geneen—via Svengali-like manipulation at the CIA—with arranging Allende's overthrow.

Then the global economy went into a serious recession from 1974 to 1975. Geneen was taken by surprise. Everything started to unravel for this corporate Alexander. Never before in his career had everything tanked at once. In the past, if the U.S. economy was weak, ITT could count on its European holdings to offset those losses, and vice versa. But ITT did not reach Geneen's revenue goals for those years, and its stock experienced a rapid decline. Any dreams Geneen had of staying on as CEO after he reached his mid-sixties went out the window with the 1970s recession.

A fight erupted over who his successor would be, and in 1978 Geneen's choice, Rand Araskog, took the corporate reins. To Geneen's consternation, Araskog proceeded to sell off many of ITT's key pieces. The ultimate blow came in 1995 when Araskog split the parent company into three units. The company that retained the ITT Corp name was involved in defense electronics and fluid technologies such as pumps and valves. Then two years later, to ward off an unsolicited takeover bid—ITT was now the prey instead of the hunter—ITT Corp itself split into three new companies. Geneen's behemoth had been atomized.

When Ray Kroc, the creator of the McDonald's empire, was once asked why he did not expand into new ventures, he replied that his company would stick with what it knew best until he could be guaranteed that every restroom in his numerous restaurants was sparkling clean. Kroc did not allow himself to be diverted from his goal by the lure of acquisitions or personal glory. Perhaps if Alexander had taken Parmenio's advice and not sought to become "Lord of Asia" by pushing into Afghanistan, Uzbekistan, and even India, overextending his resources and depleting the goodwill and patience of his army, his empire might have survived intact after his death.

●　　●　　●

When Alexander died at Babylon, his successors fought over his treasury, his body, and finally even his armor. They preserved the body in honey and then placed it in a glass sarcophagus to be shipped to Macedonia. The sarcophagus was hijacked by one of Alexander's generals and transferred to a mausoleum in the Egyptian city of Alexandria.

Alexander's "half-witted" brother was renamed Philip III and placed on the throne to serve as a puppet until things settled out. Then he was murdered. Alexander's mother, the women he had married, and the children he had sired as well as his mistresses and eunuchs were all murdered. Alexander's generals, many of them his boyhood friends, initially divided up the empire peacefully but soon began to fight among themselves. Peace would not come to the lands Alexander conquered until the advent of the Pax Romana three centuries later.

Ambition and the desire for immortality destroyed Alexander the Great. His story is the tragedy of what happens when a leader achieves power and wealth equal to his passion, something the Greek historian Plutarch warned about when he wrote: "No beast is more savage than man when he is possessed of power equal to his passion." Alexander failed because he came to believe his own propaganda, and he lacked the self-control to keep his success within a sane perspective. He was weak within and not strong enough to carry the weight of his success. Almost all his time was spent fighting to acquire new territory; nearly none of it was spent in consolidating and ruling what he had conquered. Alexander refused to accept the fact that success in large part can be due to a combination of ability, circumstances, and luck— factors that often converge in the career of a leader for a brief period when his stars are aligned.

Young Alexander often impetuously destroyed the very things he had fought hard to achieve. He was blinded by his ego and failed to learn the lesson a simple Indian ascetic tried to teach him on the banks of the Indus River: Power is ephemeral, all glory is vanity, and in the end all that any man controls is the small piece of land on which he stands while he lives.

Next we turn to the other side of the Mediterranean world and to a later time period for a look at a civilization that produced a leader with a different management style: Hannibal of Carthage.

part **III**

6

CARTHAGE

A Businessman's Paradise

According to one of history's oldest legends, a Phoenician noblewoman of exceptional intelligence and beauty founded the city of Carthage on the Mediterranean coast of North Africa. Her name was Elissa, and she had fled Tyre, her native city on the coast of what is today Lebanon, after her husband, the king, was murdered by her ambitious brother. With a band of loyal followers and chests filled with gold, she sailed the Mediterranean searching for a place to make a new start.

Elissa's ships followed the North African coast west until they came to the shores of what is today Tunisia. Captivated by the natural beauty of the land, the queen decided to settle there. The site was well protected by high hills and offered a natural harbor with a narrow entrance to the sea. To the east and west lay Egypt and Spain, and directly across the sea to the north were Sicily and Italy. Guided by the ageless dictum that in real estate location is everything, Elissa envisioned a prosperous city at this virtual crossroads of the Mediterranean sea trade.

A local African chief, seeing this woman leading her band of refugees along the shores of his kingdom, mockingly told her she was welcome to all of his land that she could fit within the hide of a bull. To the laughter of the natives and the astonishment of her people, the queen accepted the offer and ordered the sacrifice of a prize bull. When the ritual had been completed, Elissa ordered the hide carefully removed from the slaughtered animal and set about cutting the hide into thin strips. From these strips she fashioned a long and delicate thread, which she used to delineate the parcel she had chosen for her city. Outwitted and humiliated in front of his tribe, the chief had no choice but to concede the parcel, which Elissa named Carthage from a Phoenician word that means "new city." To salvage his pride, the African proposed marriage, but the queen rejected him with the reply that she had a city to build and no time for a man.

What Elissa could easily have bought with gold and silver she chose instead to win in a contest of wits. With quickness of mind and an inclination to bargain, she outsmarted the chief and demonstrated the traits that would characterize the people of Carthage as they came to control the commercial interests of the western Mediterranean.

The same legend also weaves together the founding of Rome in a romantic entanglement that turned sour. According to the legend, the founder of the Roman people was a Trojan prince named Aeneas, who had fled the destruction of his city by the Greeks. He wandered the Mediterranean until a storm drove his ships to seek shelter at Carthage. There the destinies of Rome and Carthage became entwined as Elissa and Aeneas became lovers. The queen gave everything to the man she called her husband until the god Apollo appeared to Aeneas in a dream and ordered him to leave Carthage and sail to Italy, where he would found a race that one day would rule the world.

In the darkness before dawn, the Trojan prince deserted the bed of the queen while she slept. When Elissa awoke and discovered her lover was gone, she ordered a funeral pyre to be prepared on the roof of her palace. Before the masts of the Trojan ships had disappeared beyond the horizon, Elissa looked out to sea and cursed the man who abandoned her. She prayed that there would always be war between their people, and then took her life. Her spirit descended into the underworld, where, according to legend, she waited for her champion to appear and take revenge upon the Romans. Centuries later, Elissa's prayer was answered and her curse fulfilled when Hannibal crossed over the Alps. All Italy trembled as his elephants trampled the Roman legions and his mercenaries burned the countryside.

Legends aside, archaeological evidence indicates that the people who settled Carthage came to North Africa around 800 BC, probably from the Phoenician city of Tyre. They were a seafaring and commercial people who established trading stations, or *emporia*, throughout the Mediterranean. These emporia were small settlements strategically located along the coastlines where there was commercial activity and bargains could be struck with the local people. Goods were often stored there until they could be loaded on ships and taken to Tyre. Carthage probably developed from one of these early trading stations.

Carthage prospered as a commercial center for the western Mediterranean and developed into an architectural marvel. Ancient commentators described it as the "richest city in the world" and the "jewel of the Mediterranean." It was protected by a combination of natural and man-made fortifications against the storms and marauding pirates who swept in from the sea to the north, and the hostile tribes who inhabited the deserts to the south.

Within the confines of the city, archaeological evidence reveals the Carthaginians constructed a double harbor to accommodate both warships and merchant vessels. This system, unique to Carthage, allowed ships to be safely moored in large numbers and dry-dock operations to be undertaken throughout the year. Seaborn commerce was becoming a big business in the Mediterranean, and the Carthaginians utilized the most advanced naval designs to produce large fleets. The Carthaginian navy became the strongest in the Mediterranean, and the citizens of Carthage took pride in serving in the fleet as a matter of civic duty.

At the highest point in the city, the Carthaginians constructed a citadel named the Byrsa, from an ancient Greek word meaning "hide." There they established their government, erected magnificent temples to their gods, and built splendid palaces for their nobles. In the lower portions of the city, surrounding the harbors, they constructed tenements to house the thousands of artisans, laborers, shopkeepers, and sailors who made their economy thrive, and massive warehouses to store their goods.

Everything of value in the ancient world flowed into Carthage. Gold and ivory as well as the hides of animals were shipped to Carthage from locations along the west coast of Africa. From central Africa came elephants that would be trained and utilized in both war and commerce. Silver, iron, lead, zinc, mercury, and copper came from mines in Spain; tin was brought in from as far north as Britain. Marble was imported from Greece to build temples and the palaces of the wealthy.

The Carthaginians sold a wide array of goods throughout the Mediterranean world, everything from weapons, linen, wool, vases, and glassware to ornaments made of ivory and precious stones. They traded at a profit and managed to control in one way or another almost everything of value that was carried on any ship in the western Mediterranean. They manipulated foreign competition in a way that allowed their merchants to buy cheaply and sell at inflated prices. Carthage brings to mind a twenty-first-century entrepreneur's dream-come-true: modern tax-free Dubai.

By the third century BC, the Carthaginians had established a monopoly on trade in the western Mediterranean. Less powerful city-states in southern France, Sicily, and Italy were excluded from competition by treaty or by the menacing presence of the Carthaginian navy. The Carthaginians also made money from the land that surrounded their city. There were large tracts of dense forests, and many Carthaginians established large plantations in the countryside to harvest and mill timber for use in shipbuilding and construction. A wide belt of prosperous estates developed with vast fields of grain, pasture for cattle and sheep, vineyards, and olive groves. The Carthaginians worked nearly all the land that could be cultivated, and their estates, known as *latifundia,* spread across North Africa, extending as far east as modern-day Libya and as far west as Morocco.

As in most of the ancient world, slave labor made Carthage profitable. The Carthaginians became efficient taskmasters and ruled those who worked on their estates and in their colonies with a heavy hand. Those who toiled under the yoke of Carthage had little chance to win their freedom or share in the wealth of the empire.

As the centuries passed, the Carthaginians developed a society that became a blend of cultural and religious elements, some of them unique to their Phoenician heritage and others reflecting their own experiences in North Africa. Perhaps more than any other ancient people with the exception of the Egyptians, the Carthaginians were intensely religious, and they engaged in a practice found nowhere else in the ancient world: the sacrifice of infants.

High upon the Byrsa, in a sacred quarter of the city called the Tophet, the Carthaginians erected a massive bronze image of a fearsome god. With outstretched palms, he accepted the condemned and dropped them into a raging inferno. Archaeological evidence for this practice is indisputable. In the excavated ruins of the city, large deposits of calcified remains have been positively identified by forensic specialists as the bones of infants.

What purpose did the ritual play in the religious life of the Carthaginians? Theories abound. The practice might have been a form of population control, euthanasia, a test of loyalty to the city, or a gesture to appease the god in times of famine, pestilence, plague, or war. Whatever the reason, scholars are confident that the Carthaginians were among the most religious and superstitious people in the ancient world. Worship in their society was compulsory and actively regulated by priests, who wielded considerable influence in the political life of the city.

In spite of their wealth and commercial success, the Carthaginians never developed into one of the great civilizations of the Mediterranean. Although their accomplishments are impressive, their time at the top was short, lasting less than five hundred years. They never rose to the artistic, cultural, and intellectual level of their neighbors in Egypt, Greece, and Italy. The upper classes of Carthage adopted

Greek styles of dress and language, but the society seems to have applied no more than a thin veneer of Hellenism to what appears to have been a largely materialistic culture.

What we know about the government of Carthage comes to us through Greek and Roman sources. According to the Greek philosopher Aristotle, Carthage was a plutocracy. The government consisted of an executive or magistrate, a senate of wealthy merchants and landowners, and a popular assembly. Ruling magistrates for the city, as well as generals and admirals, were elected annually by the senate, usually on the basis of their social status.

Before the rise of Rome, the Greeks were the primary competition for the Carthaginians in the western Mediterranean. They founded cities on the eastern coast of Sicily and along both coasts of southern Italy, but never presented a major challenge to Carthage. Greek influence there waned in the heyday of Alexander the Great, since Greek interests were focused in Asia Minor and Persia. By the beginning of the third century BC, Carthage had undisputed control of the western part of Sicily, Sardinia, the Balearic Islands, and Spain.

Things changed when the Romans crossed into Sicily in 264 BC. They started a series of conflicts that would become known as the Punic Wars. The wars lasted intermittently from 264 BC until the final destruction of Carthage in 146 BC. The first was a struggle over control of Sicily. The scope of the second and third was wider, and determined not only who would rule the ancient world but who would come to ultimately influence the very course of Western civilization.

During the First Punic War (264–241 BC), Hamilcar Barca, the father of Hannibal, commanded the forces of Carthage in Sicily. The war was fought to a stalemate, but the Carthaginians lost their hold on the island and were forced to retreat to North Africa. The end of this war did not stop the fighting but ushered in a period of domestic warfare more savage than the fight in Sicily against the Romans had been. The Carthaginians had hired mercenaries to do their fighting for them and at the end of the First Punic War twenty thousand of them demanded to be paid. The Carthaginians, however, balked at paying the mercenaries their full due because they had lost the war.

As groups of mercenaries arrived in Carthage from Sicily and joined those who had come before, a volatile mix of Iberians, Gauls, Ligurians, Balearic Islanders, Greeks, and Africans, impatient for their pay, began to form outside the high walls of the city. Negotiations between the emissaries of the Carthaginian senate and the leaders of the mercenaries dragged on for weeks. From the secure heights of their city walls, the Carthaginians threw down worthless promises and insults upon the agitated mercenaries. Finally, the mercenaries began to loot and burn the countryside, starting a war in which, according to the Greek historian Polybius, "both sides could not content themselves with acts of mere human wickedness but assumed the ferocity of wild beasts and the vindictiveness of insanity."

The mercenaries convinced a number of African tribes to join them, and revolts against the Carthaginians flared up across North Africa. Estates were looted and burned, and the citizens of Carthage found themselves forced for the first time in their history to fight their own battles. Desperate, the senate entrusted command of a new citizen army to Hamilcar Barca, the man who had led the war against the Romans in Sicily. The fighting was fierce and the atrocities terrible. There seemed no way to end the war short of the complete annihilation of one side by the other.

In 238 BC, after three years of fighting, Hamilcar brought matters to an end when he lured the greater part of the mercenary force into a gorge in the mountains outside Carthage. There the mercenaries, exhausted by hunger and fatigue, were trapped and trampled by Hamilcar's elephants. The few who survived were crucified outside the walls of Carthage.

Rome remained relatively neutral throughout the mercenary war in North Africa, selling supplies to both sides and even allowing Carthage to recruit small numbers of mercenaries in Italy. Roman traders provided the Carthaginians with supplies and made handsome profits just as the Carthaginians had done in earlier conflicts. Then in 237 BC, as the mercenary war was ending, the Romans seized the island of Sardinia in a blatant display of their new strength.

Worn out by years of struggle and having no warships left to fight with, Carthage was in no position to challenge Rome. Even though voices in the senate called out for another war, Carthage gave up Sardinia and paid additional indemnities to Rome. Carthaginian resources were nearly depleted, and a large portion of their territory was lost as they reluctantly submitted to the reality of a new power alignment in the western part of the Mediterranean. The Romans seized Corsica next as Sardinia, Corsica, and Sicily together formed the first Roman provinces outside Italy.

To compensate for their losses, the Carthaginians turned to Spain, an undeveloped land rich in natural resources and manpower. Hamilcar became the governor and founded prosperous cities along the coast, including Cartagena (New Carthage) and Barcelona (Camp of the Barcas). The success of Carthage in Spain caused the Romans to become interested in the potential of the western Mediterranean and set the stage for the second war, which began in the spring of 218 BC. As we will see in the next chapter, because of Hannibal's brilliance as a commander and the ineptitude of the Romans, Carthage had the initial advantage, but time, attrition, and unlimited Roman manpower turned the tide, and Rome eventually won the war in 202 BC.

Even though the Romans won the Second Punic War, their fear of Carthage set the stage for the third and final conflict in 149 BC. The Romans put Carthage under siege, and for three years the city managed to hold out until Roman legions finally breached the walls. Legend has it that the Roman fear and hatred of Carthage was so great that a curse was placed over the smoldering ruins of the city and salt plowed into the ground so that nothing could ever grow there again.

But neither the curse nor the salt destroyed the resilience of the city or the spirit of its people. By the time of Julius Caesar, a hundred years later, Carthage was once more an important commercial center, but this time in a new world dominated by Rome. Carthage no longer controlled vast foreign territories but had become a place where veteran soldiers from the Roman legions retired and grain was shipped to Rome to feed the idle proletariat. By the first century AD, Carthage had been completely integrated into the new Roman Empire and even produced an emperor.

7

HANNIBAL OF CARTHAGE

Innovation

"What do you think the Alps are? They are nothing more than high mountains. Their heights are not insurmountable to men of determination. We came to conquer Rome, now steel your hearts and climb."
—HANNIBAL

With those words, Hannibal (247–183 BC) rallied his army to follow him over the French Alps and challenge Rome for mastery of the Mediterranean. Few images in history have managed to capture and hold the imagination over the centuries quite like that of this bold African commander, perched on a monstrous elephant and leading his long column of weary soldiers through the snow and over the ice-covered peaks.

When it comes to leadership, Hannibal was cast in the mold of Alexander the Great. Like Alexander, he believed that ability, discipline, and motivation, plus a dash of self-interest, would inspire those who followed him to do anything—even march a thousand miles from Spain, fight Gauls along the way, scale the Alps in winter with six thousand horses and thirty-seven elephants in tow, rest for a couple of weeks, and then spend the next fifteen years fighting the Roman army in its own backyard.

Both Hannibal and Alexander were focused leaders, but their mo-

tives, management styles, and objectives differed. Alexander, as we have already seen, was the ultimate boss. He formulated plans and issued orders, and no one on his team challenged him and lived to brag about it. Hannibal was also the unquestioned authority in his army, but with a different temperament and approach. He combined the self-assurance and drive of an Alexander with the tempered, more self-effacing and consensus-building approach of a Xenophon. Hannibal was a leader, competent and effective, who understood limits and the importance of input and feedback from those he commanded.

Alexander and Hannibal differed as well in what they wanted to achieve. For Alexander it was all about conquest and glory. Hannibal was fighting for something else: to preserve a way of life for his people. In fact, Hannibal was not really fighting Rome at all; he was fighting history. For centuries his native Carthage had reigned supreme in the western Mediterranean, reaping all the profits. But times were changing, and the ancient world was about to enter a new era, one in which Carthage was not destined to play a major role. Carthage had passed its prime, and Rome was on the rise. Hannibal could not change the inevitable realignment of power that was coming, but he believed he could at least forestall the end and buy Carthage a few more years at the top.

If Hannibal had won his war against Rome—and he came very close—the foundations of our civilization today might have been very different. The Carthaginians were descendants of the Phoenicians, who inhabited the Syrian-Lebanese coast and spoke one of the Semitic languages (linguistically similar languages from the Middle East, such as Hebrew or Arabic). Because Rome became the dominant culture in the ancient world, Western civilization is Latin in its foundations today, and not Semitic.

Hannibal and Alexander also differed in what each one had to work with. As we saw in Chapter 5, Alexander started out with a meager war chest but quickly accumulated a plush financial cushion that allowed him to absorb any temporary setbacks. Hannibal, in contrast, was always working from a deficit, and similar to Xenophon, he was in short supply of nearly everything all the time—soldiers, money, and supplies.

Like both Alexander and Xenophon, Hannibal was fighting far from home in his enemy's backyard. He was vastly outnumbered and commanded an army of mercenaries who had to be paid. Political and material support from home were meager because factions in Carthage opposed his campaign and believed they could work out an accommodation with Rome that would be less costly than a war. When Hannibal began his campaign, he had nearly everything going against him, yet he managed to achieve his objective and tie down the Roman legions in Italy for fifteen years, allowing Carthage to go on with business as usual.

Hannibal had the edge over his adversaries because he was able to think outside the box. Time and again he was able to defeat larger and better-equipped Roman armies by doing the unexpected, the unconventional, and what the rest of the world thought impossible—such as crossing the Alps in winter. The Romans believed the Alps were an impassible barrier, and because of that were lulled into a false sense of security. They thought the mountains would always protect them, and although they knew Hannibal was coming, they were sure it would be by way of Sicily. So they concentrated their forces in southern Italy and underestimated the resourcefulness of one of history's greatest tactical geniuses.

HANNIBAL GOOGLE

When it comes to leadership and innovation in business, one striking example of doing something in the Hannibal style is Google, founded by Sergey Brin and Larry Page. In the mid-1990s this unlikely duo—Page grew up in the Midwest and Brin is an émigré from Russia—met in a computer science doctoral program at Stanford. They were both entrepreneurs and saw an opportunity in the new but very competitive field of computer search engines. In 1998, they dropped out of academia to start Google in a friend's garage. The rest is geek history.

When Brin and Page started their collaboration more than ten years ago, at least seven companies were competing in the search area of the Internet, including giants Microsoft and Yahoo. The young entrepreneurs used a Hannibal-like approach not only to beat Google's larger competitors but to overpower the playing field to such an extent that Google is now literally drawing in billions of advertising dollars not just from Internet information sites but from the traditional media as well. How did they do it?

Pulling back the curtain in front of Google's operation reveals the secret: one million cheap computers called servers networked together like the cells of a brain to form the world's most powerful supercomputer. Unlike competitors, Google did not go in for powerful individual servers; instead, Brin and Page figured that massing small inexpensive servers would give Google more capability to power its search algorithms than its competitors had. Because the servers are so inexpensive, when one breaks down it is junked and replaced instead of fixed.

Another of Google's innovations was to position its server farms next to sources of cheap electricity, such as hydroelectric power in the Columbia River Gorge on the border between Washington State and

Oregon and wind power in Council Bluffs, Iowa. This allows the firm to save enormous amounts of money on hardware costs and to direct financial resources into hiring bright people. Brin and Page recognized that brain power is always a better investment than faster and bigger boxes.

When Hannibal left Spain in the spring of 218 BC, he had nearly 100,000 men under his command. Six months later when he came down from the Alps, he had less than 30,000. Some had turned back early in the campaign. Many had died at the hands of the fierce mountain tribes who lined the route in ambush. Others perished from exposure or fell to their deaths from the high precipices as the long Carthaginian column slowly struggled over the mountains. Those who survived the ordeal and made it into Italy are described in ancient manuscripts as "shadows," half dead from hunger and cold, all their strength beaten out of them by the Alps. In spite of everything, Hannibal kept his soldiers motivated and moving in the direction he wanted them to go. The miracle is that anyone survived.

Hannibal's crossing of the Alps and his years in Italy were relatively brief episodes in the larger and longer conflict known as the Punic Wars. But what he accomplished has become one of the great stories of history. The losses and suffering have been buried by the mystique and romance that surround his name. No one today ever asks whether he won or lost his war with Rome. People only know that Hannibal did the impossible, and for that he stands out as one of history's greatest leadership figures.

HANNIBAL'S BEGINNING

Hannibal was born into an aristocratic family just as the First Punic War (264–241 BC) was coming to a close. Hamilcar Barca, his father, had led the forces of Carthage in a long struggle to retain control of the island of Sicily, and later he established an empire for Carthage in Spain. Before the First Punic War began, the Carthaginians were the undisputed naval force in the western Mediterranean and controlled a piece of nearly everything that moved by sea. Their only competitors had been the Greeks, but after the death of Alexander, the Greeks ceased to be major players.

The Romans were the problem. Rome was a young republic at the time and eager to begin building an empire. As the Romans expanded south through Italy, they crossed the straits of Messina and entered Sicily, a closely guarded Carthaginian economic resource and sphere of influence. That's when the trouble started. The island of Sicily was valuable real estate because of its position in the middle of the Mediterranean Sea. The Carthaginians used it as a base from which to control commercial traffic, and the island's rich volcanic soil provided a steady supply of grain. The Romans were new at the game of acquisitions, but they were ambitious and hungry. They took on Carthage in the first war for control of Sicily and in spite of heavy casualties persisted until they fought the conflict to a draw.

The First Punic War dragged on inconclusively for years. Finally, the peace faction in the Carthaginian senate, tired of the continuous drain on the city's finances and looking to develop new areas for investment in North Africa and Spain, signed a treaty with Rome and pulled the rug out from under Hannibal's father in Sicily.

Hamilcar returned to Carthage an embittered man. He hated the Romans for their arrogance and believed he could have won the war if the politicians at home had supported him. Making matters worse, the senate refused to pay his mercenaries, and Hamilcar found himself in a new war, against the very men he had commanded in Sicily.

When the war against the mercenaries ended, the Carthaginian senate sent Hamilcar to Spain to build them a new empire. Over the next two decades, Spanish gold, silver, and iron mines produced enormous wealth for Carthage, and the Celtic tribes provided the cheap labor to work them. New cities sprang up along Spain's southern Mediterranean coast, such as Cartagena and Barcelona. Everything came together for Hamilcar in Spain: He established a dynasty for himself and a larger and richer empire for Carthage than the one lost to Rome.

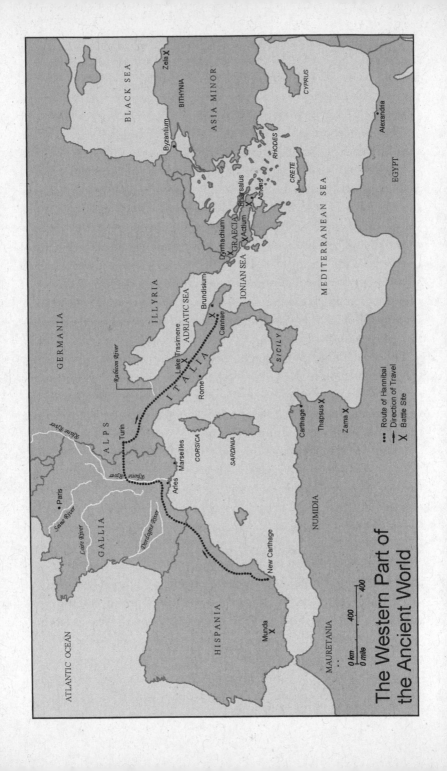

The Western Part of
the Ancient World

ATLANTIC OCEAN

GERMANIA

GALLIA

Paris

Seine River

Loire River

Rhine River

Dordogne River

Rhone River

HISPANIA

Munda
X

New Carthage

Arles

Marseilles

CORSICA

SARDINIA

Turin

A L P S

Rubicon River

Lake Trasimene
X

Rome

I T A L I A

Cannae
X

Brundisium

ILLYRIA

ADRIATIC SEA

IONIAN SEA

Dyrrhachium
X
GRAECIA
Actium
X
Pharsalus
X
Athens

SICILY

MEDITERRANEAN SEA

CRETE

RHODES

CYPRUS

Byzantium

Zela X

BITHYNIA

ASIA MINOR

BLACK SEA

EGYPT

Alexandria

Carthage

Thapsus X

Zama X

NUMIDIA

MAURETANIA

0 km   400   400
0 mile

•••• Route of Hannibal
⟶ Direction of Travel
X Battle Site

But prosperity did not diminish Hamilcar's hatred for the Romans. He took Hannibal, the oldest of his three young sons, before the altar of a vengeful Carthaginian god and made him swear to wage "eternal war" against the Romans. The boy pledged to sacrifice everything—family, wealth, even his life—to destroy Rome. This oath became the personal demon that Hannibal carried within him for the remainder of his life, and history would record that no oath by a son to his father was ever more faithfully kept or proved to be more costly in human life and suffering. Like Alexander, Hannibal was the product of a domineering and driven father, one who set the expectations and condemned him to a violent end.

LIKE FATHER, LIKE SON?

An interesting parallel to a modern-day CEO who did not have the opportunity to achieve the success of either a Hannibal or an Alexander but whose fate was set by a hard-driving father is Augustus Busch IV. In 2006, Busch took over from his father, Augustus III, and became CEO of the family-owned brewery, Anheuser-Busch, by far the largest in the United States. Young Busch became the sixth member of the family dynasty to run the company.

In the spring of 2008, InBev, a Belgian-based, Brazilian-owned brewery, made a $52 billion unsolicited bid for Anheuser-Busch. Busch's initial reaction was to tell his distributors that the company would never be sold on his watch. One reason he resisted selling was to show his father, Augustus III, that he was capable of succeeding with the company on his own.

Like Hannibal, Busch was looking for his father's respect and admiration, declaring in an interview with the *Wall Street Journal*, "His love and respect will be mine when I am successful." As the younger Busch had moved up in the company hierarchy, he found it difficult if not impossible to impress his father favorably and show he had what it took to run the company. "I never had a (traditional) father-son relationship," he said. One reason might have been his reputation as an irresponsible playboy. During his college years, Busch was involved in an automobile accident that killed a female companion, and he fled the scene.

Busch never had his chance to impress his father. The family owned only 4 percent of the company stock, and the InBev buyout became a done deal over his objections. Ironically, Anheuser-Busch became a target for a takeover because Busch did not move aggressively enough in the overseas markets—a strategy that his father always resisted. The influence of Hannibal's father motivated Hannibal to take on Rome and do what his father couldn't. In contrast, the younger Busch failed to prove that he could equal the accomplishments of his father.

HANNIBAL ASSUMES COMMAND

Hannibal's father was killed in western Spain and was immediately succeeded by his son-in-law, Hasdrubal, "the Handsome." The story is that Hamilcar was out riding with his three young sons when they were ambushed by Celtic horsemen. Hamilcar saved the boys by offering himself as bait to the Celts and diverting them.

Hannibal was too young to assume command when his father was killed. But a few years later, when Hasdrubal was assassinated by a household slave, Hannibal came into his own. At the age of twenty-six, he became commander of the army and de facto ruler of Spain. He was well prepared for command, having spent his formative years in the army camps.

As a leader Hannibal had learned never to ask more from his soldiers than he was willing to give. In the field, he set the pace and the example, enduring the elements, sleeping on the ground, and eating what his soldiers ate. Hannibal demonstrated remarkable self-control in his personal habits, always eating and drinking in moderation and putting work before comforts and distractions. His clothes and armor were remarkably modest for a leader of his stature; there were no elegantly crafted breastplates of gold, like the ones Alexander wore, no chest full of decorations, and no magnificent horses to ride. Hannibal was a leader who put his mission over his personal comforts and resisted being corrupted by wealth and success.

Unlike Alexander, Hannibal never felt compelled to prove himself on the battlefield. He believed his duty was to command and his responsibility was to formulate and execute the strategy and tactics that would enable his army to win. But, like Xenophon, he always retained a common touch that allowed him to connect with those he led. Hannibal never thought of himself as a king or god, only as a leader with a mission to accomplish.

WHAT REAL LEADERS DO

One leader in the Hannibal style was A. P. Giannini, the man who created the largest bank in the United States, Bank of America. Giannini consistently employed innovations of Hannibal-like daring in banking and learned his business the hard way, the way Hannibal learned soldiering.

Giannini started working in the produce business at age fourteen in San Francisco before the turn of the twentieth century. He became a partner in the business at nineteen and by the age of thirty-two had secured a place for himself on the board of a local savings bank. From this post he taught himself the nuts and bolts of the banking business. He quickly realized that banking presented major opportunities for expansion in ways overlooked by this traditionally hidebound industry. Giannini wanted the bank he worked for to extend loans to immigrants, but his conservative colleagues thought the idea too risky and even harebrained. Bankers tended to view immigrants as people with no credit history and risky, but Giannini believed a bank could make a lot of money from servicing small loans to the millions who were flooding into America eager to start their own businesses.

Giannini resigned from the local bank in 1904 and started his own bank—the Bank of Italy—across the street. He actively solicited deposits and made loans by ringing doorbells and even from starting conversations with strangers on the street. His unconventional methods appalled traditional bankers.

Giannini was not just aggressive but, like Hannibal, a leader who could adapt to situations and develop innovative ways of doing things. When a devastating earthquake shook San Francisco in 1906, Giannini realized that the intense heat from the resulting fires would make it impossible to open the steel doors of bank vaults for weeks afterward. Thinking quickly, he removed the gold and securities from his vaults before the fires spread, hid them under vegetables in a horse-drawn buggy, and drove to his home outside the burning city to store them. Weeks passed before other banks could open their vaults, but within days, Giannini laid a plank across two barrels at the San Francisco wharf, and started making loans and taking deposits. Then a year after the earthquake, another disaster struck: the financial panic of 1907. Giannini survived that as well because he always kept large amounts of gold and cash on hand as a safeguard.

Both the earthquake and the panic taught Giannini that banks had to be big and geographically diversified to thrive. So he opened Bank of Italy branches by buying small banks, creating the first bank chain in the United States that crossed state lines. He even used his network to go into the insurance business, changing his company's name to Bank of America.

Giannini didn't hesitate to lend money to new, unknown, or even risky industries. Bank of America helped to finance California's fledgling wine industry and bankrolled movie studios during Hollywood's infancy. When Walt Disney ran over budget making his first feature-length cartoon, *Snow White,* Giannini provided the financing to finish the project. Even though he became financially successful, Giannini, like Hannibal, was never in it for the money. He never paid himself more than $50,000 per year, and near the end of his successful career when his directors voted him a surprise $1.5 million bonus, he promptly donated the money to the University of California.

While Rome ultimately defeated Hannibal, the banking establishment was never able to destroy Giannini, although his competitors did succeed in pressuring the government to force him to divest himself of the insurance arm of his business and restrict him from making more bank acquisitions across state lines. During the bank holiday of 1933,

President Franklin D. Roosevelt ordered all banks in the United States closed while regulators determined which ones would survive and which would be closed permanently. When Giannini found out that some large competitors were lobbying the U.S. Treasury to close Bank of America, he went to Washington and successfully persuaded regulators not to cave in to the pressure. One reason Giannini was so successful was because he was his own boss and like Hannibal could respond to conditions and circumstances as he saw fit. Giannini did not have to dance to anybody's tune but his own.

LEARNING THE LESSONS OF COMMAND AND CONTROL

Hamilcar taught Hannibal how to command soldiers, and his brother-in-law Hasdrubal taught him how to rule. Though not a king, Hannibal was nevertheless a monarch in Spain. He married a Celtic princess in what was probably an attempt to strengthen his alliances with the Spanish tribes who served as his primary source of manpower, but according to the ancient sources, she became the only woman in his life and bore him a child.

As the ruler of Spain, Hannibal did not limit himself to military and political affairs. He surrounded himself with scholars and took the time to learn Greek for its cultural advantages and Latin so he could better understand his enemy. Like Alexander, he took a Greek historian with him when he invaded Italy to record what happened, but unfortunately those manuscripts were lost centuries ago.

Historians have never been able to determine exactly why Hannibal began the Second Punic War: Perhaps because of the pledge he had made to his father or because he believed war between Carthage and Rome was inevitable for economic reasons. Whatever the reasons, Hannibal took the initiative. He was too good a strategist to allow the Romans to make the first move and compel him to fight on their terms, so he formulated a plan to protect Carthage and at the same time curtail Roman expansion in the Mediterranean. Central to that plan was an invasion of Italy by way of France.

Hannibal's strategy for conquering Rome rested on his perceptive assessment of his enemies' political strengths and weaknesses. Italy was not a unified country at the time, and Rome was not yet the leviathan most people imagine when they think of the empire portrayed in Hollywood films. By the end of the third century BC, Italy was a land of semiautonomous city-states and tribes held together by the Romans in a loose confederation. In the north were the Gauls, semibarbaric mountain tribes who valued their freedom and viewed Roman encroachment with alarm. In the south were the Greeks, recently subjugated by Rome in a brutal war and as fearful of Roman domination as the Gauls.

The rest of the Italian peninsula, essentially the center, was populated by native Italians living on farms, in villages, and in small cities tied to Rome by treaties that required them to pay taxes and to serve in Rome's legions. Hannibal believed that if he successfully challenged Roman authority in Italy and demonstrated that the Romans could be defeated on the battlefield, many of these city-states might desert Rome and join him. Hannibal anticipated that if the confederation started to break apart, Roman legions would be dispatched from one end of Italy to the other in an effort to hold it together, and they would be too busy trying to keep their own house in order to menace Carthage.

Once Hannibal had decided on war with Rome, he began to build his army. When it came to wars on land the Carthaginians preferred to let others do the fighting for them while they made money. They were merchants; and although they maintained a small army in peacetime, when war was necessary, it was their practice to hire mercenaries from the surplus of unemployed yet well-trained soldiers throughout the ancient world. It was a cost efficient method of waging war because the mercenaries could be hired in time of need and when the need passed sent on their way with no further expense to the hiring authority.

Hamilcar had led mercenaries during the First Punic War, and Hannibal did the same in the second. Both father and son drew their infantry from the Greek city-states, cavalry from the Bedouins of the northern Sahara, and slingers from the Balearic Islands, off the coast of Spain (slingers were soldiers skilled in the use of a version of the sling that David used to slay Goliath). In addition, Hannibal recruited from the fierce Celtic tribes of Spain and France. Although these soldiers spoke different languages and followed different customs, they were drawn to Hannibal, as they had been to his father, as much by his reputation as by their desire to make money in his war.

Hannibal was always leary of the men he hired. They were professional soldiers from the lower classes of society who were driven to fight by a combination of poverty, desperation, and greed. His task as a leader was to mold them into a cohesive, disciplined, and loyal fighting force. He knew that he had to motivate them to follow him for something more than the money they would receive; otherwise, he eventually would lose them through desertion. They had to believe in him and his mission, so he framed what he wanted to accomplish in idealistic terms: the liberation of Italy from Roman domination. The combination of an idealistic cause and the chance to make money at Roman expense proved irresistible. But Hannibal didn't leave it at that. He trained, rewarded, and led his mercenaries so well, both officers and soldiers, that those who survived remained with him for years.

●   ●   ●

Similar leadership qualities are apparent in the early years of Walt Disney's career: creativity, an extraordinary ability to inspire, and fearless pursuit of unprecedented and seemingly impossible opportunities. Disney did not lead mercenaries and elephants over the Alps, although it would have made a great cartoon. He was a truly ingenious innovator in his field and relied on many of the leadership techniques that brought Hannibal success. In the 1920s, Disney was only one among a number of producers creating cartoon characters for cinema. The Fleischer brothers, for example, were creating Betty Boop and Popeye the Sailor. Competition was fierce, but Disney managed to find an edge when he applied a new technology—sound—to his cartoons. Synchronizing sound and action, he created *Steamboat Willie* in 1928, the first Mickey Mouse cartoon, which put him out in front of all his competitors and compelled critics to take a serious look at cartoons as an art form.

Like Hannibal, Disney innovated and led by example, working harder and longer than anyone in his young company. The hours were arduous, but Disney made sure his employees enjoyed facilities and amenities that were better than those offered by any other company in the business. He knew how to inspire. When he presented an idea for a full-length cartoon feature, such as *Snow White,* he didn't just talk about what he had in mind but acted out all of the key characters to his colleagues, enabling them to visualize what he wanted every scene to be.

Snow White in 1937 and *Fantasia* and *Pinocchio* in 1940 brought critical acclaim and commercial success to Disney. But the films created expectations among his staff that exceeded what Disney could deliver. The result was a bitter animators strike in 1941 that lasted for nearly five weeks. Although Disney artists were well paid and worked under the best conditions in the industry, there was discontent. Many had worked extra hours in the drive to finish *Snow White,* often for free; but despite the fact that the film was an enormous financial success, they received pink slips instead of bonuses.

After the strike, Disney lost his intense drive for innovative animation. His heart was no longer in it. The industry and critics no longer viewed him at the vanguard of a uniquely American art form, cartoons; instead, he was seen as a motion-picture manufacturer churning out high-quality products in a glossy but formulaic house style. Even though the strike and its aftermath seemed to temper Disney's passion for cartoons, he found new outlets for his creativity. Disney turned first to television and then later to the development of theme parks. With Disneyland he revolutionized the whole concept and redefined how Americans and their children vacationed.

Unlike Alexander and Disney, Hannibal never faced a mutiny. Even though Hannibal did not have the resources to pay his men as well as Alexander or Disney paid theirs, they stayed loyal to him, and their loyalty confirms how effective his leadership style must have

been. Hannibal invaded Italy with a relatively small army of mercenaries, yet the devastation that they inflicted on Italy, both physical
and psychological, proved to be far greater than could have been
imagined from their small numbers. The scars they left on the Roman
psyche remained for decades and affected the course of Roman economic and political development for centuries afterward.

THE CROSSING

Hannibal won a number of important battles against the Romans in
Italy, but his greatest accomplishment was his crossing of the Alps in
218 BC. Battles in the ancient world tended to be decided quickly,
usually within a day, but it took Hannibal nearly two months to get
through the Alps and two weeks to make it over the pass and down
into Italy. Every facet of his leadership was put to the test as nature
and the Celtic tribes inflicted heavier casualties on his army than any
battle he would ever fight. Yet Hannibal brought his army through intact and ready to face Rome. Alexander, in contrast, was devastated
when he led his army through the Gedrosian Desert, and after nearly
two months he emerged from his ordeal with an army on the verge of
mutiny and an empire in chaos.

The exact route Hannibal followed over the Alps has never been
conclusively determined. Julius Caesar tried to trace it, and Napoleon
pondered it. Theories abound, and the subject continues to draw
interested and enthusiastic audiences at conferences worldwide.
Hannibal's intended route probably was along the Mediterranean
coast, where the mountains are lower and weather conditions more
predictable. Unexpected developments forced him to follow a more
difficult path farther north and over higher elevations. What caused
Hannibal to deviate from the easier route was the unexpected landing of a Roman army at the Greek coastal city of Massilia (Marseilles)
while he was crossing the Rhone River somewhere between the modern French cities of Orange and Arles.

Roman ships transporting soldiers to northern Spain had put into port because of rough weather, and their commander immediately dispersed some of his cavalry units to reconnoiter the area. The Romans came upon Hannibal's scouts, and there was a brief skirmish. When the scouts reported the Roman presence, Hannibal's officers implored him to mobilize for battle, but he refused. His focus was Italy, and he knew that a loss to the Romans along the Rhone or even a stalemate could mean the end of his campaign while a win would gain him little beyond a temporary boost to morale. By avoiding battle, Hannibal demonstrated an important component of leadership: understanding which battles are important to win and which would simply waste resources and deflect attention from the objective.

Some of Hannibal's soldiers grumbled about cowardice, but he was thinking strategically. He ordered the army to move rapidly north along the river to avoid the Romans. Unfortunately, it cost Hannibal precious time and forced his army to cross the Alps at the onset of winter and at higher and more dangerous elevations than he had initially intended. As a result, his casualties were higher than they might have been had he crossed farther south—something which illustrates that decisions are not always easy and the costs can be high. Nevertheless, Hannibal reached Italy with an intact army.

Former News Corporation president Peter Chernin is a good example of a modern leader who focuses on the main objective and does not allow himself to become sidetracked. By just about any measure he is one of the most powerful leaders in the entertainment industry. Chernin ran Fox Broadcasting, the most-watched TV network in America, directed the largest movie studio in the industry, judging from 2008 box-office receipts, and oversaw a clutch of cable channels and an expanding array of Internet sites. He voluntarily left in June 2009, when his contract expired, and is now running his own production operations, which are being financed by Murdoch's company.

Fox television chairwoman Dana Walden told *Forbes* magazine in early 2008 about her own introduction to Chernin and his Hannibal-like way of focusing on objectives. In May 2001, Walden's group, the Fox television production arm, which creates shows not only for Fox but for other networks as well, had just sold two dozen shows for the fall

season, more than ever before. Walden and her partners felt like conquering heroes.

Chernin's reaction to their success was, "Congratulations, you're
ruining your business." Walden was stunned, but the message was clear:
Forgo those short-term sales and go after new, potentially more profitable markets. Walden saw the handwriting on the wall. "If we weren't
prepared to reinvent our company," she said, "we were going to die a
slow death." In other words, Chernin wanted her to focus on broader
markets and to innovate—to think outside the box: Will a show sell
well on DVDs even if it does not get high ratings on television?
Chernin inspired Walden and her partners to bring back *Family Guy,*
which had been canceled for the second time in 2002 but was enjoying new life as a cult hit on DVD. Since its return, the show has sold 17
million DVDs, including several straight-to-DVD movies.

CROSSING THE ALPS AND OTHER IMPOSSIBLE TASKS

There are scores of passes by which to cross from France into Italy,
but only a handful come close to matching the descriptions of Hannibal's pass found in the writings of two ancient historians: Polybius, a
Greek, and Livy, a Roman. Polybius lived during the second century
BC. Modern historians consider him to be a valuable source because
he claims to have followed Hannibal's route over the Alps. Livy lived
about a hundred years after Polybius, and while his history of Hannibal does not add anything new to the story, it confirms much of what
Polybius wrote.

Polybius and Livy agree that certain characteristics of Hannibal's
pass made it distinct from other Alpine passes. Less than a day's
march (about 15 miles) from the pass, Hannibal's column was ambushed by mountain tribes in a particularly narrow and difficult defile. After a day and night of hard fighting, Hannibal and his soldiers
were able to extricate themselves and regroup around an enormous
rock. The next day they followed the valley to its end, where they
came to what the ancient sources describe as a "great white wall." The
only way out of the valley was up and over one of the highest and most

dangerous passes in the Alps. The sources tell us the pass was so high there was snow on its summit all year, and the view from the top seemed to extend over all of Italy. The pass led down into the valley of the Po River, which Hannibal and his army followed to a large city, probably early Turin, inhabited by a people called the Taurini.

Given this information, all of the passes in the French Alps except one can be ruled out immediately. Most are too low to have snow on them year-round, offer no view of Italy, or do not lead directly to Turin. One pass in a remote section of the Alps meets all the criteria—the Col de la Traversette, which at 10,000 feet is the highest and one of the most difficult passes in the southern French Alps.

Even under ideal summer conditions the Col de la Traversette can be hard to reach, temperatures can plummet unexpectedly and sudden snowstorms reduce visibility to several feet. Summer storms and lightning strikes add another element of unwanted complexity to the mix. It is hard to believe anyone could take an army, much less elephants and horses, over this pass even under the best of conditions. The climb is very difficult, and up until fifty years ago the area was frequented by smugglers traveling between Italy and France and had a reputation as a place to be avoided because of "the ease with which triggers are pulled."

Although the pass used to be impossible to reach from October until late June because of the snow, as a result of global warming it is sometimes accessible even in winter. Under perfect conditions, it can take an experienced climber three hours to reach the summit. Halfway up from the valley floor there is a wide plateau that seems suitable for the base camp the ancient sources tell us Hannibal established for his army while his engineers stabilized the route ahead. Once the route to the pass was prepared, Hannibal sent the infantry over first, then the horses and pack animals, and finally the elephants.

Some of the problems that climbers encounter today, even in summer, are similar to what Hannibal's soldiers experienced. Most notable is the treacherous footing along the ledges. According to the ancient sources, the long column of men and animals trampled the snow into slush as they moved up the mountain, and it was so cold that the slush froze into a deadly layer of ice. A slip or momentary loss of footing could result in a slide, and a slide down the slopes or over the precipices brought certain death. The last third of a mile to the top is the most difficult because it involves climbing a steep snow chute that in places pitches between 45 and 60 degrees.

At the summit, the pass is only 30 feet wide, but it offers a spectacular view of Italy. The entire country opens before the climber. In the valley below, the Po River is visible, winding its way toward Turin in the distance. The view is inspirational. According to Polybius and Livy, Hannibal stood on a precipice and pointed it out to his tired and despondent soldiers as they passed him on their way over and down the other side.

The descent into Italy took the heaviest toll in casualties. As the engineers moved forward, they found sections of the path blocked by an avalanche. First they tried to climb over and around those sections, but so many men fell to their deaths that the effort had to be abandoned. Eventually, Hannibal's engineers were forced to chisel out a new ledge, using fire to heat the rock and sour wine (vinegar) to crack it.

When the army reached the lower elevations, the soldiers were finally able to rest. The climate was temperate and food plentiful, so Hannibal arranged entertainment—ostensibly to raise morale but also to make an important point. The soldiers were assembled in a great circle around some Gauls who had been captured in recent fighting along the route. Hannibal gave the Gauls weapons and ordered them to fight each other in matched pairs, gladiator style. He promised that the victors would be allowed to return home and the defeated would be freed from their imprisonment—by death.

At first the Gauls refused to fight because many of them were kinsmen. But when the reality of their dilemma set in, the contests began. Hannibal's soldiers were impressed by the bravery of the combatants, and when the fighting ended, Hannibal explained that they had witnessed men in desperate straits excelling because they had no other options. Like the Gauls, he told his men, they, too, were compelled by circumstances to excel. They could not turn back because the mountains were sealed by winter snows. Ahead of them was sure to be a Roman army that could not be avoided. They were caught between the proverbial Scylla and Charybdis—a rock and a hard place.

Hannibal explained that what they faced was more than an issue of survival. Defeat at the hands of the Romans would mean a cruel death and an unmarked shallow grave in Italy. Victory could mean glory and wealth for each of them. In case motivational speeches and dire predictions were not enough, Hannibal appealed to the self-interest of those he led. As Alexander had done, he promised each man in his command enough gold, silver, and slaves for a new start in life plus the opportunity to settle on tax-free land in Italy, Africa, or Spain. He concluded by telling his soldiers that retreat for them was not an option. Either they all moved forward, or they died where they stood. Then he ordered the army to break camp and move out onto the plains of Italy.

MOVING INTO ITALY

When the Romans realized that Hannibal had crossed the Alps, they sent an army north in a desperate attempt to stop him. The Roman legions outnumbered Hannibal's mercenaries. But most of their soldiers were inexperienced citizen-conscripts and farmers, poorly trained and led by politicians concerned with using the war to advance their careers at Rome. They were no match for the resourceful Carthaginian tactician, with his experienced infantry, skilled cavalry, and charging elephants.

Hannibal's first victory came in 218 BC at the Trebbia River, not far from where he had come down from the Alps. He exploited the ego of an inexperienced and pompous Roman commander who was looking for a quick victory. Hannibal goaded him into leading a suicidal early-morning charge through a freezing river and up a steep embankment against entrenched infantry. When the Roman soldiers who survived the charge tried to retreat, they fell into a carefully laid ambush Hannibal had set behind their lines.

The second Roman defeat came a year later at Lake Trasimene in central Italy. Hannibal enticed another impetuous Roman commander into a carefully laid ambush between the lake shores and the mountains. In short order the ambush turned into a massacre as the inexperienced Romans panicked and fled into the waters of the lake for refuge. When they tried to emerge, hands raised in surrender, Hannibal's cavalry slaughtered them in the shallows.

When word of the defeat at Trasimene reached Rome, there was panic. The road to Rome lay open and undefended. The cry "Hannibal ad portas" went up in the city—Hannibal is at the door. Terrified, the Romans resorted to what was for them a very uncharacteristic practice: human sacrifice.

Hannibal's officers begged him to march on Rome. They were only hours away from the city, but he steadfastly refused. One of the senior cavalry commanders lashed out in frustration, saying that Hannibal might know how to win a battle but he did not know how to win a war. Hannibal, however, knew a siege was something he could not afford to risk, as it would tie him down. To be successful against the Romans, Hannibal knew he had to remain mobile.

Bypassing Rome, Hannibal moved farther south, where in 216 BC he won his most spectacular victory of the war: Cannae. The Romans sent an army of eighty thousand to the eastern coast of Italy in a desperate attempt to overwhelm him by the sheer weight of their numbers. The army, the largest the Romans had ever assembled, was under the command of two generals—one competent, the other arrogant. Unable to set aside their differences and present a united front to those under their command, one general issued orders on odd-numbered days, the other on even-numbered days. The result was predictable: confusion.

While the Romans were marching in circles in response to contradictory orders, Hannibal was planning when, where, and how to fight. He positioned his army so that the rising sun on the morning of the battle would blind the Romans, and he checked the direction of the prevailing wind to ensure that the inevitable dust raised by the movement of so many men and animals would blow into the faces of the Romans as they advanced. This attention to detail, in combination with Hannibal's overall tactics, made the difference when the armies engaged. Hannibal won his battles because he exploited every advantage that terrain, weather, and psychology could afford him. Without doubt, he was a master of innovation.

TAKING ACTION IN A CRISIS

Blessed with insight like Hannibal and with charisma like Alexander, Lee Iacocca knows how to inspire and motivate people facing a crisis. His ability to get people to "believe" was never better demonstrated than in the late 1970s and early 1980s when he saved Chrysler Corporation. Hannibal said retreat is never an option, and Iacocca wholeheartedly agreed.

When Iacocca took over Chrysler in 1978, the company was broke and desperate. Something had to be done. He had been president of Ford Motor Company in the 1970s, and his record there in developing popular new models such as the Mustang was legendary. But Henry Ford II disliked Iacocca and did not intend to step down as CEO and let him take the helm. Instead, in spite of his success and ability to innovate in the areas of product design and marketing, Iacocca was dismissed by Ford in 1978.

Chrysler went after him. They struck a deal by which Iacocca agreed not to take a cent unless he turned Chrysler around. Just as Hannibal was driven from within to destroy Rome, Iacocca had a strong desire to prove that Ford was a fool for booting him out. So desperate were Chrysler's finances that Iacocca persuaded the federal government to provide the company with loan guarantees, arguing that a weak American economy could not afford the collapse of a major automobile manufacturer—a forerunner of the current bank, insurance, and auto industry refrain of "too big and too crucial to fail" that has resulted in the government pumping billions of dollars to keep banking, insurance, and automotive giants like AIG, GM, and Chrysler afloat. Just like today, Iacocca's request set off a political firestorm in Washington. But in 1980 Congress agreed to guarantee Chrysler $1.5

billion in loans if the company could come up with $2 billion on its own through cost cutbacks and concessions from unions, dealers, and creditors.

Iacocca persuaded the United Auto Workers to accept layoffs and wage cuts to save the company. Unprofitable model lines were eliminated from production as operations were streamlined and plants were closed. Iacocca knew that he had to boost revenue, so he bet everything on a new line of models, including what turned out to be the immensely profitable minivans and compact K-cars, models that Henry Ford II had rejected when Iacocca attempted to develop them at Ford.

To boost Chrysler's image, Iacocca went public, appearing in commercials with the line "The pride is back." Iacocca persuaded and cajoled American consumers, union rank and file, bankers, and car dealers in a way that Hannibal would have understood. Just as the Romans couldn't believe Hannibal crossed the Alps in winter without losing a single elephant, hardly anyone thought Iacocca could save Chrysler even with government-guaranteed loans. But by 1983 Chrysler had paid off all the debts, some of them years before they were due, and the company became immensely profitable. Iacocca was earning his money, but no one begrudged him a penny of it.

Effective leaders like Hannibal and Iacocca never lose sight of the importance of managing details. *Forbes* magazine once asked Iacocca if auto industry productivity suffered because of the charge that production-line jobs were dull and repetitious. Iacocca replied, "That's a lot of crap. It's always painted like we've got these guys in chains and we're beating their brains out. That's wrong. It's all subjective. Many days the president of Ford is bored stiff and I've got stuff I'd rather not do but that's life." The point—a successful leader attends to many unglamorous, tedious details that often turn out in the long run to be essential to achieving success.

LESSONS FROM CANNAE, THE MOTHER OF ALL BATTLES

Cannae was Hannibal's greatest battlefield victory. He proved once more that he was a master of innovation and a brilliant tactician when he faced a Roman army that outnumbered his forces perhaps three to one. Hannibal exploited a fundamental weakness in human psychology: specifically, the tendency to stop thinking rationally and start reacting emotionally when you are elated by what you think is imminent victory. When the two armies came face-to-face at Cannae, Hannibal placed his less reliable auxiliary forces in the front line and held his best infantry units and cavalry in reserve. When the front line collapsed, exactly as Hannibal anticipated, the overconfident Romans pushed through the center.

Elated by what they thought was going to be an easy victory, the Romans had no regard for the security of their exposed flanks and no idea what was about to happen to them. At that crucial point Hannibal ordered his infantry reserves to close on the Roman flanks while his cavalry rode to the rear to cut off any escape. Unable to maneuver, the Roman legions were pressed together so tightly that many of them could not draw their weapons to fight. Nearly fifty thousand Romans perished at Cannae that day, and the battle is known as the worst defeat in Roman history and Hannibal's greatest moment as a field commander.

After Cannae, Hannibal remained in southern Italy, burning cities, towns, and villages in an attempt to break apart the Roman confederation. He was always short on manpower and supplies. Both his brothers tried to reach him with reinforcements, and both died for their efforts. One led a relief column, complete with elephants, over the Alps, but the Romans were waiting when he came down the other side, cut off his head, and sent it to Hannibal as a warning of what was to come. The other brother died of wounds after a losing battle with the Romans in northern Italy.

But the Romans recovered, just as they had at the Trebbia River and at Lake Trasimene. They learned from their mistakes and changed their strategy to avoid large pitched battles, relying instead on time and attrition to work in their favor. Roman legions became more effective in smaller operations and directed their efforts toward keeping members of their confederation in line rather than taking Hannibal on.

The Roman strategy slowly began to work, and the course of the war shifted in Rome's favor. Only a few of the Italian city-states ever joined Hannibal, and by the closing years of the war he was no longer the formidable force he had been fifteen years earlier when he first came down from the Alps. His numbers were down, and his elephants, which had terrified the Roman infantry at the beginning of the war, were all dead, most of them taken by disease. But Hannibal had succeeded in keeping the Romans tied down in Italy, and Carthage remained untouched, the city's inevitable fall postponed for years.

Over time, the quality of the Roman officers improved as appointments were made on the basis of merit and ability instead of family ties and political connections. A new generation of officers came to maturity in the field, men who were not politicians looking to advance their political careers but professionals pursuing a career in military service. Scipio Africanus was one of them.

Scipio was only eighteen when he witnessed the slaughter at the Trebbia as a young cavalryman. A few years later, both his father and two uncles were killed fighting Hannibal. All three had been generals, and their deaths raised questions in Scipio's mind about the old, Roman approach to warfare against Hannibal: confronting him head-on, on his terms. The Roman senate placed Scipio in charge of a legion even though by law he was too young to qualify for the position. Then they approved his radical idea to draw Hannibal out of Italy.

The Romans desperately wanted to be rid of Hannibal, so Scipio proposed an attack on Carthage. It was risky because Hannibal was roaming southern Italy at will and could move against Rome at any time. But Scipio predicted that when the Carthaginians saw Roman legions landing on the shores of North Africa they would panic and send for Hannibal to save them. He was right. When Scipio landed in North Africa a few months later, the Carthaginian senate ordered Hannibal home.

Hannibal saw Scipio's plan for what it was, a ruse to get him out of Italy. But, like his father before him, he was a soldier and obeyed orders. The last battle of the war came at Zama in 202 BC. Scipio chose the place—the desert outside Carthage—and employed Hannibal's own tactics against him. He formed alliances with the desert tribes of the Sahara so he could utilize their cavalry; then, using a combination of infantry, cavalry, and elephants, defeated the master at his own game.

WHEN THE COMPETITION BEATS YOU AT YOUR OWN GAME

In business it happens all the time: Entrepreneurs and their companies achieve great success with an innovative product or approach only to have competitors figure out ways to outdo them by using their own creations and innovations. Xerox Corporation is a classic example. It invented the modern copier and brought it to market in 1960. Protected by an army of patents, it had nearly the entire market at the time, and its trademark name was transformed into an everyday verb used by millions of people when they want to copy something.

How to beat Xerox? American competitors Kodak and IBM tried to take on Xerox directly and failed. Several Japanese companies utilized a different approach: They turned out inexpensive and technologically simple copy machines and focused on the low end of the market. Those machines gradually improved, and the Japanese moved up the food chain, producing models that appealed to a larger and more sophisticated customer base. By the turn of the twenty-first century, Xerox was on life support as Canon and Ricoh took away market share with copiers that performed better and cost less. Although Xerox succeeded in making a comeback, it remains a far cry from what it was a couple of decades ago.

Scipio in victory proved remarkably generous. He spared Hannibal and Carthage but imposed a heavy schedule of reparations on the city to compensate Rome for the cost of the war. Hannibal was appointed magistrate for seven years, from 202 BC to 195 BC, and Carthage prospered under his leadership. He paid the Romans what was due them each year—usually early and more than they required. But Carthage still made many Romans nervous. Among them was an influential con-

servative senator named Cato, who had survived the carnage at Cannae and could not rest until Hannibal was dead and the city destroyed.
Cato ended every one of his speeches in the senate, no matter what
the topic, with the refrain *Carthago delenda est*—"Carthage must be destroyed."

Mounting pressure from the Roman senate eventually resulted in
an arrest warrant for Hannibal on charges of conspiring with Antiochus, king of Syria and an "enemy of Rome." Antiochus was a de-
scendant of one of Alexander's generals and an impediment to
Roman plans for expansion in the Middle East. Hannibal fled to the
king's court, where he became a "consultant" on Roman warfare.

Antiochus fought two battles against the Romans and was defeated. Hannibal moved to Crete and tried to live as inconspicuously
as possible but soon drew the attention of the local leaders. He won
their confidence when he showed them a number of large amphorae
that appeared to be filled with gold coins. He asked the Cretans to
guard his treasure until he was ready to leave, and they were only too
eager to accomodate. Hannibal sealed the neck of each jar in a public ceremony and then supervised their placement in the local temple
for storage.

Over the next few months the Cretans lost their interest in Hannibal other than to remark that his garden was overgrown and cluttered
with overturned statues. When Hannibal decided it was time to leave,
he asked them to safeguard his gold until he sent for it. They assured
him it would be safe and allowed him to move his belongings, statues
and all, from his villa to a waiting ship. Once Hannibal left port, the
Cretans broke open the clay jars in the temple, only to find them
filled with worthless metal ingots. Hannibal's gold was safely aboard
his ship at sea, stored in the bronze statues that had once littered his
unkempt garden.

On the run once more, Hannibal returned to consulting, this time
in the service of the ruler of Bithynia, a remote kingdom in northern
Asia Minor (an area of present-day Turkey across from Istanbul). The
Bithynian king, Prusias, like Antiochus, was eventually drawn into
conflict with Rome. One evening at dinner he complained that his

kingdom was short on fighting men but had an abundance of venomous snakes. If he could transform snakes into men, the king said, he could defeat the Romans. Hannibal urged him to innovate with what he had. So at Hannibal's suggestion Prusias sent his subjects into the countryside to gather all the snakes they could find. Snakes by the hundreds were placed in small and medium-size clay pots that were sealed with wax, perforated, and stored aboard the king's ships like cannon balls.

As the Roman ships sailed within range, the pots were placed onto catapults and hurled onto their decks. When the pots shattered, the agitated snakes disappeared below to find refuge among the galley slaves chained to their oars, and pandemonium ensued. Prusias won his battle, but the Romans returned to win the war. The defeated king gave up Hannibal to save his own life.

The Romans tracked Hannibal into the interior of Bithynia and cornered him in a remote village. He was sixty-four and tired of running. Nearly his entire life had been spent fighting the Romans, and he had no one left and no place to run. Rather than be captured and executed for the amusement of the crowd at Rome, Hannibal took his own life (in 183 BC), dying as he had lived—on his own terms even when the price was high. The Romans, finally free of their nemesis, went on to conquer the rest of the ancient world, leaving one of history's greatest commanders buried in a shallow unmarked grave.

To accomplish what he did against the Romans, Hannibal demonstrated an irresistible will, intense focus, and a disciplined approach. He had a singleness of purpose and the ability to inspire unquestioning loyalty in those who followed him. All those qualities were embodied in a mind that in terms of military strategy, tactics, and understanding of human psychology bordered on genius. He was a mixture of the best and the worst—or, as one Roman historian commented, *"inhumana crudelitas, perfidia plus quam Punica, nihil veri nihil sancti,"* which means that Hannibal displayed inhuman cruelty when necessary, had no respect for truth if it got in his way, and had no fear of the gods. He was capable of cruelty if circumstances called for it and was willing to sacrifice honor and religion. According to Polybius and Livy, he could be among the kindest and most compassionate of men and at the same time the cruelest, merciful when moved and callous if necessary, indifferent to the suffering of thousands and caring for the pain of one. For this Carthaginian commander, the end clearly justified the means.

Hannibal was an extraordinarily daring innovator. He not only conceived effectively original strategies but also had the ability to bring these "unthinkable" concepts to fruition despite immense, unforeseeable obstacles. In the corporate world that translates into doing what has never been done before in industries where giants like Rome already exist. There are risks. Some companies suffer the end that Hannibal—and, decades later, Carthage—ultimately experienced: death and annihilation. But numerous firms have exhibited dazzling successes equal to Hannibal's when hit by powerful counterattacks. They survived and came back, maybe not always as their former, glorious selves but as industry leaders nonetheless.

Hannibal relied on three primary leadership strategies: He responded to attacks with brilliant counterattacks and paid attention to detail. All three strategies have been utilized, with varying degrees of success, by contemporary leaders in the corporate world.

●   ●   ●

One example is Michael Dell, an eighteen-year-old college freshman who went from putting together computers in his dorm room to building the number-one company in the PC-maker world by the time he was thirty-five (2001). The PC business is ferociously competitive. Participants face constant attacks from price cutters and others coming up with new wrinkles and advances. How to get the advantage? Dell decided on a strategy that, like Hannibal's crossing of the Alps on elephants to attack Rome, was bold in its simplicity but risky and difficult to carry out. He cut out the retailers and wholesalers and dealt directly with customers.

Dell Computer became one of the fastest-growing companies in history handling corporate customer inquiries and orders by phone and over the Internet. Corporate IT departments loved Dell's sales and service because they knew exactly what they wanted and felt very comfortable dealing directly with the company. The results were spectacular. Dell dominated the highly competitive field the way Hannibal dominated the Romans on the battlefield. By 2004 Dell had sales reaching $60 billion.

But Dell's competitors worked to come up with more sophisticated and appealing products. They streamlined production, and Hewlett-Packard actually beat Dell to the punch in first using low-cost chips obtained from a company called Advanced Micro Devices. When it came to marketing, competitors knew that Dell's strength lay in selling to the corporate world, so HP and some of the others focused on the consumer market.

In 2004, Michael Dell stepped down as CEO. Despite having achieved Hannibal-like success, he was hit with a staggering setback, just as Hannibal had been. Once he was out of the management loop, Dell watched in dismay as his creation began to falter. By 2007 the company was in serious trouble as its stock collapsed, losing almost 60 percent of its 2004 value. There were embarrassing product failures as Dell laptops began overheating and even catching on fire. The company was late in spotting crucial market trends, such as the potential of the consumer market to expand much faster and be more profitable than direct sales to businesses and government agencies.

Michael Dell came back. Others in the computer industry who returned from retirement and tried to rescue their troubled companies, such as Gateway's Ted Waitt and Vonage's Jeffrey Citron, failed. But Michael Dell was like Hannibal—persistent and innovative. One surprise from the newly returned corporate commander was his announcement that Dell Computer was going into the retail business, creating what he hoped would be new and exciting products for the average consumer.

Starbucks is another company that prospered as a result of innovation. Coffee is a staple of American life. Anybody can make it, and countless retailers sell it. The industry didn't lack successful brands such as Maxwell House and Folgers or successful retailers such as Dunkin' Donuts or even Chock full o'Nuts. What made Howard Schultz of Starbucks different was that he transformed a mundane, cheap and essentially boring product into a special luxury for tens of millions of people. He brought excellent coffee and a European-style coffee-house mind-set to mainstream America. Like Hannibal, Shultz understood something about human psychology: People need a little something extra, a daily luxury or indulgence, to get them through the day, and they will be willing to pay for it. He made Starbucks cafes places where people can enjoy excellent coffee, espresso, and tea in a relaxed setting (except during the morning rush hour, when people line up to get their lattes and donuts or pastries before work). Even when consumers were complaining about the price of gasoline at the pump, they were willing to belly up to a Starbucks counter and spend ten times more per fluid ounce on a cup of coffee. Only the bone-crunching recession that hit full force in late 2008 put a real crimp in Starbuck's sales.

The company paid careful attention to detail, brilliantly handling the logistics of buying coffee beans from all over the coffee-growing world, creating an enticing array of different coffees and teas, and delivering and handling perishables ranging from high-margin sandwiches and fruits to donuts, pastries, and cookies. Starbucks didn't just sell coffee; it transformed America's thinking. The words *latte* and *Frappuccino* became part of the everyday vocabulary of millions of Americans as they adopted Starbucks terminology for sizes—"tall" instead of *small,* "grande" for *medium,* and "venti" for *large.* Unlike most restaurants, which want their customers in and out quickly, Starbucks took pride in encouraging customers to linger. Cafes multiplied because Starbucks management realized that the more outlets there were, the more people would find it convenient to grab a cup of coffee and a snack. Sales surged as outlets sprang up almost overnight everywhere from Athens, Georgia, to Athens, Greece. Dunkin' Donuts was left in the dust. Imitative chains emerged, but Starbucks easily beat off these competitors and almost all of the imitators failed. Starbucks had become a global icon. Schultz felt comfortable enough with what he had accomplished to turn the operating reins of the organization over to others.

But the new management lost its way, more interested in expansion than in focusing on the product and on the competition. Schultz grew increasingly concerned about the direction in which the company was moving. Though still the industry leader, Starbucks was no longer unique. Dunkin' Donuts woke up, introduced numerous new coffee creations as well as noncoffee beverages, and expanded its food offerings. McDonald's realized that coffee did not have to be a bad version of what the airlines served. Quality improved. In Europe and elsewhere McDonald's even opened Starbucks-like outlets right next to the traditional McDonald's stores. Local competition proliferated and took business from Starbucks. It soon seemed that every town had a favorite coffee house that locals swore was superior to Starbucks.

Starbucks stock dropped almost 80 percent from its 2006 highs. Shareholders and customers became disgruntled. Schultz took back control in early 2008 and curtailed expansion to focus on what had made Starbucks successful in the first place: good coffee and tea in the right atmosphere.

Few businesses are as competitive as athletic wear, yet Kevin Plank, the founder and CEO of Under Armour, saw an opportunity and ran with it. Plank was a football player in college and noticed that his teammates routinely went through several sweat-soaked T-shirts during practice or a game. Amazingly, makers of athletic gear had never thought to do something about the perspiration problem, but Plank did.

He visited a nearby fabric store and found a synthetic material similar to what was being used in compression shorts designed to keep injured muscles warm and relaxed. He paid a tailor to sew seven prototype shirts and then tested them on some of his fellow athletes. At first his teammates thought the shirts were a little too lingerie-like, but after trying them, they became believers. The shirts felt good against their skin and kept them comfortable and almost sweat-free.

Plank continued to improve his product and then established a network of friends and contacts to sell the shirts to college teams around the country. Business took off as the product line grew. Scores of professional and collegiate teams became customers.

Under Armour expanded and now sells not only perspiration-absorbing athletic apparel but also footwear and accessories (including football cleats). While Nike and other traditional businesses in the athletic-wear industry are going hard after Under Armour, Plank still has a Hannibal-like ability to innovate and sell. UA, in fact, has become something of a fashion icon, especially among young people, who gladly pay a high price for the item not only because of its unique attributes but because it shows that the wearer appreciates high quality. Sales are approaching $1 billion, and the company is expanding overseas. Plank has yet to meet his Scipio.

During the twentieth century, the food business underwent a massive transformation, from traditional family farms and ranches supplying the nation's produce and meat, to agribusinesses. The result has been a highly efficient supply chain that draws from all over the globe for its products. Mega giants in the industry dominate everything—the land crops are raised on, the plants that process food, the trucks that transport it, and the stores that sell it. Real prices have declined over time, but in the minds of consumers, concerns about quality, nutritional value, and freshness remain. The food industry is a notoriously competitive business with razor-thin profit margins. Traditional supermarkets are lucky to survive, and they make just one cent on every dollar of sales. The $500 billion annual market is dominated by Wal-Mart, the nation's largest grocer, with over four thousand stores.

Into this fray plunged John Mackey, the founder and CEO of Whole Foods. Mackey was an innovator and visionary who, like Hannibal, detected weaknesses in the empires that dominated the market and exploited them to his benefit. He was able to look ahead and see that natural foods could be the wave of the future. Most of the natural foods stores in existence in the late 1960s and early 1970s were small, visually unappealing, and poorly managed. Sensing an opportunity, Mackey started small. Using a few thousand dollars borrowed from family and friends, he opened a health-food store in a garage in Austin, Texas, in 1978. He sold produce from local farmers, as well as nut loaves and multigrain bran muffins made by nearby hippie bakers. Everything was strictly vegetarian, just like Mackey himself.

Mackey had a knack for selling, displaying, and managing. In his first year of operation, sales reached $300,000. Two years later, the first large Whole Foods facility opened. Even though Mackey was a vegetarian, he sold natural beef and other products in an attempt to attract a wide range of customers. Mackey's store was neat, and his employees were well trained, helpful, and knowledgeable about what they were selling. Whole Foods broadened its market by reaching out beyond the "hard-core organic foodies" to a much more diverse clientele. Mackey's customers did not have to be true believers in the organic food movement to feel welcome in his stores. Everything came together, resulting in increased sales.

As the demand for organic food exploded in the United States, Mackey expanded his company, maintaining margins that put the industry to shame. But natural food was pricey, and wags joked that because of the steep prices at Whole Foods the company should be renamed "Whole Paycheck." Despite the carping and rising prices, the company expanded and prospered. Mackey has dealt with competing chains the way Hannibal initially handled Rome. Whole Foods absorbed Bread and Circuses, Fresh Fields, Wellspring Markets, and Wild Oats.

When it comes to corporate management, Mackey sees himself as a kind of democratic renegade. The Whole Foods "Declaration of Interdependence" includes high-minded principles such as "satisfying and delighting our customers" and building "team member happiness and excellence." In his dealings with the people who work for him, Mackey takes a Hannibal-like approach. Whole Foods employees are "team members," coworkers vote on who stays and who goes after mandatory probation periods, and bonuses are pegged to performance. Mackey's approach to managing his people is based on a combination of peer pressure and self-interest. If you are not good enough, your team will vote you out, not the boss. Mackey has a personal antipathy toward labor unions, once commenting that having a union in your shop "is like having herpes, it doesn't kill you but it's unpleasant and inconvenient."

Always thinking ahead, Mackey is offering online shopping as he continues to try to bring organic foods into the American mainstream, where it still accounts for less than 3 percent of the $500 billion annual market. True, the prices at Whole Foods are not the bargain prices available at Wal-Mart and elsewhere, but Mackey tapped into a clientele of well-educated, health-conscious urban professionals and suburbanites who are willing and able to pay for quality food grown locally and naturally.

Another area that Mackey has successfully tapped into is the demand for ethnic foods. With the growth of immigration in the United States and a general awareness that there is more to food than pot roast and boiled potatoes, Mackey has used globalization to offer a wide variety of foods from around the world, such as Mexican and Thai, in his stores.

No Scipio has appeared on the horizon to challenge Whole Foods' domination of the natural foods market yet, although recently Wal-Mart, sensing opportunity, announced it would be making a foray into the natural foods business. But even before the crash of 2008, Whole Foods' stock had fallen on unnaturally hard times, plunging some 80 percent from its highs of four years earlier. One big factor: The rising costs of obtaining the food it sells made Whole Foods' already high prices look even higher. This inflation was quickly followed by the economic slowdown. Same-store sales growth fell by two-thirds. As times get tighter, people become less willing to buy premium, high-quality perishables. That's why Whole Foods is making serious efforts to attract more price-conscious customers. A new program called Whole Deal offers, among other things, money-saving coupons. Also, to help the bottom line, the company is pushing hard a growing array of high-margin, private-label products.

The lessons of Hannibal are not limited to innovative thinking. He was also a stickler for details, a quality that Anne Mulcahy has exhibited in her successful turnaround of Xerox. In 1999, the company consolidated thirty-six administrative centers into a mere three, thereby saving millions of dollars. At the same time, Xerox reorganized its sales division. The simultaneous consolidation and reorganization turned out to be a disaster. The company's billing system began failing as invoices were sent out for products and services that customers had never ordered. Sorting out the mistakes proved expensive and took months of valuable time. The resulting chaos cost Xerox dearly as customers fled to competitors. Anne Mulcahy was put into the CEO's chair with a mandate from the board of directors to get Xerox back on track.

As boss, Mulcahy had Xerox managers apply the principles of Six Sigma, a data-driven technique for finding and eliminating defects in business processes. Mulcahy recognized that the effort would have to be companywide; otherwise, the exercise would be incomplete or have unintended, even negative consequences for some parts of the organization.

The goal was straightforward: remove any unnecessary steps in making or doing things, work out the bugs, and make the process user-friendly to people long accustomed to the traditional way of doing things. Any quality improvement system worth its salt, however, involves scores of analytical methods. Training executives and managers to run it can take an enormous amount of time and energy. Applying a new system means ascending a steep learning curve, which can become tedious and expensive. Also, there is the problem of overcoming people's basic reluctance to do things differently.

But attention to detail often proves crucial, as the following example from Xerox illustrates. A critical part in a new $500,000 printer was unexpectedly wearing out too quickly. The culprit turned out to be the oil on the roller. Xerox managers worked with the company supplying the oil maker to refigure the formula, and the problem got solved. Because of Six Sigma, top management at Xerox did not need to bone up on the chemistry of oils; under Mulcahy's leadership, the organization had in place systems and lower-level managers able to deal quickly with such problems.

● ● ●

Hannibal is one of those leaders in history who is valued more for how he did things than for what he did. Whereas Cyrus and Alexander conquered and built empires, Hannibal did the impossible: He climbed mountains no one thought could be crossed, and he took on an adversary no one thought could be beaten. The Romans outnumbered Hannibal, yet he managed to outwit them at nearly every juncture by thinking ahead, managing details, and responding in a focused way to their attacks. He held things together for over fifteen years until his adversaries figured out how to fight the master on his own terms.

With Hannibal out of the way, Rome moved to take first position on the stage. Rome stepped forward to take control of the ancient world with new leadership and new ideas. Two of those leaders, Julius Caesar and Augustus, are the subjects of our next chapters.

part **IV**

8

THE ROMAN REPUBLIC

The Ultimate Multinational

Of all the great empires in the ancient world Rome lasted the longest and had the greatest influence on Western civilization. Its history stretches over twelve hundred years, from the legendary founding of the city by Romulus in 753 BC until its destruction by the Vandals in AD 476. Archaeological evidence, however, indicates habitation or settlement in the area of Rome from at least the first millennium BC. What started as little more than a primitive sanctuary for criminals and runaway slaves in the seven hills of a remote region of Italy called Latium eventually grew to become the largest enterprise in the ancient world.

For the first several centuries of its history, Rome lay dormant, largely ignored by the major powers of the time. But the Romans, by virtue of their strategic location, their reserves of manpower, and their natural inclination toward political and military organization, were destined to emerge from their seclusion and play a dominant role in the affairs of the ancient world.

Roman history can be divided into three periods: the monarchy, the republic, and the empire. The first period begins in 753 BC with the legendary founding of the city and ends in 509 BC when the last Etruscan king was driven out by a disgruntled aristocracy. During this period, Roman society evolved from *gentes*, clans whose members had

a familial bond and claimed descent through the male line. Each clan
was headed by a wealthy older male in a pattern of primitive feudal
governance that continued for centuries. At some point, these clans
came together under one king and took control of a large region of
the western coastal plain of central Italy bounded on the north by the
Tiber River and on the east by the Apennine Mountains

According to legend, the first Roman king was Romulus, a descen-
dant of the prince Aeneas, who escaped the destruction of Troy during the Trojan War. Romulus established a settlement on the Palatine,
the most defensible of the seven hills of Rome. His twin brother
Remus founded another settlement on an adjacent hill, the Aventine.
In a dispute over who would rule, Romulus killed his brother and established his authority over the Romans as their first king.

According to literary accounts based on legends, the early Romans
were mostly criminals and runaway slaves who needed women. In an
act of hospitality, Romulus invited a neighboring tribe, the Sabines, to
dinner, and after serving their guests copious amounts of wine, the
Romans seized the Sabines' wives and daughters. In no condition to
offer any defense, the Sabine men were driven out of Rome. A few
days later, sober and armed, they returned to retrieve their women,
but they found to their consternation that their wives and daughters
refused to leave.

After the death of Romulus, Rome was ruled by a succession of six
kings, each of whom appears to have been absolute in his authority. But
unlike the Egyptian pharaohs or the Persian kings, the Roman kings
were not worshipped as gods. The Roman monarchy seems to have
been based not on a dynastic divine right to rule but on a legal concept
that the Romans termed *imperium,* the king's unquestioned authority to
inflict capital punishment on any subject who refused to obey him.

The Roman king was the leader of his people in war and the
guardian of their safety in peace. His jurisdiction included cases of
treason and murder, both punishable by death. The symbol of his
authority became a bundle of sticks wrapped around an ax and
known as the *fasces.* The sticks symbolized the king's power to punish
any of his subjects by whipping and the ax his power to behead. The

fasces remained the official symbol of executive power in Italy until the death of Mussolini at the end of the Second World War, and they can be found today behind the rostrum in the U.S. House of Representatives and on old dimes!

The powers associated with the king evolved into the constitutional foundations of Roman law. The concept of imperium reflected the conservative Roman belief that discipline and order took precedence over liberty. Self-discipline, order, and simplicity were important to the early Romans and enabled them to systematically bring the entire Mediterranean world under their control.

The only restriction on the authority of the Roman kings appears to have been a common-law carryover from the early days of the clans that allowed each Roman male citizen, or *paterfamilias,* the right to rule his household as he saw fit. The paterfamilias could kill or sell into slavery anyone in his household who disobeyed him or questioned his authority, including his wife and children. A Roman male had the right to divorce his wife at will and dispose of her property. The role of the paterfamilias in the early years of Roman history was as strong and ingrained as the notion of imperium and came to influence the development of family law in Western civilization as reflected in the adage "A man's home is his castle."

The last of the Roman kings was an Etruscan, Tarquinius Superbus, known as the "arrogant." The Etruscans occupied the area north of Rome known today as Tuscany, and during the second half of the sixth century BC, they established control over the Romans. As Rome prospered and Roman influence extended into central Italy, the Romans chafed under the dictatorship of the Etruscan king. The resentment became a crisis when the king's son raped the wife of a respected Roman nobleman and the distraught woman, unable to bear the trauma, took her own life. Her funeral galvanized public opinion against the king and his son, and they were subsequently driven from Rome.

With no king to rule them, the Romans entrusted the functions and powers of the former monarchy to two annually elected magistrates called *consuls*, and Rome became a republic. The consuls were nominated by an advisory board of nobles known as the *senate* and elected by a popular assembly of all Roman male citizens. The consuls administered the affairs of the city, and the Republic became the most democratic period in Roman history. Political power over the next five hundred years was shared to varying degrees by the senate, the annually elected magistrates, and the popular assemblies.

Roman society during the Republic evolved into a two-tier class system, but there is evidence that the distinction between *patricians* and *plebeians* might have developed even earlier during the monarchy. All males who qualified for citizenship in Rome were assigned to one of the two classes based on their birth.

Those Romans born into wealthy aristocratic families were known as patricians and may have been descended from the old Etruscan nobility. Many patrician families, especially during the last years of the waning Republic, took particular pride in tracing their lineage as far back as the mythical founding of Rome. Some, like the family of Julius Caesar, even claimed descent from the gods. The patricians became the privileged class, the landholding nobility, and they exercised considerable political, social, and economic influence in Rome for centuries.

Romans who were born into modest or even impoverished circumstances but still qualified for citizenship were known as plebeians. They constituted the laboring classes—farmers, tradesmen, artisans, and laborers who became increasingly important as the city expanded and prospered. The patricians oversaw their estates in the countryside and ruled Rome, while the plebeians did the work that made the city run. Plebeians plowed the fields that grew the food, built temples and government buildings, paid their taxes, and in time of war came forward to fill the ranks of Rome's legions. As the Republic prospered and transitioned into an empire, many plebeian families accumulated significant amounts of personal wealth and began to play important roles in government.

The foundation of the Roman government was its constitution. It was not a written document but a set of beliefs, traditions, and laws that evolved over time. Roman government became a flexible system of overlapping popular assemblies, an advisory senate with no legal authority, and magistrates responsible for carrying out the executive functions necessary to run first the city and later the empire.

The popular assemblies were the most democratic institutions in Rome. Because of their size and the infrequent nature of their meetings, however, they had little impact on the daily workings of government beyond providing a forum in which every citizen could express approval or disapproval of what the government officials were doing. The senate was the most influential and stable of all the governing entities but had no legal authority. Composed of patricians and later wealthy plebeians, it came to represent the interests of the landed aristocracy and the commercial classes. According to legend, the senate was established by Romulus as an advisory board, composed of the most influential men around him. In fact, the Latin word *senator* is derived from *senex*, which means "old man," and senators came to be known as *patres*, or "fathers of the country."

During the period of the Republic, the senate's main purpose was to advise the consuls on the running of the city. Eventually, as Rome expanded throughout the ancient world, the senate also provided advice on foreign affairs. As a deliberative body, it was conservative. Although it had no constitutional power to pass laws and could only recommend actions on the basis of custom and usage, the senate came to direct the Romans in their most important matters of state.

The senate became powerful for two reasons. First, it was a permanent body that Romans could turn to in times of crisis when quick decisions needed to be made. Its conservative nature made it stable, and it served as a counter against two potentially disruptive political forces: (1) the whims of the people, which could manifest themselves periodically in the popular assemblies, and (2) a consul who might seize control of the army and attempt to become king. Thus a balance of power developed in Rome through a system of checks and balances that centuries later would influence the very foundation of U.S. constitutional law.

The second reason why the senate became powerful was that appointment carried lifetime tenure, and it became the place to which all magistrates retired after the expiration of their terms of office. As a result, the senate embodied a wide range of collective experience in all matters relating to the running of the city and later the empire—military, legal, financial, and political. Yet the senate was small and cohesive enough to get things done quickly and efficiently.

A very close tie developed between the magistrates who carried out the daily administration of the city and members of the senate, because they came from the same aristocratic, propertied class and had the same financial interests at heart. A consul made his decisions knowing that at the end of his term he would take his place in the senate, so cooperation became paramount.

The senate became the means by which the heads of the ruling families in Rome controlled the city and its administration. Then in the fifth century BC, the increasingly restive plebeians made demands for political reform. The popular assemblies took a more active role, resulting in Rome's first written law code—the Twelve Tables. A commission of prominent Roman legal scholars, the *decemviri,* or "ten men," traveled to Greece to study the Athenian law codes of Draco and Solon. When they returned, they drafted a code that gave plebeians increased civil and property rights, protections against judicial abuses by the consuls, and a stronger voice in directing the affairs of the city.

As a result of these reforms, many of the social, economic, and political barriers that had existed between patricians and plebeians for centuries were lowered. Because patricians depended on plebeians to provide the labor that made the city run and prosper, they chose accommodation and compromise in dealing with demands instead of repression and possible civil war. That is not to say that there were no periods when the Romans did not fight among themselves. They did on occasion. But in general during the early and middle years of the Republic, there seems to have been a willingness among both groups to resolve their differences within a framework of political cooperation and accommodation.

As a result of the reforms, plebeians were able to marry into the patrician class and gain access to the senate and the consulships. The concessions came during a period when the Republic was embarking on a series of domestic and foreign wars that would carry Rome to the pinnacle of power in the ancient world and plebeian cooperation and support were crucial.

This spirit of cooperation between the classes was especially strong from the fifth through the third centuries BC as Rome first unified Italy and then set out to build an empire in the western Mediterranean. The willingness to resolve differences in the common interest enabled the Romans to focus their resources on the conquests that would bring them great wealth and power. The problems between the classes that proved fatal to the Republic would develop toward the close of the second century BC as Rome became successful, powerful, and prosperous.

The Roman consuls were at the top of the *cursus honorum*—"course of honors"—a hierarchy of publicly elected officials, or magistrates, who directed the daily operations of the city and led the armies in time of war. Consuls could issue edicts as well as convene the senate and the popular assemblies to ratify their requests for laws. Each consul could veto the actions of the other. While the consuls were elected by the popular assemblies, the senate maintained control over them by deciding who was eligible to run for the office. Initially consulships were reserved for candidates from the patrician class, but over time wealthy plebeians were able to win election to the post.

As the plebeians gained in political and economic influence, they succeeded in creating an executive position to rival the consul: the *tribune*. Elected by the popular assemblies, tribunes were not technically a magistracy and did not hold imperium. They were elected as ombudsmen, to protect the plebeian class from exploitation by the senate and the consuls. A tribune had the legal authority to stop any actions of the senate or the consuls that he considered harmful to the plebeians by exercising a veto. By the second century BC, there were ten tribunes and they had become as powerful as consuls, and although the office was reserved exclusively for members of the plebeian class, some patricians sought it through sham adoptions into plebeian families.

There were two unique positions at the highest end of the administrative spectrum in Rome: *censor* and *dictator*. The censors were patricians elected by the popular assemblies every four or five years to serve an eighteen-month term. There were two, and they were responsible for compiling an official list of everyone who qualified for Roman citizenship on the basis of moral suitability and economic status. The censors' power lay not in their counting of the numbers but in their determination of each citizen's status. The level of a Roman's personal wealth determined his eligibility to remain in, or qualify for membership in, the senate and determined his place in the popular assemblies and election to the magistracies. Citizens could be removed from one class and reassigned to another with a loss not only of status but of political power.

Censors oversaw public morals and occasionally enacted laws to curb the Romans' growing love of luxury. They banned inappropriate behavior in public and even limited the number of guests at dinner parties and the serving of foods considered too decadent for consumption by sober, disciplined, honest Romans. The role of the censors was to keep the Romans on the right moral track by reminding them of the *mos maiorum,* the values and simpler ways of their forefathers. With prosperity, however, the Roman appetite for excess in every form grew—from food to violence—and eventually the office of the censor became an anachronism and disappeared in the early years of the Empire.

The dictator was the most powerful executive position in Roman government. In times of crises resorting to a dictatorship was determined by the consuls in consultation with the senate, and a candidate was elected by the popular assemblies to rule for no more than a six-month period. During his tenure the dictator could suspend the deliberations of the senate, overrule any actions of the consuls, and disband the popular assemblies. The Romans appointed a dictator only when they needed quick and effective solutions to serious political or military problems, and he became the personification of the traditional Roman belief that in times of crisis political discipline and expediency take priority over liberty.

As mentioned previously, the executive functions at Rome were organized into a hierarchy of public offices. From the lowly *aedile* tending to the upkeep of the city's bridges to the lofty dictator in whose hands was entrusted the very safety of the city, all candidates for public office had to begin their climb on the lowest rung of the cursus honorum. The only exceptions were the tribunes, who were elected directly by the popular assembly.

A patrician who aspired to power and desired to make his fortune in politics had to begin at the bottom of the political ladder and work his way up. Climbing the ladder was expensive because candidates had to spend large amounts of money at each level to win votes. Name recognition was important, and candidates often sponsored public spectacles, circuses, gladiator fights, and banquets to curry favor among the electorate. The cursus honorum became the instrument by which the senate regulated the entry of those they called "new men" into the realm of Roman political power. The senate set the minimum age requirements for holding each office, established term limits, and selected the candidates, while the popular assemblies actually voted on them.

Once the Romans had their political house in order, they undertook to build an empire through small, measured steps, first in Italy and then, as events unfolded in their favor, in Sicily, Spain, France, North Africa, and Asia. They came to control a vast empire almost by default, but once they developed a taste for empire feeding it became insatiable. The Romans began by establishing control over the tribes and cities that surrounded them. Italy was a mixture of independent city-states, tribes, and clans with diverse cultures that stretched from Gauls in the north to Greeks in the south. The Romans undertook to unite them into one people, initially by military conquest, and then by the development of a common system of law, politics, and language.

War was the primary means by which the Romans took control of Italy and eventually most of the ancient world, but it was not their only method. At first they were not powerful enough to rely solely on military force to bring their neighbors under their control. Nor did they believe that force was the only way to conquer. Diplomacy and willingness to extend the benefits of Roman citizenship to other

Italian cities and tribes played as important a part in the process of consolidating power as force. The Romans offered many of their neighbors an umbrella of protection as well as varying degrees of alliance, ranging from simple friendship to full citizenship, which could be adjusted up or down, depending on the cooperation and "good behavior" of the allies.

With each alliance or conquest in Italy, the Romans increased their pool of manpower and resources. Over time this development generated its own momentum and built for them a strong political and economic base. Allies were granted rights and privileges, including the protections of Roman law, and some allies became *cives sine suffragio,* which means they had access to all the private and civil rights of Roman citizenship but did not have the right to vote or stand for election. The conferment of even this partial franchise became a privilege eagerly sought by many who came under Roman sway either through treaty or by conquest. Time and again the Romans demonstrated in dealing with their neighbors a particular skill that combined judicious applications of force, negotiation, and accommodation. This gave many cities and communities throughout Italy an incentive to support Rome in order to enjoy the economic benefits and prestige of citizenship.

The Romans built a confederation of neighbors throughout Italy who with few exceptions remained loyal to them in times of crisis and provided a broad base of support on which to undertake the conquest of the ancient world. The support from the members of this Italian confederation proved crucial in Rome's wars of empire, first with the Greeks in southern Italy and then in three wars with Carthage.

By the beginning of the third century BC, all of central Italy had been incorporated into a Roman confederation. Only in the north and in the extreme south were the Romans uneasy with the inhabitants. The Gauls inhabited the Alps and the broad plains of northern Italy and gave the Romans reason for concern. They were fierce though undisciplined fighters who had nearly destroyed Rome when they attacked the city in 390 BC. The Gauls would be a continual source of trouble, and not until the first century AD would they be brought completely under Roman domination.

In the south, the Romans had to deal with the former colonies of the Greek city-states. Many of these cities were older than Rome itself, and there were so many of them that southern Italy and Sicily became known as Magna Graecia. In 280 BC, the Romans undertook a series of wars against some of these city-states that became known as the Pyrrhic Wars, after the king who led the Greek forces. In the initial conflicts, Pyrrhus defeated the Romans but lamented his victory afterward because the costs far outweighed the benefits, creating the modern term *Pyrrhic victory*.

The wars against Pyrrhus brought the Romans into contact with the military tactics of the more sophisticated Hellenistic world. The Romans were an intelligent and tenacious people who learned from defeat and remained focused on their long-term objectives. They refined their tactics on the battlefield, and by the end of the decade, in 270 BC, Roman armies had extended their control to the southern tip of Italy. The Pyrrhic Wars proved to be the first test of the strength of the new Roman confederation, and it held together as the Roman allies provided much of the manpower that helped defeat the Greeks.

Warfare played a central role in the civic and religious life of many ancient cities, but nowhere did it become more important than in Rome. Especially during the final years of the Republic, warfare became deeply entrenched in the Roman psyche and shaped the highest political offices by determining the careers of Rome's greatest leaders. The consuls assumed responsibility for planning and leading campaigns of conquest, and their battlefield successes from Spain to Syria and from Egypt to Britain affected their political careers.

Warfare was a seasonal activity. Roman citizens reported for military service in the early spring and often were able to choose the consuls under whom they wished to serve and the theater of operations. The Roman legions drew recruits from both classes, the officers and cavalry from the patricians and the infantry from the plebeians. Most recruits seem to have joined out of a sense of duty, but there was also the potential for significant personal gain.

Military operations usually began in the late spring after the rains had subsided and before the first crops could be harvested. They lasted until the onset of winter, when the Roman soldiers returned home or moved into winter quarters to await spring—a systematic pattern of warfare that enabled the Romans to eventually gain control of Italy and most of the ancient world.

After the conquest of the Greek cities in southern Italy, in 264 BC the Romans became involved in a conflict with Carthage on the island of Sicily that expanded into the wars, which were described in detail in the prior chapter on Hannibal. No other conflict did more to redefine the Romans and bring them to the pinnacle of the ancient world, yet at the same time planted the seeds of the Republic's destruction. The wars ended in the middle of the second century BC with the destruction of Carthage as Rome emerged as the most powerful state in the Mediterranean.

Macedonia, an ally of Hannibal, surrendered after the Second Punic War and became the first Roman province east of Italy. The once powerful Greek city-state of Corinth resisted Roman domination and was destroyed in 146 BC. Athens, seeing the handwriting on the wall, cooperated and was designated a Roman ally. Roman troops moved from Greece east into Asia Minor and south into Egypt. In the remnants of the old empire of Alexander the Great, the Romans opened a new and even more successful chapter of conquest and profit.

Over the next century, the Romans gained control of nearly every state in the Mediterranean. The governance of the provinces in Spain, France, Greece, and Asia Minor became a variation of the system that existed on the Italian mainland. Some cities and kingdoms voluntarily entered into a client-patron relationship with Rome and received the protection and prestige of an alliance. They were exempted from all taxes, and their citizens were granted full Roman rights. Some states were simply annexed through conquest and placed under direct Roman rule, with no freedom and a heavy, even oppressive, tax burden. Others became protectorates under Roman supervision—a flexible arrangement that allowed Rome to collect tribute but left the question of rendering costly military assistance to the discretion of the Roman senate on a case by case basis.

As a result of the conquests, almost every conceivable luxury that the ancient world had to offer flowed into Rome, creating prosperity that only fed an appetite for more. As the empire grew, the Roman senate was confronted by a multitude of problems and demands as emissaries from foreign nations came to present their requests. Provincial and Italian dependents as well as allies looked to the senate when they had problems that needed solutions. To govern these provinces, the senate put in place a system designed to exploit their resources, and as a result, the administration of the provinces became a big business. Because there was an immediate need for a code of regulations, the senate issued *lex provinciae*, a code for the administration of the provinces, but left the details of administration to the governors, as long as the taxes were paid.

Each year the senate determined which newly conquered territories would be governed by men of consular rank. The primary duties of a proconsul, or governor, were to defend the province from invaders, keep the local peace by administering justice in his courts, and, most important, collect taxes. Appointments were made almost exclusively on the basis of family connections, bribery, and influence. Governorships became guarantees of wealth, and former consuls flooded the senate with their requests.

The Punic Wars put Rome on the road to empire, but they also exacted a heavy price at home. They transformed the Roman economy and way of life, setting the stage for the demise of the Republic. The war with Hannibal had been particularly costly, in fact the most costly in Roman history. Small farmers, the economic backbone of Italy, were ruined and dispossessed. No longer able to make a living from their land or pay their property taxes, they watched helplessly as their land was taken and incorporated into estates owned by the Roman aristocracy.

These estates, or *latifundia*, became vast commercial enterprises worked by slaves brought in from all parts of the new empire. Landless and unemployed, the small farming class, as well as discharged soldiers with nothing to do and nowhere to go, began to migrate toward Rome, seeking solutions to their plight. The number of impoverished and disgruntled people demanding opportunity grew to alarming proportions. In the years to come, they would redefine Roman politics in an effort to reap some of the benefits of the new empire.

After the Punic Wars, Roman politics at the highest levels became polarized. On one side was the conservative class favoring the continuation of priviledged senatorial rule. On the other was a new breed of wealthy plebeians known as *equites*, or knights, who wanted a greater say in how Rome was ruled. This class had become wealthy by exploiting the commercial and military opportunities that developed as Rome expanded overseas, and many had made fortunes through their control of contracts to supply goods and services to the legions. At the same time, the poorer classes were making stronger demands on the political system through the popular assemblies and their ombudsmen, the tribunes. In combination with the equites, who courted their favor, the poor of Rome began to influence the election of consuls, who, needing their votes, pandered to them through the games and festivals.

Stresses in Roman society brought about by rapid economic and political changes reached dangerous levels in the last century BC as the Roman Republic experienced the worst period of civil disorder and political violence in its history. The years from the end of the Third Punic War until 27 BC, when Augustus took control, were a time of serious class conflict not just in Rome but throughout Italy.

Reformers came forward with demands for a redistribution of the land. Some of them, like the brothers Tiberius and Gaius Gracchus, were disaffected political aristocrats from mixed patrician and plebeian families, who because of a sense of social conscience championed the causes of the impoverished classes. They gained political power through the office of tribune and tried to reduce the power of the aristocrats in the senate and redistribute the wealth. They attempted to revive the class of small farmers who had been wiped out by the large latifundia, and their efforts at political reform and land distribution brought a violent reaction from the senatorial class. Roman politics became polarized between supporters of reform and supporters of the status quo.

In addition to its internal issues, Rome faced serious problems outside of Italy. The Greek city of Massilia (Marseille), which had allied itself with Rome during the Second Punic War, asked for aid against barbarian invaders who were migrating into the Rhone River valley. Roman armies established a base in southern Gaul at Aquae Sextiae (Aix-en-Provence) in 122 BC, and the area around Massilia was organized into a new Roman province called Gallia Narbonensis.

In 111 BC in North Africa, the Romans were drawn into a war with a defiant African king, Jugurtha. The conflict dragged on inconclusively for four years until the exasperated senate entrusted command of the legions in Africa to Gaius Marius. Marius returned to Rome a popular war hero, dragging the king behind him in chains. As a result, he was elected consul an unprecedented five times. When trouble with the barbarians broke out in Gaul again in 102 BC, Marius took command of the legions and defeated a large concentration of migrating tribes outside Aquae Sextiae.

Marius continued as a war hero and champion of the common people. As commander of the Roman army, he recruited men from the lower, impoverished classes and offered them careers in military service. He trained them to professional standards, and they became disciplined and loyal, not to the senate and people of Rome but rather to Marius alone!

Shortly after Marius stopped the Gauls outside Aquae Sextiae the Roman allies throughout Italy revolted. Cities that had supported Rome with troops and money during the Punic Wars felt exploited and excluded from the prosperity of the new empire. They had fought with the Romans and had helped build the new empire, and even though they were being assimilated in language and customs into the Roman culture, they felt relegated to second-class political and economic status.

Their dissatisfaction became so great that in 90 BC they revolted and established a federation of cities called Italia. The revolts were put down by Marius and his assistant, or quaestor, Sulla in a brutal two-year conflict that became known as the Social War (from the Latin *socii*, meaning "allies"). The war lasted until 88 BC, when the

Roman senate reluctantly agreed to bestow full Roman citizenship on all Italians and extend to them the benefits of participation in the political system.

The Social War temporarily diverted the Romans from their pressing internal problems, which surfaced again with renewed intensity. Although Marius and Sulla had served together, they were political rivals. Sulla came from an impoverished aristocratic family, Marius from the upper commercial class of the plebeians. Both had armies behind them, but Sulla won by occupying Rome and forcing Marius to flee to Africa.

Sulla changed the Roman constitution. He stripped the popular assembly of much of its legislative authority and curtailed the power of the tribunes. Confident that his power was secure with his conservative allies in the senate, he set out for Asia Minor to begin a new round of imperial conquests.

While Sulla was away, Marius took back Rome. Now it was the liberals exacting revenge on the conservatives. Sulla returned to Italy in 83 BC and was met on the shores by two young supporters, Pompey and Crassus, each with his own private army. A savage civil war ensued, and a triumphant Sulla took Rome in 81 BC and had the senate declare him dictator for life.

To curtail the power of the people, Sulla crippled the office of the tribune and packed the senate with his supporters. He undertook a series of bloody purges, which came to be known as the *proscriptions,* and by 79 BC, he felt confident that he had placed Rome back on a conservative track. He retired to the countryside and died a natural death the following year. With Sulla's death the Republic entered its final and most agonizing period.

Pompey, Sulla's young protégé, developed a consuming ambition to reach the heights of political power in Rome and had a knack for changing political sides. Sulla had given him the title *magnus,* or "great one," before he had even won a battle, and Pompey's family had become wealthy by taking advantage of the proscriptions to buy up the properties of the condemned at distressed prices. As he began his political ascent, Pompey maintained his popularity with the com-

mon people because of his military exploits and kept favor with the aristocrats because of his conservative stance. Pompey's goal seems to have
been to gain entry into the priviledged and prestigious patrician class.

Pompey's first military success in his own right came when Sertorius,
a governor in Spain, rebelled against Roman authority. Sertorius was a
liberal reformer and undertook to make Spain an autonomous democratic state. He established a senate on the Roman model, opened
public schools, and accepted Spaniards into his new regime as citizens.
In 80 BC, the senate sent Pompey, who was too young at the time to
hold even the lowest political office at Rome, to crush the revolt.

Pompey returned a hero and then undertook to help Crassus put
down the final stages of a slave revolt that had broken out in southern
Italy. Like Pompey, Crassus was an ex–Sulla man who had become extremely wealthy through his political connections in the senate and
his real estate transactions. Because Rome had no public fire department, Crassus formed a private one. When a fire broke out in one of
the crowded wooden tenements in the city, he would hurry to the
scene and offer to buy the property from its distressed owner as it
burned—hence the term *fire sale*. Once he had obtained the best
price, his men would put out the fire and Crassus would have the
property rebuilt and promptly sold.

Pompey had joined Crassus to put down the revolt of a Thracian
slave named Spartacus, which had started in 73 BC. For nearly two
years, Spartacus led an army of runaway slaves and criminals who
looted, murdered, and burned the Italian countryside. Spartacus defeated the first Roman legion sent against him, and it took the combined efforts of Crassus and Pompey and the duplicity of Cilician
pirates to finally end the war in Rome's favor.

The victory in Spain and the triumph over Spartacus made Crassus
and Pompey popular. Even though they were peers in vanity and ego,
they chose to cooperate and were elected co-consuls for 70 BC. Then in
an unexpected turnabout, they became the darlings of the reformers
and the bane of the conservatives. Under the consulship of Pompey
and Crassus, the power of the senate was curtailed, and the office of
the tribune was restored to give more political power to the plebeians.

Pompey was not content to remain at Rome. He wanted to win even more military glory, and an opportunity presented itself in the eastern Mediterranean. Piracy had been a problem there for decades and was seriously hampering the profitable Roman sea trade. Cicero, Rome's greatest orator and lawyer, persuaded the senate to pass a law giving Pompey extraordinary powers to subdue the pirates. The new law, *lex Gabinia*, gave Pompey control over the entire Mediterranean Sea.

The pirates were defeated in 67 BC, and the senate rewarded Pompey by putting him in charge of the new Roman war against Mithridates, a king in Asia Minor. The senate approved another law, *lex Manilia*, which gave Pompey dictatorial powers over Asia Minor, Armenia, and Syria. He became for all intents and purposes a king in the eastern Mediterranean, and using the legions under his command, he reorganized the provinces there. Pompey returned to Italy at the head of the largest army in Roman history and to the greatest welcome ever given a Roman general. He was immensely popular.

A new class of men had now emerged to lead Rome—men like Marius, Sulla, Pompey, Crassus, and, later, Julius Caesar. These were powerful new political figures who benefited from the inflow of wealth from the overseas provinces and exploited the anger the dispossessed Roman urban poor felt toward the rich. As consuls, they led legions of professional soldiers who became loyal to them, not to the government in Rome.

Political power in Rome had traditionally rested with the aristocrats; now, it lay increasingly with the families of the new commercial class. The attainment of high political office became the main goal of these families because it meant prestige, power, and more wealth. Individuals captured office not so much on the strength of their political philosophy and policy but on the appeal of their personalities, charisma, and conquests. Rome began to be dominated by men who were self-seeking, larger-than-life figures who won the support of the masses through the distribution of free food, olive oil, and wine, and the sponsoring of public entertainment. Surpluses that flowed to Rome from the fertile fields of its provinces overseas—Carthage, Sicily, Sardinia, and Numidia—allowed free distributions to the restless and unemployed urban proletariat. This class continued to grow in Rome, and candidates for public office competed for its support.

The Roman games, *ludi Romani*, first appeared in the early years of the Republic as day-long religious festivals. By the end of the Republic, they consisted of elaborate circus performances, horse and chariot races, animal hunts, and gladiator fights that could last as long as two weeks. Admission was usually free and financed from a combination of funds from the public treasury and contributions by men seeking public office. Sponsorship was valuable because it allowed a candidate to preside over the games and increase his public exposure at election time.

This new breed of power seekers exploited their appeal as war heroes and projected themselves as champions of the common people. They were ambitious and pursued power and glory through the performance of great deeds in the service of the Roman people. The most effective way to reach the heights of political power in the last century BC became by leading Roman legions against foreign kings, barbarians, and Oriental potentates, then returning in triumph and sponsoring games and festivals with the money. Military success was the fast track to the top, and the desire for it produced a class of ambitious men who undertook quasi-private wars to gain wealth, popularity, and political influence.

When there were no foreign enemies to fight, they turned on each other and succeeded in destroying the Republic through a series of civil wars that started in Italy and spread throughout Greece, Egypt, North Africa, Asia Minor, and Spain. Two of those men, Julius Caesar and Augustus, are subjects of the next chapters.

9

JULIUS CAESAR

Ego and Ambition

"When the gods wish to take vengeance on a man for his crimes they usually grant him considerable success and a period of impunity, so that when his fortune is reversed he will feel it all the more bitterly."
—JULIUS CAESAR

Ambition is among the strongest and most creative forces in the arsenal of human psychology and frequently the reason things get done. It also is one of the most dangerous—that drive to grab the biggest slice of the pie before anyone else and sometimes even the entire pie. Julius Caesar (101–44 BC) had plenty of ambition. Early in his career he happened upon a bust of Alexander the Great. Comparing himself to the great king, Caesar lamented that he was the same age as Alexander had been when he died but that by age thirty-two Alexander had conquered a world and so far he had done practically nothing. Vowing that would change, Caesar entered the Roman political arena and the rest is history.

The word for "king" in German is *kaiser,* and the word for "supreme ruler" in Russian is *czar.* Both come from the Latin word *caesar,* confirmation of this ancient leader's profound impact on history. In today's communications age, Julius Caesar would be a highly effective CEO. He was a superb orator who could appeal to a wide array of constituents, from common citizens to soldiers to officers to aristocrats to

merchants to foreign leaders and women. He was an excellent writer and an amazingly capable executive, who successfully undertook enormous endeavors fraught with risk. Caesar had a natural talent for sizing up situations, knowing when to push and when to hold back. Throughout his career, he learned from his mistakes. Only at the end of his life, at the height of his success and power, did hubris, ego, and the daggers of his assassins converge to destroy him.

Ambition is not all bad. Healthy doses can pay off. The trick to mastering ambition is recognizing the rewards when they come your way and then deciding when enough is enough. Left unchecked, ambition can cross the line, mutating into arrogance and avarice, two of the most destructive of human impulses. When ambition crosses that line, the result, as we will see in Caesar's case, can be a compulsiveness that leads to self-destruction.

Interestingly enough, it seems that for every person driven by ambition, a hundred seem content or complacent enough to accept what they have and walk away. Take, for example, Steve Wozniak, cofounder of Apple Computer. At age thirty-four, Wozniak chose to take his profits in 1985 and walk. Today, his partner, Steve Jobs, is still at it, the innovative force behind exciting products such as the iPod and the iPhone. What makes a Wozniak walk and a Jobs stay on the treadmill? Successful ambition, as Jobs demonstrates, seems to be a healthy mix of energy and determination, well-defined goals, and an ethical framework to keep within honest parameters.

THE DARK SIDE

Julius Caesar was the consummate politician of his time, a gifted writer, and one of history's great military commanders. He was a man of action—equally skilled with the persuasive word, the pen, or the sword—yet also a tragic example of the consequences of unchecked ambition. Although Caesar set standards for success and leadership that continue into our own age, he also shows us—like Alexander before him—that unbridled ambition is capable of turning on and destroying anyone, no matter how powerful and seemingly untouchable.

Caesar projected a sense of sovereign self-assurance. There was no question that he was the boss and considered himself the only man for the job. Of course, Caesar was not the first person to live with the delusion that he alone could handle the top job. But in his case, that sense of self-worth turned out to be a double-edged sword. It mesmerized his followers and galvanized his enemies. Throughout his career, Caesar gave the impression that he always knew where he was going and what he was going to do when he got there. That impression eventually proved to be his undoing as it mutated into an imperious arrogance that cost him his life.

●   ●   ●

A recent example of an executive who let ambition warp his sense of judgment and perspective is Edward Finkelstein, a highly respected and successful retailer who shocked the corporate world by presiding over Macy's bankruptcy in 1992. When Finkelstein joined R. H. Macy & Company as a young management trainee in 1948, the company was one of several nationally known department store chains, its most famous rival being Gimbels.

By the 1960s, Macy's had become stagnant, but its bright star was

Finkelstein, who was proving to be a superb retailer through his management of the company's Bamberger's stores in New Jersey. Finkelstein transformed dowdy, uninteresting Bamberger's into a place to shop where consumers were eager to spend their time and money. He spiffed up the facilities and offered attractive merchandise, soon gaining a reputation in the retail world as a wunderkind. It was no surprise in 1980 when Finkelstein took the helm at Macy's.

Macy's did well until 1985, when Finkelstein decided to take the company private through a leveraged buyout. The company would borrow massive amounts of money to buy out existing public shareholders, leaving as owners a handful of Macy's managers along with private equity funds that invested in the business. Eventually the company would go public again by selling its stock, and the managers and private equity funds would reap huge profits. At least that was the plan.

Thanks to his success, Finkelstein was revered by Macy's managers. That intense admiration deepened when he allowed hundreds of them to buy stock in the recapitalized company; significantly profitable participation in such deals was usually reserved for a handful of top executives. The devotees of this retailing Caesar believed that in just a few years, the value of their investment would increase sixty- to ninetyfold. But that did not happen. Intoxicated by his success, Finkelstein started making mistakes.

To boost profits, Macy's began pushing its own private labels despite the fact that customers still wanted traditional brands. Consumers preferred prestigious labels or at least merchandise with names they recognized. Private labels in department stores often connote "cheap." But Finkelstein kept the prices on Macy's private labels so high that even customers who, to save some money, might have overlooked the stigma of in-house brands chose not to buy them.

Even though Macy's was heavily in debt from the initial stock buyout, Finkelstein tried to buy Federated, a collection of department stores that included Bloomingdale's and I. Magnin. Finkelstein lost that battle in 1988 to Robert Campeau, a leverage-buyout artist from Quebec; but as part of an agreement with Campeau, Macy's did get to purchase

Bullock's and I. Magnin. Macy's debt, already extremely high, ballooned even more. The new debt schedule that resulted from the acquisitions meant that absolutely everything had to go right, there was no margin for error. But the 1989 Christmas season was disappointing, losses mounted, a national recession occurred in 1990–1991, and the red ink became a flood.

Finkelstein enjoyed playing his executives off against each other, and as conditions worsened, he behaved as if temper tantrums and bellowing would make Macy's debts disappear. Company morale suffered as a result, and Finkelstein's image tarnished. He aggressively promoted two of his sons, and some of his key executives began leaving. Finkelstein became increasingly aloof, even watching the Macy's Thanksgiving Day Parade in his private viewing stand instead of with his top executives.

After another disastrous Christmas retail season and crushed by debt, Macy's filed for bankruptcy in early 1992. Instead of listening to any criticism of his stewardship or suggestions for improving the situation, Finkelstein shouted his critics down and refused to take any responsibility. He blamed forces beyond his control since his ego would not allow him to admit that he bore even marginal responsibility for the bankruptcy.

Macy's creditors finally did to Finkelstein what the senate did to Caesar. They finished him off. But, Finkelstein's story, unlike Caesar's, has a relatively happy ending. Federated, which Finkelstein had tried to gobble up only a few years before, bought Macy's in 1994, and a considerably humbled Finkelstein became a well-paid consultant to the new enterprise.

IF YOU ARE GOING TO CROSS THE RUBICON, MAKE SURE YOU KNOW WHAT YOU'RE DOING AND WHERE YOU'RE GOING

Much of Julius Caesar's success can be attributed to the fact that he was focused and decisive and knew how to get things done quickly. Nothing illustrates the interaction of these qualities more forcefully than Caesar's decision to lead Roman legions under his command across the Rubicon River in 49 BC. It was a defining moment not only for Caesar but for history. By crossing the Rubicon, he not only defied Roman law but began a civil war that transformed Rome and changed the ancient world.

As Caesar prepared to cross the river on the night of January 10 in 49 BC, he reflected in solitude for a while, then turned to his commanders and gave the order. When they reached the other side, his first words were *Alea iacta est* (the dice have been thrown). Since that fateful night, the phrase "crossing the Rubicon" has come to mean willingness to undertake a major and risky course of action from which there is no turning back. It is a move that requires foresight, strength of character, and willingness to accept the consequences of one's actions, both good and bad. Caesar knew that he was about to plunge Rome into civil war and that as a result he would either become master of the ancient world or be killed. He was willing to accept either outcome.

"Crossing the Rubicon" means embarking on a course of action from which you cannot turn back. What is the lesson here? Be sure to think before you act and to understand fully the implications of what you are about to do—the rewards as well as the costs for yourself and others. Once you decide on your plan and take action, don't look back or second-guess yourself. Execute your plan to the best of your ability and let the chips—or dice—fall where they may. When Caesar crossed that river in 49 BC, he released the dogs of war, and once out they could not be restrained but had to run their course.

CAESAR'S BEGINNING

Gaius Julius Caesar was born into an obscure and relatively impoverished family of Roman patricians. His father died when Caesar was in his early teens, and the family was left with little money or political influence. Young Caesar took pride in his aristocratic lineage, and he told everyone who would listen that his family could be traced back to the very founders of Rome and even to the patron gods of the city.

Ultimate success, the top spot, came relatively late in Caesar's career.

He was in his late forties by the time he attained the consulship, Rome's highest political office, and in his fifties when he took power as dictator after the conclusion of the civil wars. Cyrus and Alexander, by contrast, were leaders who came to power early in their careers and by force of arms. Caesar used force only at the end. To position himself to become dictator or perhaps even king, he had to make his way up from the bottom of the Roman sequence of elective offices known as the *cursus honorum.*

Caesar came of age during a time of political and economic dislocation in Rome and throughout Italy. The war with Hannibal the century before and the rapid acquisition of an empire had changed everything for the Romans. Small farmers had fallen on hard times and were rapidly being displaced by large plantations worked by slaves and owned by wealthy absentee landlords. The importation of cheap grain from Roman provinces abroad and the easy availability of slaves to do the work destroyed the traditional economy. Lower- and middle-class tax-paying Romans found themselves impoverished and unemployed with few prospects for the future. With nothing left to tie them to the countryside, large numbers were migrating to the city searching for opportunities.

By the first century BC, the stresses in Roman society had reached dangerous levels. Prosperity was increasing because of imperial expansion, but only two classes were reaping the benefits: aristocratic patricians and *equites,* or knights, a new commercial upstart group from the plebeian class. Because little wealth was flowing down to the poor, Rome entered into a period of severe civil disorder and political violence.

Marius—the popular war hero and a liberal force in Roman politics for a more equitable distribution of the empire's wealth—was Caesar's uncle by marriage (Caesar's aunt Julia was Marius's wife). The resistance of the conservative patrician class to Marius's reforms drove Rome into civil war (88 BC). When the war ended, Marius was firmly in control and Caesar's political career got its start. Young Caesar married Cornelia, the daughter of Cinna, Marius's liberal co-consul.

Still in his teens, Caesar was appointed to his first quasi-political post, as a priest of Jupiter.

In 82 BC, the political pendulum at Rome swung once more from left to right. A new leader, Sulla, took control of the city and re-structured Rome in the interests of the aristocratic class. He took away the free grain ration from the poor, abolished the rights of Roman citizens to be tried by their peers in the popular assemblies, and established minimum age requirements for holding public of-fice (like any good conservative, Sulla believed that older men made wiser and better leaders than younger ones). Then, not content merely to reform Roman politics and the welfare system, he under-took a purge of the liberal element in government through a pro-cess known as *proscription*. Lists of individuals and families considered dangerous to the state were published in public places. The lucky ones were allowed to go into exile; the rest were executed and their property was sold for pennies on the dollar to Sulla's officers and closest friends.

Because of Caesar's relationship to Marius and Cinna, his name came up for inclusion on the lists. As Sulla pondered his fate, friends and family prevailed on the dictator to spare "a mere boy." Sulla re-luctantly agreed, but with this caveat: "Take him; only bear in mind that the boy you are so eager to save will one day deal the death blow to the cause of the aristocracy; for in this Caesar there is more than one Marius." Sulla saw in young Caesar the potential for him to be-come a popular reformer, a leader who could rally the masses behind him as his uncle Marius had done and endanger the interests of the aristocratic class.

As a condition of sparing Caesar's life, Sulla required him to di-vorce Cornelia. When Caesar defied the order, Sulla stripped him of his priesthood and his wife's dowry. Impoverished and fearful, young Caesar got as far away from Rome as he could by securing a minor po-sition on the staff of the Roman governor in Asia Minor. He spent the next several years in Rome's eastern provinces (81–75 BC), keeping a low profile.

After Sulla died, Caesar returned to Rome. On his way back, he was captured by pirates who ran a lucrative business capturing Romans and holding them for ransom. They proposed a modest ransom of 10 talents (around 600 pounds of gold or silver) for Caesar and incensed at what he considered a cheap price for his life, demanded they increase the amount to 50. He remained a captive on a remote island while the ransom was being raised and to pass the time, wrote poetry, exercised, and dined with the pirates. He recited some of his verses at dinner, including lines in which he threatened to return one day and crucify them all. The pirates loved his poetry and attributed his threats to youthful bravado. Misjudging and underestimating Julius Caesar would later cost them their lives.

Once the ransom was paid and he was released, Caesar made good on his promise. He returned to Asia Minor, obtained a small fleet of warships from the Roman governor, and hunted down the pirates. Captured and condemned to death by crucifixion, they pleaded with Caesar to spare them because of the good times they had shared. Touched by their pleas, he ordered their throats cut before they were crucified to minimize their suffering on the cross.

THE POLITICAL CLIMB TO THE TOP, RUNG BY RUNG

When Caesar returned to Rome, he entered politics, determined to reach the top of the cursus honorum. In 69 BC, he was elected *quaestor,* military paymaster and commissary officer. This position was one of the lowest rungs on the political ladder. In the same year, Caesar's aunt Julia died, and he transformed her funeral into a political event. In her eulogy, he revived the memory of her husband, the popular reformer Marius.

The funeral was the first time since Sulla had proclaimed Marius a public enemy years before that anyone had dared to mention his name in public. Plebeians in the crowd shouted their support for Caesar until he went on to tell the crowd that he was descended from the kings of Rome and could trace his lineage to the goddess Venus. Talk about kings did not go over well with the plebeians. Rome had been a republic for nearly five hundred years, and there was no more hated word in the Roman lexicon than *rex,* or "king."

Death came again to Caesar's household, this time taking his wife, Cornelia. Once again he used a family funeral to speak about Marius and the need for political and economic reform to benefit the people of Rome. Caesar was eager to climb higher on the cursus honorum, but running for office was expensive, so he turned to Marcus Licinius Crassus, one of Sulla's ex-generals and a very wealthy Roman. Sulla had been a mentor to Crassus, and Crassus became a close ally of Caesar. With his help, in 65 BC Caesar was elected *aedile*, the magistrate in charge of public building projects, entertainment, and the grain supply. A step up on the ladder, this high-profile position required him to sponsor games, gladiator fights, plays, and other spectacles, all of which he did with an eye to winning the favor of the people and advancing to the next rung.

By virtue of his patrician background and election to the aedileship, Caesar was eligible to sit as a junior member of the senate. He spoke frequently on behalf of the poor, and crowds assembled outside the chamber to support him. Conservative senators voiced their fears that a revolutionary movement might be brewing "because of the hopes the poor fix upon Caesar." Then, in what was possibly a political move to curry favor with those aristocrats, Caesar married Pompeia, granddaughter of the arch-conservative Sulla. By 62 BC, he had been elected *praetor,* an understudy to the consul and the second-highest political office in Rome.

During the period when Caesar was praetor, Clodius, a patrician playboy, pursued his young wife, who, according to some of the ancient sources, was "not unwilling." Each year the Romans celebrated the festival of Bona Dea, the goddess of women, in the homes of the city magistrates. One of the homes selected that year to host the festivities was Caesar's. The occasion was exclusively reserved for women, and it was unlawful for a man to attend the ceremonies or even be in the house while they were going on. The most important rites took place at night with considerable revelry and music, for Bona Dea was the mother of the wine-god Bacchus. When Caesar and the men of his household left, Clodius entered disguised as a woman. He was discovered and the next day, word spread throughout Rome, and the incident escalated into a scandal.

Clodius was indicted for heresy, but before the trial could begin, Caesar divorced Pompeia. At the trial, Caesar testified that there had been no affair between Pompeia and the accused. Why, then, the prosecutor asked, had he divorced her? "Because the wife of Caesar must be above even suspicion," Caesar arrogantly replied. Clodius was acquitted.

In 61 BC, at the end of his term as praetor, the senate appointed Caesar governor of the province of Spain. Governorships were highly sought because they provided opportunities to make significant amounts of money through tax collections and other forms of extortion. Caesar surprised everyone by proving to be a popular and able governor. When his term in Spain ended, he returned to Rome to register for the next round of elections.

Although he had done well in Spain financially, Caesar liked to spend. He built houses for himself in Rome and spent considerable sums entertaining and sponsoring public spectacles—all with an eye to elections. Caesar needed money to run for the city's highest political office, the consulship, so he turned again to Crassus and to a second powerful figure in Rome: Pompey.

After his victories in Asia Minor, Pompey returned to Italy at the head of the largest army in Rome's history. He had made lavish promises of land and pensions to his veterans, and he needed to find a way to make good on them. His opponents in the senate had blocked most of his requests for money and land, so he was receptive when Caesar approached him with a proposition for a mutually beneficial political alliance with Crassus. The three formed an alliance, known as the First Triumvirate, to advance their interests. The first goal was to get Caesar elected consul, which would allow the *triumvirs* (three men) to circumvent the aristocrats in the senate and run things in Rome to their own advantage. They would have executive power in Caesar, an army with Pompey, and money with Crassus. It was an unbeatable combination. To cement the alliance, Pompey married Caesar's only child, Julia.

Then in 59 BC, Caesar formed another political alliance. He took as his third wife Calpurnia, the daughter of the president of the senate. From the senate floor conservatives railed that it was "intolerable to have the highest magistracies of Rome prostituted by marriage alliances and to see men helping each other to power, armies and provinces by means of their women." Nevertheless, relying on his popularity, the deep pockets of Crassus, and the intimidating presence of Pompey's soldiers, Caesar was easily elected consul. His co-consul was Bibulus, an aristocrat so intimidated by Caesar that he retired within the walls of his villa and passed the time engaging in "aviary augury."

Caesar's first move as consul was to present a proposal to the senate designed to carry out his part of the bargain with Pompey: allotments and distributions of land for his veterans. Catering to his own constituency, Caesar proposed generous grants of public land for Rome's urban poor. When opposition from aristocratic landowners in the senate threatened to defeat the proposal, Caesar bypassed the senate and appealed directly to the people of Rome in the assemblies.

From that point on, Caesar got everything he wanted and in the process became very popular with ordinary Roman citizens. He distributed public land throughout Italy, released debtors from a significant part of their obligations, and reformed the system of tax collection. These actions infuriated the aristocrats, who not only held most of the land in Italy but also collected the taxes and held the debts of the poor. Then, to make matters worse for the aristocrats, Caesar undertook to reform the administration of the provinces and end corruption among the provincial governors.

As consul Caesar presided over the senate. In dealing with those who opposed him in the chamber, he became heavy-handed and impatient, adding new names to his already long list of enemies. One of them was Cato, a highly respected patrician senator who was the spokesman for the aristocracy and, along with Cicero, a champion of republican values. On one occasion when Cato rose to speak out against some of Caesar's proposals for reform, Caesar had him dragged from the senate and imprisoned. This act, however, stirred so much outrage even among the common people that Caesar rescinded the order and shipped Cato off to Cyprus to head up a provincial reorganization commission. When another senator, Lucullus, dared to criticize Caesar, Caesar turned on him with such ferocity that the man fell to his knees on the senate floor and begged forgiveness.

When Caesar's consulship came to an end, he asked the senate to award him the governorship of Gaul (France) for five years instead of the usual one-year term. He considered Gaul the one place in the empire where he could achieve a military triumph that would exceed anything Pompey or Crassus had ever achieved. Only a small portion of southern Gaul, along the present-day French Riviera, was under Roman control; the rest was unconquered territory and held the potential for tremendous wealth. Not coincidentally, Gaul's proximity to Rome would allow Caesar to keep a close eye on political developments at home.

Conservatives in the senate tried repeatedly to block his appointment, fearing that he would use Gaul to enrich himself, raise an army, and threaten the Republic. That was exactly what Caesar intended to do. Backed by his father-in-law, Piso, his son-in-law, Pompey, and his old friend Crassus, he succeeded in pressuring the senate to award him not only a five-year governorship of Gaul but also the governorships of Cisalpina, the Roman province in northern Italy and Illyricum across the Adriatic Sea in northern Greece and present-day Albania.

The years Caesar spent campaigning in Gaul became the defining moments of his career. He was forty-three when he became governor, and he would spend the next ten years waging a war to showcase his ability as a military commander and win glory in the eyes of the Romans. Caesar needed his war not only to build his financial reserves and military but also to cover his political bases. Victory in war was the way ambitious men in Rome acquired popularity and gained the standing that invariably translated into political power at the highest levels. It was also the way to build a personal army. Pompey and Crassus had used conquest and victory to rise quickly in their careers. Caesar intended to surpass them and become supreme ruler not only of Rome but of a world larger than the one conquered by Alexander nearly three hundred years earlier.

Caesar made good on his promises to himself. He brought the entire area from the Spanish Pyrenees to the French Alps under his control and made two successful incursions—one across the Rhine River to attack the Germans in their own territory, the other across the English Channel to invade Britain. He sent vast amounts of treasure as well as hundreds of thousands of captives to Rome in a successful effort to remain popular with the people. Even though he was in Gaul, Caesar remained immensely popular in Rome as he financed new building projects, entertainments, and distributions of grain. He sent dispatches to Rome chronicling his exploits, which were published and widely circulated. Today those dispatches form the basis of Caesar's famous literary work *The Gallic Wars*. Forced to acknowledge his overwhelming popularity as a conqueror and the vast amount of money and large numbers of slaves he kept flowing into Rome, a reluctant senate proclaimed a two-week public holiday in his honor.

Caesar's political problems in Rome, however, were not behind him. In 59 BC, just before the end of his consulship, a motion had been brought before the senate to hold an inquiry into his conduct. Caesar had managed to avoid the investigation by arguing that as governor of Gaul he was immune from any type of civil or criminal prosecution. It was a valid legal point as long as he remained in government service. However, once he became a private citizen, he would lose his immunity, and his enemies in the senate were eagerly awaiting that day.

In an effort to head off his political problems, Caesar brought Pompey and Crassus together at Luca, a town in northern Italy, and prevailed on both of them to seek election as consuls in 55 BC. It was agreed that after their co-consulship ended in 54 BC, Pompey would govern Spain for five years and Crassus would govern Syria. With his associates as consuls, Caesar would be guaranteed a second five-year term in Gaul and protection from senatorial prosecutions. Pompey and Crassus easily won the election and proceeded to bully the senate into extending Caesar's term as governor to 50 BC.

In 54 BC, Caesar's daughter Julia died in childbirth at the home of Pompey. The death of her infant followed a few days later. Both Pompey and Caesar grieved, but her death loosened their bonds of kinship and unraveled their political alliance. The First Triumvirate came to an end the following year when Crassus was killed in Syria. He had set out for his province early, eager to win fame in a campaign against the Parthians, but he was ambushed in northern Iraq and killed. The Parthians filled his severed head with molten gold and sent it back to Rome as a warning against any further incursions into their territory.

The Roman Republic now began a slow drift into anarchy, and for nearly three years street gangs operating in the guise of political clubs terrorized the city. Some of the most violent were headed by Caesar's political allies and by their rivals who supported Pompey. There were frequent clashes between them in the streets, and in one brawl the meetinghouse of the senate was burned. In response, the senate passed emergency legislation giving Pompey authority to restore order. The rioting had moved them closer to Pompey and the perceived security of his army.

Caesar recognized the danger to his political position in the sudden shift of alignments at Rome, and in a move to provide for his own security, he reinforced his army beyond the number authorized by the senate with new recruits from Gaul. Caesar trained them in Roman battle tactics and promised citizenship in return for their loyalty. Then in 51 BC he sent a request to the senate to prolong his command in Gaul until the end of 49 BC so he could run for the consulship the following year. Caesar still needed the protection of his office to avoid prosecution by his enemies in the senate.

One of Caesar's centurions appeared before the senate to convey his request for an extension of his command. When the senators denied the request, the centurion slapped the handle of his sword and said, "If the senate will not give its approval, this will." Pompey sat silent. A motion was made that Caesar be recalled before the expiration of his term as governor, and then a second motion was made that he be required to appear in Rome if he intended to campaign for the consulship.

Roman law required candidates for public office appear in person to campaign. Caesar was certian that if he returned as a private citizen he would be indicted on charges of abusing his authority during his terms as consul and as governor. He had used physical force for political ends as consul, even embezzling money from the public treasury (normal behavior by Roman politicians at the time). He had exceeded his authority when he invaded Gaul, increased the size of his army without senate authorization, and violated Roman law when he sought to evade prosecution by prolonging his governorship. There was no way Caesar would return to Rome to face any charges without an army behind him. However, he made several attempts to reach a compromise with the senate by offering to resign the governorship of Gaul and his other provinces as soon as he was elected consul. But the senate rejected his proposal and nominated new governors to replace him.

The senate's action amounted to an order that Caesar surrender to his political enemies. When the tribune Mark Antony, Caesar's closest political ally, threatened to veto the measure, he was driven out of Rome. Antony joined Caesar, who had established his camp north of the Rubicon River, the boundary between the province of Gaul and Italy proper. According to Roman law, Caesar could not cross that river at the head of his army. He had to relinquish his command and enter Italy as a private citizen. As such, he was subject to arrest. When the senate learned that Caesar was at the Rubicon, it declared a state of emergency and immediately handed military control of Italy and Spain to Pompey.

As the divide between Caesar and Pompey widened, Caesar attempted to narrow it by offering Pompey his sister's granddaughter in marriage, even though she was already married. In return, Caesar asked for the hand of Pompey's daughter. Pompey refused on both counts, and the situation came to a dangerous impasse. Once more Caesar offered to compromise. He would surrender his command if

Pompey would do the same, and both would become private citizens again and run for the consulship. Pompey refused, arguing that he had been appointed by the senate and was operating in accordance with Roman law. It was Caesar, he argued, who had to comply with the law and surrender his command.

Meanwhile, Pompey remarried, and his new father-in-law was Scipio, an influential aristocratic senator and an enemy of Caesar. In the senate, Scipio proposed that if Caesar did not lay down his arms immediately he should be declared a public enemy. When the senate split on the matter, Scipio and his supporters cried out that against an enemy of the Republic like Caesar. The time had come to take up weapons, not cast votes.

In response Caesar offered to surrender his army with the exception of two legions if the senate would allow him to stand for the consulship in absentia. The senate refused. When moderate voices expressed their fear of impending civil war, Pompey boasted that Rome need not fear Caesar because "Magnus Pompeius" (the great Pompey) had only to stamp his foot and he could fill Italy with his armies. Cato the Younger, great-grandson of the Cato who had fought Hannibal and staunch defender of Rome's traditional conservative values, threatened to impeach Caesar the moment he set foot in Italy.

From a legal point of view, Caesar was guilty of starting the civil war when he crossed the Rubicon at the head of his army in violation of Roman law. But hard-line conservatives in the senate who refused to compromise and insisted on his recall and trial also bore responsibility for what happened. The animosity of many of them toward Caesar and their insistence on deposing him made compromise impossible.

When Antony reached the Rubicon and related what had transpired in the senate, Caesar made his decision to cross the river and march on Rome. Over the next several years, civil war touched every part of the Mediterranean world—from Spain and North Africa, to Greece, Egypt, and Asia Minor.

Aristocrats in the senate sided with Pompey because they believed he could be used against Caesar, not because they liked him. Cato, Cicero, and other conservatives supported Pompey as the lesser of two evils. They saw the senate losing its authority and dignity to opportunists who contended for power and wealth for their own ends, not for the good of the Republic. They believed that in fighting Caesar they were saving an old order from the destructive new wave of popular democracy embodied in him.

Caesar commanded fifty thousand of the most skilled and loyal soldiers in the Roman army when he crossed into Italy. He had molded them over the last ten years into the best infantry in the ancient world; they were disciplined, experienced, well equipped, and capable of moving quickly from one theater of operations to another. Most of all, they were loyal to Caesar, and in return he provided them with everything from the best equipment money could buy to generous retirement packages, grants of land, and promotions. When Caesar crossed the Rubicon, Pompey had no legions in Rome, but he had the numerical advantage because at his disposal were all the military resources of the Roman Empire from Spain to Asia Minor.

CAESAR TAKES OVER

As refugees arrived at Rome with word that Caesar was moving south with his army, panic swept the city. On the senate floor, Pompey was criticized for allowing Caesar to become so strong, and senators mockingly urged him to begin stamping his foot and fill Italy with his legions. Instead of taking decisive action to counter Caesar's advance, Pompey issued an edict declaring a state of anarchy, then left Rome for Illyricum in northern Greece, where one of his armies awaited him.

Caesar entered Rome less than sixty days after crossing the Rubicon, without fighting a battle. He conferred in a gentle and affable manner with the senators who had remained, urging them to send a deputation to Pompey and find a solution to the crisis. Some of them underestimated Caesar's resolve, and when he asked for the keys to the public treasury they refused. But when Caesar threatened to execute any who continued their "troublesome interference," they produced the keys, and he took control of Rome's gold supply.

Instead of pursuing Pompey to the east, Caesar headed west to

Spain and defeated Pompey's forces there in a series of battles. Pompey's soldiers who survived were either dismissed from military service and sent home or allowed to enroll in Caesar's legions. With Spain secured, Caesar returned to Rome, where the senate implored him to reach a settlement with Pompey. But Caesar was finished with proposals for compromise. In his mind, Rome would have only one ruler at the end of the civil war. The senate proclaimed Caesar dictator, and he turned his attention east to the final showdown with Pompey.

Pompey had assembled his army at Dyrrhachium, on the Adriatic coast of northern Greece. He was in a secure position behind fortified walls and well supplied by convoys of his ships. Caesar crossed the Adriatic in April of 48 BC and laid siege. Pompey launched a surprise counterattack, forcing Caesar and his army to withdraw. Pompey had taken the initiative and briefly enjoyed an advantage, but he failed to follow up, thereby allowing Caesar to recover. Caesar commented that "Magnus" still knew how to win a battle but did not know what to do with his success. At a second battle in central Greece, at Pharsalus, Caesar won a decisive victory, and Pompey fled to Egypt. When Caesar reached Alexandria, a wicker basket was handed to him as a gift from the young pharaoh, Ptolemy XII. It contained Pompey's head. When Caesar saw it, he wept and remarked that he had not wanted things to end like this between them.

The Romans had long coveted Egypt as a province to add to their empire. Fighting soon broke out between Caesar's army and the forces of the pharaoh, during which the great library of Alexandria was burned. After executing Ptolemy, Caesar turned the administration of Egypt over to his new mistress and political ally, Cleopatra, and her younger brother Ptolemy XIII. In 47 BC, Caesar led his army north into Asia Minor, where Pharnaces, a client-king of Rome, had taken advantage of the civil wars to declare his independence. Caesar defeated the king in a quick battle and sent the senate a three-word report: "Veni, Vidi, Vici" (I came, I saw, I conquered). The battle of Zela in northern Asia Minor was classic Caesar—quick, thorough, and decisive.

That same year Caesar pursued the remnants of Pompey's army to the shores of North Africa, where the mercy he had shown earlier toward the defeated was now replaced by slaughter. No quarter was either asked for or given. At Thapsus, a city situated on a headland of the Tunisian coast, most of Pompey's remaining officers were killed or, like Cato, committed suicide rather than surrender. The final battle of the civil war took place at Munda, in Spain, where Caesar cornered Pompey's two sons. With their defeat, he became undisputed master not only of the Roman Empire but of the entire Mediterranean world.

Caesar returned to Rome to celebrate his triumphs, carrying the head of Pompey's eldest son as a trophy. He was welcomed into the city as a hero, and senators fell over one another to gain his favor. He treated those who had opposed him and now asked for pardon with mercy and even generosity, a quality that the Romans termed *clementia.* Caesar declared there would be no proscriptions against his former enemies, and many of them were allowed to resume their former offices and recover their property lost during the civil wars. It was a remarkable course of action for a conqueror to take, and it indicated Caesar's genuine desire to reunite all Romans, but under his leadership.

In the summer of 46 BC, the senate proclaimed Caesar dictator for ten years, then in 44 BC "dictator for life with divine honors." Caesar took to wearing a purple robe and a laurel crown. In the senate, he sat on an elaborate throne instead of on the *sella curulis,* the traditional simple chair that had been used by consuls for centuries. The senate renamed the fifth month of the year July in his honor, and coins were issued bearing his portrait. All over Rome statues were erected in his honor, and the distinction between *res humana,* "the living man," and *res divina,* "the god," became blurred. Mark Antony was appointed high priest of a new temple where the faithful could gather to worship and praise Caesar.

Dictatorship had been established in Roman law since the earliest days of the Republic, but it was always a temporary expedient sanctioned by the senate during a crisis and intended for six months or less. Extended dictatorship went against tradition and in Roman eyes came perilously close to monarchy. When Caesar first became dictator, it was generally believed he would reform the Republic as Sulla had done and then resign. But as his power grew, he began to make unsettling remarks about the value of dictatorship and to display a growing "imperiousness of manner." In a society where freedom of speech had been the cornerstone of government for centuries, Caesar began to stifle and punish criticism.

The implications of his actions seemed clear: Rome was moving toward monarchy. Even some of Caesar's supporters and close friends feared he intended to destroy the Republic. But Caesar remained immensely popular because he had brought stability to Rome after years of political turmoil and devastating civil war. His power rested on the army, and he continued to take good care of his soldiers, dispensing generous bonuses and providing retirement packages of land and money for his most loyal veterans.

RUNNING ROME, OR "OUR LEADER IS CONSTANT AS THE NORTHERN STAR"

Caesar's first move as dictator was to reform the government. He started by filling vacancies in the senate resulting from the civil wars, and he increased the number of senators to nine hundred. At his insistence, the senate enacted legislation conferring citizenship on the Italians and Gauls who had been his allies, and he appointed many of them to serve in the senate. The number of magistrates who carried out the administrative duties of the city and the empire was substantially increased. Caesar provided that except in the case of the consulship, half of the magistrates should be appointed by the assemblies while he appointed the remainder. Then, in a show of his clemency and reconciliation, he admitted to elected office and to the senate the sons of men who had opposed him on the battlefields.

His second move was to rebuild Rome's infrastructure. Because Rome's population was now over a million and the city was overcrowded, maintaining public safety and order was difficult. Public works projects were begun to relieve congestion and improve services. A highway was constructed from the Tiber River across the Apennine Mountains to the Adriatic Sea. In Greece, Caesar ordered the construction of a canal through the Isthmus of Corinth, and shortly before his death, he began plans to drain the marshes around Rome to create more usable land.

To feed the poor, Caesar ordered the distribution of free grain and cooking oil, and he imposed tariffs on imports to stimulate domestic production. He enforced an old Roman law against imported luxuries, going so far as to place his agents in marketplaces to report on items sold in violation of the prohibition. A form of rent control was instituted for all Romans with the adjustment of rent tied to their income levels.

Doctors and teachers from all parts of the empire were encouraged to resettle in Rome with immediate grants of citizenship and stipends. Caesar funded public education and libraries. Then, as conditions improved, he put many of Rome's poor to work by requiring the owners of the largest estates to have one-third of their workforce composed of Roman citizens and to pay them a fair wage. As a result, many of Rome's urban poor were taken off the dole, and others were resettled in overseas colonies.

Caesar continued the state-sponsored public banquets and entertainments. There were gladiator fights, circuses, chariot races, naval battles, and plays throughout the city. The people loved Caesar because he brought Rome stability, the beginnings of prosperity, and entertainment. He had accomplished everything he set out to do. The young lieutenant who had gazed in awe at a statue of Alexander the Great twenty-four years before and lamented that at the same age he had accomplished nothing was now the most powerful man in the Roman Empire. He had conquered more territory than Alexander and had no rival or competitor on the horizon. The only enemy Caesar had was his own ego. With success came feelings of invincibility and infallibility. The ingredients were all coming together in a toxic brew that would spell the end of the ancient world's greatest conqueror.

CAESAR AND THE PERILS OF OVERREACHING

Real estate and finance are two areas of business prone to overreaching and hubris. Real estate developers by nature have to be optimistic, and their projects require careful planning and often years to come to fruition. Like Caesar, they often have to borrow to finance their projects. When money is cheap and plentiful, borrowing can be easy. They rationalize increasing leverage as an effective and quick way to generate more projects. It's easy to understand how they can get carried away in good times and overbuild. There's an old joke about developers who read in the newspaper that an area will need five thousand new housing units in the next two years. A hundred developers run out, and each of them builds five thousand units. Then when the dust settles, and most of the units are sitting unsold in a saturated market, and creditors are clamoring for their money to be repaid, the developers ask themselves, "What happened?"

What they did was let short-term success blind them to the realities of the long-term market, just as Caesar's success blinded him to what was coming his way in Rome. Developers take on too much debt because they think a strong, robust housing or commercial real estate market will continue forever—just as Caesar and Alexander thought they would rule forever. Then, as predictably as the sun rises each dawn, credit markets tighten, demand weakens, and the economy slows. Developers suddenly find themselves left high and dry, but they can be the last to realize—or at least to fully appreciate—that conditions turned and they failed to turn with them. Remember the Persian "wheel of fortune" and the advice to Cyrus a few chapters back?

The late William Zeckendorf could be termed the Julius Caesar of American real estate because he fell into that trap. His ambition and overconfidence resulted in overreach, which trumped sound business judgment and brought about his downfall.

From the end of World War II to the mid-1960s, no one personified the imaginative, innovative, risk-taking empire builder more than Zeckendorf. He is credited with developing much of the urban landscape of New York City and bringing United Nations headquarters to Manhattan. The UN had been negotiating with city authorities for a site and when the talks broke down UN officials decided on an alternative site in Philadelphia. Zeckendorf had been buying property along the East River, between Forty-second and Forty-eighth streets, amassing a 17-acre site that he planned to transform into a complex of office and apartment buildings dubbed X-City. When he heard the UN was looking in Philadelphia, he offered the organization most of his land in Manhattan and sealed the deal when he convinced a young Nelson Rockefeller to talk his father, John D., into financing the project.

Using cutting-edge architects such as I. M. Pei and Le Corbusier, Zeckendorf developed other successful projects, including Kips Bay Plaza in New York City, L'Enfant Plaza in Washington, D.C., Mile High City in Denver, and Century City in Los Angeles. The successful and flamboyant Zeckendorf became a media favorite as he backed Broadway shows and cut a familiar figure at New York's trendiest nightclubs. Politicians, business executives, and bankers all solicited his advice. Zeckendorf loved to boast that he handled as many as thirty-five telephone calls an hour while simultaneously entertaining visitors and clients in his office suites.

Thinking he would go on forever at the top of the real estate heap, Zeckendorf overextended himself financially, taking on massive amounts of debt at high rates of interest to finance a growing number of projects. His ideas were bold and imaginative, but his appetite exceeded his balance sheet's ability to support what he wanted to do. Debts began to overwhelm cash flow. Zeckendorf's empire collapsed in 1965 when his firm, Webb & Knapp, was forced into bankruptcy—the most spectacular failure in the real estate industry at the time. A decade later, when Zeckendorf's life came to an end, he was a broken man battling the IRS over back taxes.

Finance is another area of business prone to the pitfalls of Caesarlike ambition. The financial crisis that hit in the summer of 2007 is a prime example. It capped several years of increasingly reckless lending practices in the housing industry. Banks and mortgage brokers fell over themselves to write mortgages no matter what the credit qualifications of the prospective homebuyer. Incomes were not checked. No down payments were required. Appraisals didn't matter. Indeed, some mortgages didn't even require payments of principal or interest—"negative amortization" was what they called it. Lending officers were upbraided by superiors if they didn't churn out enough mortgages, quality be damned. Some brokers aggressively solicited would-be home-buyers even among the homeless. Bouts of lax lending standards are chronic characteristics of the money world as supposedly flinty-eyed financiers succumb to manias, though what we have seen in this decade is without historical precedent in size and scope.

Diners Club credit card was an extraordinary innovation when it was introduced in 1950. It was designed to help salespeople dining with clients pay their tabs without worrying about whether they had enough cash on hand. American Express, which had developed and popularized traveler's checks, jumped onto the credit card bandwagon in 1958 and targeted high-end users. Then banks entered the fray with the revolving charge cards Visa and MasterCard. But not until the 1960s and 1970s were millions of Americans persuaded to use these new plastic instruments of personal finance.

In 1977, James Robinson III, a forty-two-year-old dubbed "Jimmy Three Sticks" by his critics because of the Roman numeral he appended to his name, took over as CEO of American Express. Robinson was a courtly southern gentleman from a prominent Atlanta family and a graduate of Harvard Business School. He had worked for the blue-chip banking firm Morgan Guaranty Trust Company before joining Amex in 1970. But behind the southern charm and graciousness lurked a real Caesar.

Robinson was driven to make American Express the world's premier financial institution, and he wanted to do it quickly. Like Caesar with his eye on the ancient world, Robinson surveyed the financial world and beheld an empire of insurance companies, Wall Street brokerage houses, banks, and mutual funds waiting to be conquered. In 1981, he bought control of Shearson Loeb Rhoades for nearly a billion dollars. Shearson had become a Wall Street powerhouse through mergers engineered by Sanford Weill. Other deals followed, including the $550 million purchase of Geneva-based Trade Development Bank. This deal brought American Express into the closed realm of Swiss private banking, a small industry that catered discreetly to the richest individuals in the world.

As a result of his initial success, his company bought Republic Bank, a commercial bank, and then purchased Minneapolis-based Investors Diversified Services. IDS pedaled mutual funds, annuities, and CDs to individual investors—products notorious for their high fees. At the same time, Robinson continued to successfully promote the American Express credit card in television commercials featuring stern TV cop Karl Malden warning viewers not to leave home without it.

Robinson came very close to building a globe-girdling financial services empire. But it was not to be. His plans were undone because there was no rationale or glue to hold his acquisitions together. Robinson believed that cross-selling would generate huge profits. But it never worked. Each piece of the empire remained a separate kingdom. Wealthy clients wanted special treatment, not the one-size-fits-all products offered to middle-income consumers. Other problems developed for Robinson, including losses in Fireman's Fund, an insurance firm that he spun off in 1985.

Competition intensified. MasterCard and Visa went after American Express's high-end users. Merchants complained about the high fees that American Express charged them. A Shearson subsidiary tried to go after RJR Nabisco in a hostile takeover bid. A spectacular battle ensued, and when KKR (Kohlberg, Kravis, Roberts & Co.) took over RJR, Shearson looked like a bungling also-ran. All of a sudden, Robinson looked weak, tired, and vulnerable. The American Express board pushed him out in 1993, and his successor, Harvey Golub, quickly dismantled most of Robinson's empire.

Robinson had tried to create a global financial supermarket. But financial products and services are in no way similar to the thousands of items a real supermarket sells. Just because you get an American Express card doesn't mean you might be interested in American Express's investment banking services.

CAESAR'S END

Everything seemed to be going well for Caesar. One day as he rode his chariot into the city, some of his supporters, planted along the route, shouted out as he passed, "Rex, rex." The normally adoring crowd of people suddenly fell silent, and Caesar sensed they were ill at ease with the salutation. He cried out in response, "My name is Caesar, not rex."

Not long afterward, a number of senators approached Caesar with greetings and petitions for favors. He was seated on his throne in the senate and failed to rise when they entered, not displaying the customary sign of respect that a consul afforded to senators when they came into his presence. The apparent slight disturbed some of the senators. Instantly aware of his affront, Caesar explained that because of his illness, the "falling sickness," he was not always steady on his feet.

What Caesar referred to as the "falling sickness" was probably epilepsy, and it first appeared during his time as governor in Spain. He made no excuses for his condition, and when he suffered seizures, he used them to his political advantage. The highly superstitious Romans believed that an attack of the "falling sickness" was an indication of divine favor. Also, a provision of Roman law known as *morbus comitialis* allowed the stricken person, if he was a prominent officeholder, to use an attack as a reason to postpone elections or other important public business until he recovered. Thus Caesar adroitly transformed a potentially negative or career-killing condition into a powerful political tool.

Each year in February, the Romans celebrated the Lupercalia, a traditional festival to ensure fertility. As part of the festivities many of the magistrates ran naked through the streets. Women lined the route and extended their hands to be slapped by the passing sprinters, a gesture they believed would help ensure easy pregnancies.

During the festival in 44 BC, Caesar was seated in the Forum on his golden throne when Antony, one of the runners, approached carrying a diadem, or crown of laurel. Reaching Caesar, he fell to his knees and offered him the crown. Caesar rose and the crowd became silent. Always the consummate politician, he sensed their apprehension and rejected the offer. The people applauded, and historians have often conjectured that if the crowd had approved Caesar might have chosen the moment to proclaim himself king.

During the festival, some of Caesar's statues around Rome were decked with crowns. Offended by the sight, two tribunes removed them and arrested those they suspected of having placed them on the statues. People responded with applause and cheers at each arrest and called the tribunes "Brutus." Brutus was the aristocrat who had put an end to monarchy in Rome when he drove out the last Etruscan king in 509 BC and declared the establishment of a republic. When Caesar learned of the arrests and the removal of the crowns from his statues, he was furious and stripped both tribunes of their offices. Clearly, Caesar had been testing the political waters and when they proved frigid, he recoiled in anger.

According to Roman folklore, Caesar's murder was foretold by unmistakable signs the day before. A small king-bird with a sprig of laurel in its beak flew into the theater of Pompey, pursued by other, larger birds that tore it apart. The night before the murder, Caesar's wife Calpurnia dreamed that he died in her arms, blood gushing from wounds inflicted by daggers. The next day, she implored Caesar to remain at home, but Decimus Brutus, a senator Caesar counted among his closest friends, arrived to escort him to the senate.

Brutus was part of the plot, and he feared that if Caesar did not go to the senate that day, the conspirators would lose their opportunity. Caesar was preparing to leave Rome the next day to begin a military campaign in Asia against the Parthians. As many as sixty senators may have been involved in the plot, and among them were men with personal grievances as well as those who genuinely believed they were about to strike a blow for the Republic against tyranny.

Brutus stroked Caesar's ego by telling him that the senators were preparing to proclaim him king of all the provinces outside of Italy. Would it be appropriate, he asked, for the new king of the Roman Empire to send word that he would come back another day when his wife had better dreams? Brutus took Caesar by the arm and gently but firmly guided him toward the door. On the way to the senate, they encountered a blind soothsayer who several days before had warned Caesar to be on his guard when the Ides of March (March 15) came.

Caesar cried out to him, "The Ides of March are come," and the seer replied, "Yes, but not gone."

The senate was meeting in the theater of Pompey instead of its usual place, the Capitol. Decimus Brutus detained Antony outside the chamber. As Caesar entered, without a bodyguard, senators pressed in close, including the conspirators, begging him to read their petitions for favors. Caesar was amiable at first, but as they pressed upon him with greater urgency, he became annoyed.

Then one of the conspirators, Tullius Cimber, gave the signal for the attack by seizing Caesar's toga at the neck with both hands and pulling it down from his shoulder. Another conspirator, Casca, thrust his dagger into Caesar's neck. Caesar reacted by driving the point of his pen into Casca's arm. Casca called out, "Brothers, help me," and daggers flashed from all sides. In their frenzy, some of the conspirators wounded one another, "for all had to take part in the sacrifice and taste of the slaughter." Caesar was hemmed in from every side, and there was a dagger every way he turned. When he saw that even Marcus Brutus had drawn a dagger against him, he gave up, pulling his toga over his head and slowly sliding to the cold marble floor. Those who were not part of the conspiracy recoiled in horror, paralyzed by fear and unable to utter even a word in protest. Caesar was fifty-six when he died at the foot of Pompey's statue.

As word spread of the murder, businesses were shut in apprehension of what might be coming, and people secluded themselves in their houses. Antony and Lepidus, Caesar's closest friends, hid because they feared to return to their own homes. An ominous silence descended over Rome as Marcus Brutus and the conspirators, brandishing their blood-stained daggers, marched through the empty streets to the Capitol—proud, confident, and defiant. They had planned to drag Caesar's body with hooks through the streets and dump it into the Tiber River, then revoke his decrees in the senate and confiscate his property. But fear of Antony and the army outside Rome restrained them for the moment.

The next day, Brutus addressed the crowd that had gathered in the Forum. Brutus was respected in Rome as an aristocrat who believed in the Republic. He claimed as his ancestor the Brutus who had driven out the last Etruscan king. His mother, Servilia, had been Caesar's mistress for years, and his family had become wealthy as a result of that relationship. Even though Brutus had joined Pompey's army in the civil war, Caesar had spared his life at Pharsalus along with many of his friends. He had even restored Brutus to his place in the senate. So although Brutus genuinely desired to abolish the dictatorship, he was torn by his deep affection for Caesar.

The crowd listened as Brutus explained why Caesar had been murdered. People showed no anger or resentment, but neither did they shout their approval. The senate met later that day, and in an effort to avoid civil war, voted divine honors for Caesar and vowed not to change any of his laws or decrees. The senate also bestowed honors on Marcus Brutus and the other conspirators on behalf of the Republic and assigned them armies and governorships in the provinces. At the end of the day, they left the Capitol confident that war had been averted and matters settled to everyone's satisfaction.

Caesar's will was read at the request of his father-in-law in Antony's house. As Caesar had no living children he had named his sister's grandson, young Gaius Octavius, later to be known as Augustus, as his heir. A funeral pyre was erected in the Campus Martius near the tomb of Caesar's daughter, Julia, and all through the night people came to honor the fallen leader. The crowd grew, and when people saw the wounds on his body inflicted by the daggers of the assassins, their anger grew. Antony inflamed them further when he ordered his herald to recite the honors that the senate had bestowed on Caesar and to repeat the oath that each senator had taken to protect him.

As the night wore on, the crowd became a mob. Men set fire to the funeral pyre and then with blazing torches ran to the homes of the conspirators to avenge the death of their champion. But Brutus, Cassius, and the other conspirators had already left for their provinces and the protection of their armies. In a frenzy for revenge, the mob caught a poet in the street named Cinna and, mistaking him for Cornelius Cinna, who had been one of the assassins, tore him to pieces.

What destroyed Caesar in the end were not his assassins' daggers but his own weakness—what the Greeks called hubris. He tried to wear two hats, or a hat and a crown: to be a popular reformer and the supreme ruler of the largest empire in the ancient world. Like Alexander, Caesar became increasingly enamored with himself the more successful and powerful he became, and eventually the crown seemed to matter to him most. The more he conquered and the higher he advanced the more he came to regard himself not just as a leader of the Romans but as a living god to be worshipped by the entire ancient world.

●   ●   ●

Caesar-like figures, people who achieve great things only to meet an unexpected, abrupt, and often humiliating end to their stellar careers, are not hard to find. To some extent, we all have some Caesar in us. Many successful people in politics and business manage to keep their "secret Caesar" safely secured under wraps, but sometimes he can get loose and in the most surprising circumstances. We look next at two financial empire builders, Walter Wriston and Sandy Weill. One was able to restrain his inner Caesar and manage his success; the other was not.

When Walter Wriston went to work for First National City Bank after World War II, banking was a hidebound, lackluster, backwater business. The federal government set interest rates on deposits. Savings banks focused on individual depositors and home mortgages, and commercial banks like First National City catered to the needs of corporations. The slow pace of the business was reflected in the phrase "keeping banker's hours"—that is, starting work late in the day and finishing early.

Wriston turned that world upside down. He looked for loopholes in the law to circumvent and even break down regulatory barriers. In 1961, he created negotiable certificates of deposit with minimums of $100,000 to get around government-mandated interest rate ceilings. He went after the consumer business by setting up a holding company able to pursue activities barred to regular banks. Unlike other banks, First National City, which subsequently became Citibank and a bank-holding company Citicorp (which morphed into Citigroup long after Wriston departed), was willing to incur huge short-term losses in order to build its long-term business. The strategy succeeded, and First National quickly became the dominant financial institution in the field. Early in his career Wriston worked closely with Aristotle Onassis in financing what seemed at the time a high-risk fleet of freighters and supertankers. As a lender, he was constantly innovating and taking risks to make money, such as moving aggressively in equipment leasing. Financing tankers and leasing equipment are mundane activities now but decades ago looked to many bankers to be hair-raising undertakings.

Wriston aggressively pushed Citibank into the credit card business. The credit card is a commonplace financial tool today, but it was a rarity in the 1960s. Other banks offered plastic to their customers, but none did so with the relentlessness and expansive persistence of Citi.

Its determination was obvious in the way it dealt with the problem of state usury laws, which limited the interest rates that cards could charge people who didn't pay off their balances. The problem became especially acute as inflation soared in the 1970s. Inflation sharply increased the cost of money for Citi. Wriston persuaded legislators and government officials in South Dakota to remove those lids, and in return he agreed to set up Citi's processing facilities in the state. South Dakota became Wriston's Gaul. The state needed new jobs, and the deal was quickly consummated. Other banks followed Wriston's lead, and South Dakota became the nation's credit card capital.

Then Wriston pushed the idea of automated teller machines. He pointed out that they made possible the opening of virtual bank branches in a wide area, as well as making it easy for people to attend to their banking needs whenever and wherever they wanted. Again the banking community scrambled to catch up with the leader.

Until Walter Wriston came along, Chase Manhattan Bank had been the dominant player in commercial banking. With Wriston at the helm, Citi rapidly overtook Chase. Wriston looked to conquer foreign markets where Citi already had an impressive presence, and as he went after competitors' consumer, commercial, and investment banking

business, he applied the same combination of aggressiveness and innovation that had served Caesar well.

Not everything Wriston did in his career proved successful. He made
mistakes, when, for example, he tried to branch into insurance and acquire Chubb. His competitors, like Caesar's adversaries in the senate,
blocked the move. After the oil crisis of 1973, Citi became an aggressive
lender to developing countries such as Mexico and Brazil. "Countries,"
Wriston confidently boasted, "don't go bankrupt." But as he and other
bankers discovered to their embarrassment, countries could default
and use their position as sovereign nations to demand the renegotiation
of their loans. On their own turf they were the bosses. As a result, Citi
suffered losses in what turned out to be a high-risk investment arena.

Wriston had Caesar-like abilities and ambitions, but he never let
ambition and conceit blind him to what needed to be done, especially toward the end of his career, when he was most successful. Ego
blinded Caesar to what was going on behind his back and cost him
his life. Wriston made sure never to let an inflated self-image get in
the way of dealing boldly and effectively with any mistakes he made
and crises he encountered. No one could ever accuse this brilliant
man of a lack of self-esteem. But he was always careful to remain
within the law, never engaging in the types of financial practices that
are wrecking the industry today. For one thing, Wriston knew he was
not indispensable. He didn't try to make himself CEO of his company for life, as many strong-willed and self-centered executives are
inclined to do. Citi had a mandatory retirement age of sixty-five, and
Wriston abided by it. He recognized when it was time to go and left
on his own terms, without waiting to be pushed out of the way, as
Sandy Weill would be.

When it came time to relinquish the corporate throne in 1984, he
did so modestly, even though he could have gone out in a blaze of
glory. Citi was on the verge of being the first bank to break the billion-
dollar profit barrier. With just a few accounting adjustments, a little
tinkering with the corporate ledgers, Wriston could have reached that
number on his watch and claimed the credit. Instead he said no and
walked away.

Sanford Weill, who substantially expanded Citi, is an example of a corporate leader who could not control his inner Caesar. Weill made a name for himself as the man who could arrange Wall Street financial marriages and make them work. Traditionally when one firm merged with another, key personnel fled, leaving only the bones of the purchased company for the acquirer to pick over. Weill's creation eventually merged into American Express, where Weill lost his only big corporate battle. He thought he would succeed CEO Jimmy Robinson; instead, Robinson tossed him out in 1985.

Weill's Gaul was a company called Commercial Credit, which engaged in financing receivables from manufacturers, as well as in financing high-interest loans to marginal consumers. The company was a spin-off from Minneapolis-based Control Data Corporation in 1986. Using $7 million of his own money, Weill took charge of Control Data in 1986 and started to put together his financial empire. He relentlessly made acquisitions. His crown jewel was Travelers Corp, a major insurance company. Weill then named his new colossus Traveler's Group. In 1998, he captured what was in effect Rome when his company merged with Citicorp. At the time, Citi was the second-largest commercial bank in the United States and had an impressive presence in most countries around the world. For a while, like Caesar and Pompey, Weill and long-time Citibank CEO John Reed shared power. When the inevitable struggle for control ended in 2000, Weill, like Caesar in Rome, emerged as the sole ruler.

Soon after the ouster of Reed, Weill shelled out $27 billion for Associates First Capital Corp., a consumer-finance firm that had a large presence in Japan and specialized in the subprime segment of the credit market. Combining with Citi's other mortgage operations, Associates mutated into Citi Financial, which became the largest originator of home equity loans in the United States. Months later, the Federal Trade Commission charged Citigroup with predatory lending at Associates. Citigroup settled the lawsuit in 2002 by agreeing to pay $240 million to consumers affected by the allegedly deceptive marketing practices.

A number of state and federal investigations were launched into alleged questionable practices at another Citi subsidiary, Salomon Smith Barney. Weill also was accused of attempting to persuade an analyst there to raise his rating on AT&T, a company on whose board Weill sat. Then Citigroup was part of a $1.4 billion settlement between ten Wall Street firms, the New York State attorney general, the SEC, and other regulatory agencies. Citi paid $400 million in fines and payments, the largest amount of all the firms involved in the probe.

Weill's handpicked board began to fear that if Weill didn't leave the corporate throne the company would suffer. In a post-Enron environment, the board—prodded by some institutional investors—began to think seriously about deposing their emperor. Unlike Caesar, Weill sensed what was happening and, metaphorically speaking, fell on his sword. In 2003 he picked a successor, Chuck Prince, and then moved on. Although he didn't suffer the dramatic Caesar-like corporate assassination like others, such as the sudden and unexpected removal of Hank Greenberg by the AIG board in 2005, it was nevertheless an unexpected and unwelcome end for the man who had climbed to the top of such an immense financial empire.

With Wriston and Weill, we see two different Caesars. Both men were extremely bright and intensely ambitious. Wriston was an acute observer of the current scene and could write with the same facility as Julius Caesar. His book *The Twilight of Sovereignty: How the Information Revolution Is Transforming Our World* (1992), is a classic in the realm of finance and economic policy making.

Both also were capable of radical moves and immense risk taking. But there the similarities end. Wriston never let ego cloud his judgment when things went wrong. When dealing with a crisis, he didn't let bruised feelings over having made a mistake get in the way of dealing with it effectively. Wriston had too wry a view of human nature and of himself to think of himself as a "god." He knew he was brilliant and could spar intellectually with the best, but he never felt the need to show off.

By contrast, Sandy Weill, at the end of his career, began to believe what flatterers told him. His lifelong intense, energetic drive to achieve seemingly impossible goals, to overcome corporate humiliation that would have shattered others, and to patiently build a new empire that took him to the peak of business and civic success veered into imperiousness that brooked no dissent. He fired Jamie Dimon, his immensely able top lieutenant at Citi, and could not accept the idea of stepping down. (Dimon now heads JP Morgan Chase, which has expanded mightily during the recent financial storm as Citi has struggled.) Weill fell into the trap of self-delusion that destroyed Julius Caesar. Wriston, a corporate Caesar if there ever was one, manifestly did not.

Is Citigroup too big and unwieldy to be nimble, innovative, and profitable enough to succeed in this rapidly changing world? These questions were bubbling even before the great financial crisis began in 2007. Weill's successor, Chuck Prince, was hit hard by huge losses from that credit crisis and was ousted soon thereafter. Prince's successor, Vikram Pandit, could not save the company as Augustus would save Rome after Caesar's death. He suffered the humiliation of receiving massive Washington bailouts to help the company stay alive. And under Washington and market pressure Pandit reluctantly agreed to break up the empire. The epitaph for the Weill creation: too big to succeed.

BOLD AND RISKY ACTIONS

"Crossing the Rubicon" has almost become a cliché for taking a bold and risky course of action from which there is no turning back. Sometimes the move leads to dazzling success, but at other times it can lead to catastrophic failure. The long history of AT&T is an example.

Theodore Vail is the man who invented AT&T, the longest-lasting, most successful service-oriented monopoly in American history. His Rubicon was the belief that America could achieve the best and most widespread telephone service in the world through the creation of what in effect would be a government-sanctioned monopoly. Vail came to his Rubicon late in life. The formidable financier J. P. Morgan wanted Vail to take over then floundering AT&T, which Morgan had invested in. Morgan wanted Vail to turn the company around. As we shall see, Vail had grander ambitions and risked his career on the gamble that he could persuade Morgan to accept his unique vision, even if that meant accepting limits on what AT&T could earn on its invested capital.

Vail was born in 1845 and went to work as the general manager of American Bell Telephone in 1878 when he was thirty-three. American Bell was established soon after the telephone's invention by Alexander Graham Bell in 1876. The company's principal competitor, Western Union, was out to crush the upstart, but Vail fended off his rival by connecting local phone networks to a long-distance system that crossed state lines. Then he cofounded Western Electric to build telephone equipment for American Bell. Vail had set the company course—signing up telephone users as aggressively as possible and buying up as many small local companies as he could. With heft would come safety and prosperity.

Then suddenly in 1889, when Vail was in his early forties, he retired after a fierce dispute with the company's board of directors. As CEO he had wanted to reinvest capital to expand the business, but the directors were focused on dividends. In this regard, Vail resembles a number of contemporary high-tech entrepreneurs who do great things in their younger years and then leave the corporate world to putter around. But in 1907, Vail, at age sixty-two, came out of retirement and did his greatest work. AT&T, the successor to American Bell, had expanded over the years. But the company suffered from a reputation for bad service; staff morale was low. To complicate matters, the expiration of the company's phone patents had sparked a round of fierce competition. J. P. Morgan, the most powerful financier in America, then or ever, took control of AT&T. Vail had an image of what he thought a phone company should be: a public service company that would offer the best phone system possible to its clients, putting service first even before profits.

Morgan wanted Vail to run AT&T and make it profitable, but Vail had bigger goals in mind: making AT&T the largest, most powerful, best-run, and most service-oriented telephone company in the world. Should Vail take his chances with a financier who might decide that other priorities meant putting Vail's aggressive plans on the back burner? Could Morgan deliver on getting the capital together that would achieve Vail's dream? Giving up a comfortable retirement, Vail took the plunge. His comeback strategy sounds simple but was not easy to achieve.

Vail believed that providing nationwide service utilizing the best possible phone technology would be the only way to successfully compete against the almost 6,000 new companies that were providing telephone service to nearly 600,000 customers. To raise capital, Vail sold bonds at a discount to shareholders. He sharply increased research and development. He made it a company policy to seek out and hire smart young scientists. He instituted a research laboratory, which became the famous Bell Labs, to systematically research new technologies—even if some of the research had no direct connection to the telephone business. AT&T also aggressively bought up independent phone companies and consolidated them into state and regional phone companies.

Then Vail demonstrated his true genius: He leased the use of AT&T phone lines to competitors to achieve his goal of universal service across the country. He went to the federal government and asked for, in effect, a legal monopoly, comparing the importance of telephone service to that of the postal service. The Feds agreed and AT&T pioneered long-distance service. The company worked closely with state regulators, embracing political oversight rather than fighting it.

During World War I, the government actually took over AT&T and put it under the U.S. Post Office. Populist politicians figured that if the company did not have to generate profits, long-distance service could be made even cheaper. But with Washington in charge, the opposite happened and rates went up. The public demanded that the company be freed from government ownership and returned to the private sector—and it was. Thereafter, the real price of long-distance service dropped consistently and dramatically.

Vail died in 1920, and Harry Bates Thayer succeeded him. Thayer shared in Vail's vision, and for years AT&T remained at the forefront of innovation and service especially when compared with what was offered in other countries. That didn't stop the U.S. Justice Department in 1974 from filing an antitrust suit to break up AT&T, arguing that technology was making the old monopoly obsolete. The company settled the suit in 1982 by agreeing to divide into seven regional companies, the so-called Baby Bells, and one long-distance company, which retained the AT&T name. New players were able to enter the telecommunications field. The long-distance business remained a cash cow through the 1980s and even into the 1990s, but AT&T's management realized it was no longer a strong growth market—increasingly the opposite—and the company would have to enter new businesses if it was to thrive.

In 1997, AT&T brought in a new CEO—C. Michael Armstrong. The new chief had had a spectacular career at IBM and Hughes Electronics. AT&T's stock price soared on the news. Armstrong knew that AT&T was still burdened by many of the bad habits of its old monopoly days, including too much bureaucracy and slow decision making. Armstrong decided to put his career on the line and transform this mammoth into a high-tech version of a lithe ballet dancer.

Armstrong moved across his Rubicon, and for the first few miles afterward things went well, especially when he got the board to issue new stock options to fifty-six thousand employees: Everyone would share in the new prosperity Armstrong would create and thus be less resistant to the big changes he wanted to make. Armstrong's goals were to reduce the company head count and operating costs, market Internet services, finish the implementation of a national cellular network, and increase AT&T's global reach by competing more aggressively overseas. He froze hiring, tied more compensation to results, and even went so far as to get rid of the company's executive limo service.

Then in 1998, Armstrong did a complete about-face. He went on a spending spree, acquiring the cable company TGC for $11.3 billion, then TCI for an eye-opening $48 billion. Not long after, AT&T won a bid to snare cable giant Media One Group for $54 billion. Then in an amazing move only five months later, Armstrong announced he was breaking AT&T into four separate companies. By this point, Armstrong had a growing legion of critics who saw this plan as an admission that his cable-centric strategy, which had resulted in $125 billion in acquisitions and $55 billion in new debt, had been a mistake. The Internet was poised to do to AT&T what the barbarians eventually did to Rome.

AT&T's wireless business was growing, and Armstrong persuaded Japanese mobile giant NTT DoCoMo to invest in AT&T wireless. This move provided capital, a beachhead in Japan, and credibility for AT&T's future in the hotly competitive wireless arena. But it did not alter the fact that AT&T's own technology was inferior to the technology of many of its competitors. AT&T was a hodgepodge of ill-fitting technologies. Not long after, Comcast acquired AT&T's broadband division for $50.5 billion. Armstrong became non-executive chairman of Comcast, a small solace for his failure to make AT&T a company of Vail-like proportions in the high-tech era.

●   ●   ●

Julius Caesar and his modern parallels show us the pitfalls of over-reaching. Some leaders can do it and recover; most cannot and fail. Our next example is the man who picked up the pieces from Caesar's wreckage, learned the lessons from Caesar's mistakes, and went on to take Rome to the height of its power and glory. Augustus, the subject of Chapter 10, put together and managed an empire that worked right and, as a result of his sound management foundation, was able to remain at the pinnacle of the ancient world for centuries after his death.

10

AUGUSTUS

Stability and Moderation

"May it be my privilege to establish the state firm and secure . . . so that I might be called the author of the best government and when I die, the foundations which I have laid will remain."
—AUGUSTUS

If Augustus could be restored to life from the pages of history, his leadership skills would be highly valued and very much in demand. Today, when many large companies—especially those currently foundering in the depressed financial and automotive sectors—are in severe disarray, his ability to instill confidence and provide direction would make him as close to being the perfect CEO as anyone could be. For Augustus the most important aspect of rebuilding a failing company and then transforming it into an industry leader would be laying the right foundations. With the proper foundations in place and a sense of direction, there would be no limit to what the organization could accomplish.

Augustus was a man who by temperament proceeded cautiously in nearly everything he did. His two favorite sayings were *festina lente* (make haste slowly) and *sat celeriter fieri quidquid fiat satis bene* (that which has been done well has been done quickly enough). In both his public and his private lives Augustus was guided by a very practical point of view toward just about every problem he encountered.

The Roman Empire when Augustus took over had been pulled apart by decades of infighting among key officials. After the murder of Caesar in 44 BC, the resulting civil wars lasted for nearly fifteen years. No part of the Mediterranean, from Spain and North Africa to Egypt and Asia Minor, was left untouched. When the fighting was over, only Gaius Julius Caesar Octavianus, known in history as Augustus, was left standing.

Augustus (63 BC–AD 14) straddled two important periods, the end of the Roman Republic and the beginning of the Roman Empire—a time of political, economic, and religious transformation. Perhaps the most significant figure in Roman history, he captured power in a period of turmoil, succeeded in reviving and reforming a fractured political system, and then led the Romans forward into a new and prosperous age. Rome's "first among equals" (*primus inter pares*), as Augustus modestly referred to himself, was not a conqueror and warrior in the style of Cyrus, Alexander, or Caesar; he was an administrator. While visiting the mausoleum of Alexander the Great in Egypt, he commented that conquest is the easy and glamorous part of empire building; keeping it together and directing it is the hard part. Augustus consolidated what Caesar had conquered and through reform and competent administration established for Rome an empire that would dominate the ancient world for centuries.

The same principle by which Augustus managed Rome holds true for any business today. If the foundations are secure and if leaders have a clear vision, a company has an excellent chance to succeed. Otherwise, it is likely to become stuck in a routine and stagnate. Look at banks, Wall Street investment houses, and brokerage firms. From the late 1920s to the early 1960s, they were stodgy outfits with short workdays. Technology and innovation upended this cozy world. Countless Wall Street firms from that era folded or were submerged. By contrast, John Chambers of Cisco Systems and Larry Ellison of Oracle work relentlessly to change and expand their high-tech firms.

AUGUSTUS ON THE OFFENSIVE

Julius Caesar had no heirs except the nineteen-year-old grandson of his sister Julia. He adopted the boy and made him heir to his fortune only a few months before his murder. An obscure young man with no political experience, Augustus was in Greece undergoing military training when word reached him of Caesar's death. He returned to Rome to claim his inheritance and found the city and government in turmoil.

After Caesar's murder, two of his principal lieutenants, Antony and Lepidus, maneuvered to fill the resulting power vacuum. Both were experienced commanders who had served with Caesar for years. They had directed his armies in Gaul and in the civil wars against Pompey. Antony was the more powerful, having served as Caesar's second in command, and he considered himself Caesar's political heir.

Immediately after the murder, Antony and the senate reached an accommodation to avoid a military confrontation, but Antony violated the agreement when he used Caesar's funeral to inflame the crowd with his eulogy. A riot ensued, and the senators involved in the assassination fled to their provinces and the protection of the legions that awaited them there. Brutus, Cassius, and the other assassins commanded formidable armies in northern Italy and Greece, and when they were joined by Pompey's surviving son, Sextus, with his fleet of warships, the second round of civil wars for control of Rome was set to begin.

When Antony and Lepidus first met young Augustus, they were not impressed. He possessed none of Caesar's vitality or charisma and had no experience in war or politics. When the three came together to plan their strategy, he brought little to the table beyond his newly adopted family name, Julius. But that name gave Augustus plenty of political capital. He had been recognized by the senate as Caesar's son, and changing his name gave him considerable prestige among Caesar's legions and the people of Rome.

Soldiers loyal to Caesar held the key to control of Rome. They were angry over his murder, but they were more concerned about their future paychecks and retirement benefits. Augustus was heir to a considerable fortune, which meant he would have the funds to pay them. They pressured Antony and Lepidus to accept him because they feared their interests would suffer if Caesar's two most senior associates and his adopted son were to become adversaries. Antony and Lepidus recognized that if the army were divided in its allegiance, they would be considerably weakened in their dealings with Brutus and the other conspirators. There was also the possibility that the soldiers would fight among themselves if Antony, Lepidus, and Augustus came to blows. The army had to be kept unified, so Antony and Lepidus decided to include Augustus even though they discounted his abilities.

In November of 43 BC, the three formed the alliance now known as the Second Triumvirate. Unlike the First Triumvirate sixteen years earlier, which had been an informal political and military arrangement among Julius Caesar, Crassus, and Pompey, the second one was sanctioned by law. The *triumvirs* ("three men" in Latin) simply bypassed the senate, where there was sure to be resistance to their plans, and, invoking Caesar's name, appealed directly to the Roman people in the popular assemblies to sanction their authority in the form of a new law—the *Lex Titia*.

The triumvirate's success depended on the maintaining of a balance among the conflicting ambitions of the three aggressive men. Their first objective was to neutralize their political enemies in Rome. The old system of proscriptions was revived, and lists naming everyone who had been involved, even marginally, in the murder of Caesar were drawn up. Some three hundred senators and nearly two thousand members of the Roman commercial upper class known as *equites* were massacred as a result.

The executions were driven by a combination of political expediency, revenge for Caesar's murder, and the prospect of the large sums of money that could be raised through the sale of property taken from the condemned. Each triumvir submitted his list of who had to go. Many of the condemned had not been involved in the killing of Caesar but had simply incurred the enmity of Antony, Lepidus, or Augustus. Some who perished were family members of the triumvirs and were sacrificed as a macabre show of good faith among the three.

Among the murdered was Cicero, Rome's greatest orator and the Republic's staunchest defender of liberty against military dictatorship. He had taken no part in the killing of Caesar, but in a series of speeches he had attacked Antony from the senate floor, branding him a dangerous threat to republican liberty. Cicero had compared Antony to Caesar when it came to ambition and had accused him of wanting to become king. Cicero's severed head was placed on the speaker's rostrum of the senate as a warning to others that the triumvirs would not tolerate criticism or resistance to their rule.

By 42 BC, the Roman Empire was in a full state of civil war for the second time in less than a decade. The army of the triumvirs, directed largely by Antony, defeated the forces of Brutus and Cassius at the battle of Philippi in northern Greece, while Augustus pursued Pompey's son on the seas around Sicily. The heads of the defeated were sent to Rome and flung at the base of Caesar's statue in the senate.

When the wars against the assassins were successfully concluded, Antony and Augustus undertook to parcel out Rome's imperial holdings between themselves (Lepidus was shoved aside). Antony took the eastern provinces of the empire—Greece, Macedonia, Egypt, and Syria. Augustus took Rome, Italy, Gaul, and Spain.

Antony and Augustus were now the principal players in the struggle for power, and they sealed their pact in a traditional Roman manner: Antony divorced his wife, Fulvia, and married Augustus's sister, Octavia. The ancient world was now divided between them, two strong figures, each at the head of his own army and claiming to be the political heir of Julius Caesar.

Antony installed himself in Egypt and undertook to rule the eastern part of the Roman Empire like a Hellenistic king from his new capital at Alexandria. He had become enamored of Caesar's mistress Cleopatra, and he recognized her young son, Caesarion, as his ward.

Augustus remained at Rome and launched a vitriolic public relations campaign against Antony and his "Egyptian whore." He accused Antony of betraying traditional Roman values and miring himself in a cesspool of Eastern degeneracy and debauchery. Antony responded in a public letter to the Roman senate in which he explained at great length that he was less of a drunk and debaucher than Augustus. Then in a follow-up letter, he leveled the charge that Caesar had adopted Augustus because the younger man had engaged in "unnatural relations" with the dictator.

Public opinion at Rome began to turn against Antony, mostly because of his relationship with Cleopatra. Augustus further exacerbated the situation by issuing ominous predictions that the Egyptian harlot would persuade Antony to move the capital of the Roman Empire to Alexandria.

There was an element of truth to what Augustus said. Cleopatra was a strong-willed and aggressive ruler who sought to restore the Ptolemaic kingdom of her forefathers to its earlier place of prominence in the ancient world. Egypt had the resources to become a power once more, and Cleopatra in her own way probably posed the greatest threat to Rome since Hannibal crossed the Alps two hundred years before. Antony was little more than a means to her end, just as Caesar had been.

When Antony married Cleopatra and then divorced Octavia, it did not sit well with the Roman people or with Augustus. Antony ordered golden thrones set up for himself and his new queen and miniature versions for their three young children—Alexander, Philadelphus, and Selene. From his new throne, Antony proclaimed Cleopatra and Caesarion co-regents of Egypt and his children by her the new rulers of Asia Minor. Gold coins were issued with likenesses of Antony on one side and Cleopatra on the other, and in the tradition of Alexander the Great, Antony held himself out to the ancient world as a "second Hercules" who would father a new race of kings.

In response, Augustus played his trump card in the escalating propaganda game. He obtained Antony's will, which had been deposited for safekeeping in the temple of the Vestal virgins at Rome. Opening a man's will before his death was against Roman law and ethics, but Augustus calculated that the contents of the will would inflame public opinion more than his transgression. And he was not mistaken. The will gave him everything he needed to further turn Roman public opinion against Antony. It laid out provisions for Antony's burial at Alexandria instead of Rome and favored Cleopatra and her children over Octavia and her children when it came to inheritance. Antony, Augustus charged, was favoring Egyptians over Romans.

Antony had seriously underestimated the skill with which Augustus could manipulate public opinion against him in Rome. Antony might have been the better general, but Augustus clearly was the better politician. Even the Roman soldiers in Antony's army resented Cleopatra. Her presence in their camps, her arrogance, and the public flaunting of her affairs first with Caesar and now with Antony offended their essentially conservative nature. The situation brings to mind what Alexander the Great had faced nearly three hundred years earlier when he married the Bactrian princess Roxanne in an effort to blend Persian and Hellenic cultures.

The inevitable military showdown between Antony and Augustus took place in 31 BC off the western coast of Greece. Antony and Cleopatra had assembled a large army at Actium and were preparing to send it by naval transport against Italy, but Augustus took the initiative. Mounting a two-pronged attack by land and sea, he forced the royal couple to flee for Egypt, leaving behind most of their navy and army. Although Actium was not much as battles go, it ended Antony's threat and Augustus always regarded it as his greatest military triumph. The architect of the victory was Augustus's close friend Agrippa, who commanded the fleet. After the battle, Augustus showed remarkable leniency toward the defeated soldiers, at least toward the Romans among them. They were absorbed into his army, which numbered nearly 300,000 and was unquestionably the largest in the ancient world.

Antony and Cleopatra retreated behind the walls of Alexandria and waited for the inevitable. Nearly a year later, in July of 30 BC, Augustus arrived and his army surrounded the city. Before the battle, Augustus approached the city walls and performed an ancient Roman ritual called *evocatio*. It was psychological warfare at its ancient best. With an eerie musical accompaniment, Augustus exploited Roman superstition to its fullest. He summoned the native gods of Alexandria to turn their backs on the doomed city and take up residence in a new Roman world. When the ceremony was over, Augustus's legions mounted a furious attack against the city walls. Antony's demoralized soldiers surrendered, and the "second Hercules" retreated to his palace, where he took his own life.

Cleopatra was captured. Augustus had her closely guarded, but she managed to end her life with the bite of a small African cobra (the asp) that had been smuggled to her in a basket of figs. She died believing she would become a goddess. There was no other way out for her. Her pride would not allow her to be dragged through the streets of Rome and taunted by the same crowds that only a few years earlier had cheered her triumphal entry into the city at the side of Julius Caesar.

Augustus spared Cleopatra's three young children by Antony and sent them to Rome, where they were adopted and cared for by the generous and compassionate Octavia. However, Antony's eldest son by his first wife, Fulvia—Antony's legal heir under Roman law—was murdered along with Cleopatra's son Caesarion. Augustus could not risk allowing either of them to develop into potential rivals.

With the deaths of Antony and Cleopatra, Augustus became a very wealthy man. He confiscated the treasure of the pharaohs and annexed

Egypt to the empire as his private reserve. By 29 BC, the last of the resistance to his rule had been suppressed, and Augustus returned to Rome to celebrate his triumph. His first public act was to close the doors to the temple of Janus, the god of war. When Romans were at war anywhere in the world, the temple doors were traditionally left open. Augustus's closing of those doors marked the beginning of a period of peace and prosperity, which would become known as the *Pax Romana*. It also signaled a new phase in Augustus's career—administrator of the empire.

Augustus had spent fifteen years fighting a civil war. With no opposition left, he turned his attention to rebuilding a fractured Roman society and government. Through a methodical process of trial and error, he moved cautiously but decisively to achieve the goals he set for Rome.

HURRY UP, BUT TAKE YOUR TIME AND DO IT CAREFULLY

Alfred Sloan, who made General Motors a behemoth in the auto industry and a corporation admired around the world for its success and longevity, and Augustus were kindred spirits. In the early 1920s, General Motors was a poorly run, ramshackle collection of auto companies and nearly bankrupt. At the time, Ford Motor Company was the dominant player in the auto world, with over 50 percent of market share in the United States. No one else in the industry could manufacture a car as cheaply as Henry Ford could put out the Model T or market it more effectively.

The Du Pont family invested heavily in General Motors and installed Sloan as president with a mandate to turn it around. Sloan had become president of his father's ball bearing company in 1899 at the age of twenty-four and ran the company successfully for seventeen years before selling it to William Durant, the founder of General Motors. Sloan had watched General Motors fail and was convinced that mismanagement was the problem. He developed some strong ideas about how the various pieces of the automotive giant could be molded together into one efficient and profitable unit much as Augustus approached the task of rebuilding Rome.

For a moment, assume the role of a CEO and put yourself in

Sloan's shoes. Your market share is small, and your principal competitor, who is more than twice your size, is making cars more quickly and far less expensively. What would you do? Sloan couldn't make a car that would cost less than Ford's Model T, so he changed the rules of the game. Rather than competing with Ford on price, he devised a way to change how people looked at cars and how they bought them.

What Sloan did seems simple and obvious today, but at the time it was a dazzling innovation: Buyers of General Motors vehicles could choose the color of their cars, while Henry Ford haughtily responded that his customers could have any color they wanted—as long as it was black. As CEO, Sloan introduced the annual model change, which proved to be a brilliant marketing innovation. Cars were no longer just a means of moving from one place to another; they became a statement about success and even a comment on fashion and style. A consumer's choice of a car said something about the purchaser and where he or she was in life. By introducing an annual model change, Sloan sparked excitement and anticipation among consumers as they waited to see what the new models would look like and what the new features would be.

Sloan introduced the concept of installment buying as a way to help people afford GM cars. Traditionally people paid for their cars in full at the time of purchase. Letting customers make monthly payments was regarded in the industry as a risky idea and an invitation for abuse and massive losses. Installments might work for housing purchases, but a car was something that could easily be moved, stolen, or even wrecked. Also, new houses didn't suffer from rapid depreciation the way a car does as soon as it leaves the dealer's lot. Ford thought Sloan was "nuts" and countered with a layaway plan that allowed buyers to deposit money in an account over time and then pick up their Model T when the full price was paid.

Sloan went to great efforts to build a corporate structure that brought scientific precision to management and procurement. His organizational charts looked complex, but they made sense. They showed how a mammoth organization in which thousands of employees were making a product with thousands of parts and using immense amounts of raw materials could be set up to run smoothly and efficiently. Under Sloan, the leadership at GM, from the factory floor to the corporate board room, was able to innovate, improve, and make decisions in an informed and efficient manner.

Like Augustus, Sloan tapped key people to make sure his organization would run the way he wanted it to. One of Sloan's best picks was Charles Kettering, who headed research at GM for twenty-seven years. Kettering had cofounded Dayton Engineering Laboratories (Delco), and Sloan made that company the foundation of the GM Research Corporation and Delco Electronics. One of Kettering's spectacular breakthroughs was an electric starter, which replaced the hand crank located on the front of the car. The hand crank was inconvenient in inclement weather, and if not turned correctly could even break a user's arm. During his lifetime, Kettering held three hundred patents on various automotive-related products. In later years, after Sloan and Kettering were gone, GM's management no longer focused so intensely on innovation.

Under Sloan's leadership, GM's sales surpassed those of Ford, and GM never looked back. For decades, it remained the largest company in the world and held a commanding share of the auto market. So successful did GM become that in the 1950s and 1960s the company deliberately slowed sales of its autos so the U.S. Justice Department wouldn't file an antitrust suit and try to break up the empire, as it had done to Standard Oil and American Tobacco in the early part of the twentieth century.

In the 1970s, GM started to slip and gradually lose its place at the top. Japanese and other foreign manufacturers came up with more fuel-efficient and stylish models. In 2007–2008, Toyota surpassed GM as the world's biggest auto manufacturer, having sped by GM in profits several years before. What ultimately happened to the Roman Empire is happening to GM today—its very survival is in question. During the 2008 financial crisis, GM was forced to turn to the federal government for loans to stay alive. Like Augustus's successors—the emperors Tiberius, Caligula, Claudius, and Nero—the executives who followed Sloan could not match their predecessor's ability and foresight. Now the world waits to see if the current CEO, Frederick "Fritz"

Henderson, can pull off an Augustan resurrection for GM. One positive factor: GM remains a formidable, successful, and profitable enterprise outside North America and that might be what will save it in the short run.

When Augustus took the helm, his first task was to rebuild Roman government. He was no lawgiver in the tradition of Moses, Hammurabi, or Solon and he never produced an all-encompassing law code. Instead, Augustus modified existing Roman institutions and laws to reflect what he thought needed improvement and attention, not only in government but in Roman society as a whole. He proceeded to feel his way forward, governing first Rome and later the whole empire with patience and caution.

Once he decided on a course of action, Augustus pursued it until it was completed to his satisfaction. His directives to subordinates were often little more than pragmatic responses to what was going on at the time and what he thought needed immediate attention, such as barbarian incursions along the northern borders of the empire or civil disturbances in the Roman provinces of the Middle East. Augustus never deluded himself by thinking that he had the answers to every question. Although historians often criticize him as a leader who lacked deep philosophical insight, they are quick to praise him for his pragmatic and effective responses to problems throughout his vast empire.

CONSISTENCY, LEADING DAY-IN AND DAY-OUT

Two of Augustus's strengths as a leader were his willingness to delegate authority and his close working relationship with the senate and other parts of the Roman government. When confronted with problems that were beyond his ability to solve, he turned to two loyal friends and ministers, Agrippa and Maecenas. He was fortunate to have in them very competent subordinates who showed both initiative and discretion in carrying out his directives.

Augustus regarded stability, attained through law and order, as more valuable in the long run for Rome than the promotion of civil liberties. He believed that liberty was something that would come in time with political and economic stability. Nevertheless, throughout his reign he upheld three important principles of republican government for Rome: (1) Political power is a trust to be exercised in the interests of the people. (2) Government should be a shared responsibility among those elected to political office. (3) No ruler is above the law. Rome under Augustus became a guided democracy where he firmly held the tiller that guided the Roman ship of state through troubled waters.

Augustus was nominated by the very senate he had created and then elected consul six times by the people of Rome. The consulship was Rome's highest executive office, and Augustus used it to bring about his first round of reforms. Then, in 28 BC, in a totally unexpected move, he went before the senate and resigned. He relinquished control over all the Roman provinces with the exception of Egypt, and he placed everything, except control of the army, at the disposal of the senate and the people of Rome.

The resignation was a calculated political move to enhance his popularity and make him seem indispensable. The senators, many of whom owed their positions and wealth to Augustus, beseeched him to remain at the helm because he had brought stability to Rome and Italy. He agreed, and in gratitude the senate bestowed upon him the name Augustus to signify his closeness to the gods. The senate renamed the month Sextilis August in his honor as years before it had renamed the month Quintilis July to honor Julius Caesar. Finally, the senate awarded Augustus the appellation *princeps*, "first citizen," a general form of address used among Romans but one that had a special connotation when applied to him.

Although there was no doubt that Augustus was the boss, he was careful to avoid the title and trappings of monarchy—which he realized went against the Roman grain and had cost Julius Caesar his life. Augustus wore neither a crown nor the robes of a king. A simple broad-brimmed woven straw hat that shielded him from the harsh rays of the Mediterranean summer sun signaled to his subjects his simplicity and modesty. He projected the image of a reluctant "caretaker" of the empire, a leader motivated by a desire to serve and to uphold the principles of Republican government.

As a leader, Augustus could be friendly and approachable. He often listened with courtesy to what tradesmen, soldiers, poets, senators, or governors had to tell him. His approachability and unpretentiousness may have saved his life on one occasion while he was crossing the Alps. A Gaul who had infiltrated the royal entourage with orders to assassinate Augustus could not bring himself to push such a simple and kindly man over the cliff where he was standing admiring the view.

As a speaker Augustus lacked the flamboyant and inspiring style of Rome's greatest orators from the Republican period—Caesar, for example, or senators such as Cicero and Cato. When he spoke in the senate or in other public gatherings, he prepared his words beforehand and delivered his message from a script in a straightforward manner. His writing style was equally simple, and he often commented that it was substance that mattered, not the form.

AUCTORITAS: THE POWER TO GET THINGS DONE WITHOUT LIFTING A HAND

In addition to his hold on government and the army, Augustus relied on an intangible aspect of power to get his way, something the Romans called *auctoritas*. Difficult to define precisely, the word connotes the respect that a Roman male was shown by his fellow citizens in daily life because of his accomplishments, lineage, financial status, marriage, military service, the way he carried himself, and the people he associated with. A Roman who had auctoritas could get things done without ever having to give a direct order, and nothing mattered more to him. The loss of auctoritas, whether in the household or in public life, could be cause for suicide.

Auctoritas had no basis in Roman law, but it gave Augustus greater prestige, moral authority, and influence than any other citizen and made it possible for him to secure compliance from senators and consuls without resorting to direct orders or the use of force. Who today possesses auctoritas? One person who had it until recently was Alan Greenspan in the years when he chaired the Federal Reserve Board (1987–2006).

Greenspan dominated the financial world, whether testifying before Congress, or speaking to global financial institutions such as the World Bank and the International Monetary Fund, or the press. Even the simplest off-the-cuff remark could send stock prices higher or lower. For nearly two decades, he ruled the Federal Reserve just as Augustus had ruled Rome—with auctoritas. But in 2004 Greenspan made a fatal miscalculation. He thought the U.S. economy was much weaker than it was and pumped out excessive amounts of money keeping interest rates artificially low. When too much money is printed, the first area to be impacted is commodities. Excess money flows immediately into the market, particularly gold. Thus the Fed begat a global commodities boom. The price of gold, oil, copper, steel, international shipping— even mud—shot up. Gold—the best historical barometer of monetary disturbances—soared above its average of the previous twelve years. For nearly four years the U.S. dollar sank in value against the euro, yen, and British pound. The already booming housing market in the United States went on steroids. Housing experienced above-average price rises because of a favorable change in the tax law in 1998 that nearly eliminated capital gains taxes on the sale of most primary residences. With money suddenly so plentiful, people believed that housing prices would always go up, so lending standards were lowered. If a risky borrower defaulted, it didn't matter because the value of his house would always be a cushion. Money flooded into the housing market.

Wall Street got into the act by packaging investment-grade mortgages and selling them to institutional investors, something that had been a routine activity for years. But now Wall Street investment houses went on a gluttonous binge of packaging *subprime* mortgages, which generated high fees. Since housing prices would always go up, Wall Street and mortgage buyers reasoned there was minimal risk. Rating agencies eagerly accepted this falacious reasoning and gave triple-A ratings to this stuff, which was sold all around the world. It was alchemy: mix a bunch of junk mortgages together and—voilà!—you have a safe blue-chip security. The Fed and other bank regulators simply stood by as the balloon continued to inflate, and when it burst in 2007, Greenspan's auctoritas and reputation deflated with it.

LEADERSHIP AND LIMITATIONS

Rome under Augustus was clearly an autocracy, a form of government that had existed before for short periods in Roman history. But it was an arrangement that Romans of all classes seemed willing to live with, even for an extended period, if it maintained the facade of democracy and brought them peace, prosperity, and stability. Augustus recognized this and remained within carefully defined parameters, ruling in an autocratic manner yet remaining popular and enjoying the cooperation of the senate and the consuls.

As Rome's "first citizen," Augustus promoted the virtues of a simple agrarian lifestyle and the worship of the traditional gods. These policies resonated with a Roman electorate that looked back with nostalgia on an earlier agrarian past and was being inundated with new cults and religious practices from the East. Augustus became the champion of what the Romans called the *mos maiorum*, or old ways of their ancestors, and he undertook to set a public example of how they should curb their growing appetite for the vices and luxuries the new empire was bringing them. He believed that the early years of the Roman Republic were an idyllic period in which people were connected to the land and motivated by a sense of duty to country, religion, and family.

But Augustus also realized that the world was changing and that Romans could not afford to turn away from it and retreat inward. Isolationism was not an acceptable choice. Augustus recognized that the Roman conquests of the previous two hundred years had made the Mediterranean a smaller place. Although the Romans had conquered territory extending from one end of the ancient world to the other, they had not consolidated and developed their holdings. Regions were beginning to trade with one another—from Spain and France to Syria and Iraq. Labor markets in one part of the empire could be tapped to produce goods for sale in another, and natural resources could be mined in one place and then shipped and transformed into finished products somewhere else.

Opportunities were opening up, and Rome was in a position to coordinate, regulate, and tax everything to its advantage. With the prospects of profits to be made, Augustus appealed not only to the aristocratic class of Rome, the traditional ruling families, but to the equites, the ambitious and rapidly prospering new class of merchants and businessmen, to put aside their differences and join with him to build an empire that would enrich them all.

Augustus recognized an empire needed infrastructure, and he created it for Rome. His engineers built a network of roads that allowed the legions to quickly reach even the most remote outposts of the empire while the Roman navy patrolled the Mediterranean Sea, minimizing the activities of pirates who interfered with trade. People and goods began to move rapidly and safely, and the prosperity of the empire took off as the provinces became overseas markets for Roman investors. Augustus structured the economic integration of the ancient world so that Rome was at its center, and he did it so efficiently and effectively that all roads really did lead to Rome.

After years of civil war, the city was in need of improvement. The water and sewerage systems had fallen into a state of disrepair, and Augustus entrusted Agrippa with their restoration. Years later Augustus would write in his memoirs how he had found Rome a city of "mud bricks" and left it a "city of marble." Although this was true of the city center, known as the Forum, the rest of Rome consisted of slums of closely packed, multistory wooden tenement houses and narrow, winding, crowded streets. By the first century AD, nearly a million people were living in Rome. While there were no urban renewal projects on a grand scale under Augustus, he did provide funding for the construction of several magnificent public buildings, baths, theaters, libraries, temples, granaries, and warehouses.

Maintaining popular support is always an important political consideration, so Augustus continued Caesar's practice of sponsoring entertainment on a grand scale with free admission. In order to feed the poor, cheap grain was imported from Egypt, Sicily, and North Africa and, along with vouchers for clothing, salt, and olive oil, was distributed among Rome's lower classes, who remained, for the most part, content and therefore quiet under his rule.

On a personal basis, public aid to Roman citizens was offensive to

Augustus. He believed that the dole robbed people of their initiative and made them too dependent on the state. But he never did away with the practice because too many poor Romans had become dependent on the free distributions and enjoyed the entertainment. Augustus tried not to alienate this class because they were prone to rioting when displeased and had brought down more than one unpopular ruler in the past.

On the surface, the Augustan system of government was one of joint rule by the "first citizen" and the senate within a framework of popular approval. In foreign affairs Augustus retained supervision over Egypt, Spain, and Gaul, while the senate controlled the rest. In reality, Augustus's control of the army and the treasury ensured he controlled everything.

Augustus's constitutional authority to run the government and the empire derived from two powers conferred on him by the senate in the name of the people of Rome. The first was *maius imperium proconsulare,* which gave him the authority to override the decisions of any provincial governor or commander in the field. This power extended to the most remote outposts of the empire, but Augustus used it sparingly as long as the governors administered their provinces in a relatively honest manner, maintained order, and collected the taxes.

The second power was *tribunicia potestas,* which gave Augustus civil authority over the city of Rome and all of Italy. While Augustus relinquished the consulship, he remained a tribune, the representative of the people. This was a clear signal that he considered the source of his political support to be the people of Rome voting in their assemblies, not the senate. Tribunes had functioned in Rome since the fifth century BC as the people's representatives against abuse of authority by the senate or the consuls, and Augustus used the office to his advantage.

By the end of the Republic, the position of tribune had evolved into the most powerful of the executive offices. Tribunes, through their exercise of a veto, could literally bring Roman government to a halt until matters were resolved to their satisfaction. Sulla had curtailed the power of the tribunes during his conservative dictatorship, but Caesar restored it and Augustus expanded it. As a tribune, Augustus held the authority to order the senate to convene, to bring forward motions for debate ahead of any other senator, and even to bypass the senate and introduce legislation directly to the popular assemblies for approval.

Those two powers, maius imperium proconsulare and tribunicia potestas, became the principal constitutional vehicles by which Augustus controlled Rome and the empire for forty years. In effect, he had the last word on nearly everything, especially questions of money, the army, war and peace—but all within a constitutional framework. Thus Augustus could claim, as he often did, that he followed the law to the letter in everything he did.

SOLIDIFYING THE EMPIRE

In the last phase of his career Augustus focused exclusively on administering the empire. He did away with the old system of corrupt provincial administration that had been based on political patronage at Rome and replaced it with a competent civil service. Members of his new civil service were required to have been born Roman citizens and have a substantial net worth. They had to have successfully completed a term of military service and proved themselves to be of good character. Over the years, the civil service developed into a vast administrative network that became indispensable to the running of the empire and upon which sucessive emperors depended. This aspect of Augustus's work proved to be one of his most important and enduring accomplishments. His civil service remained the foundation for the administration of the empire for nearly four hundred years, and many of its members made important contributions to the development of Roman private law—which eventually evolved into Western civil law.

Even though Augustus presented himself as the restorer of the Republic and the upholder of the constitution, he was an absolute dictator. In every aspect of government, with the exception of the military, he allowed the senate and the consuls to retain a facade of importance in running Rome and the empire. Senators frequently consulted him and his civil service for advice on how to carry out tasks in the financial, legislative, and judicial realms, and Augustus in turn consulted them on matters of foreign and domestic policy. But even though the senate remained, together with the popular assemblies, the constitutional source of Roman authority, it could never override the wishes of Augustus because it lacked the authority and money to enforce its decisions.

Nevertheless, Augustus treated the senate with great outward respect. He never forgot that Julius Caesar's cavalier attitude toward this council of aristocratic senior statesmen had cost him his life. Augustus rose from his seat to greet senators and magistrates when they entered the chamber, and he afforded them every public courtesy. To promote cooperation and collegiality, he formed a standing committee of senators to meet with him on a regular basis and prepare the legislative agenda for the senate.

While Augustus consulted with the senators on important matters and consistently showed them the respect due their office, he also controlled entry into their order. He accomplished this through another constitutional tool, the office of *censor*. From the earliest years of the Republic, Romans elected two censors every four years. As Rome's moral compass the censors had the authority to determine who did or did not qualify for citizenship, for membership in the senate and the popular assemblies, and for public office. Their decisions were based on a combination of moral and financial judgments.

By the end of the Republic, censors were an anachronism. Augustus revived the office, which he held jointly with Agrippa, and together they used it to reduce the senatorial rolls from a thousand, the number established by Julius Caesar during his dictatorship, to eight hundred, and finally to six hundred, where it remained until the end of the empire. Admission to the senate had always depended on birth and class status, but Augustus modified that and included factors such as personal integrity, military service, and net worth.

Roman senators traditionally wore a broad purple stripe on their togas, called the *latus clavus,* as a sign of their status and a badge of honor. Augustus began to award the stripe to men of nonaristocratic birth based on his assessment of their service to Rome. This became an effective way for him to infuse new blood into what for centuries had been a closed club for the aristocracy. So although the number of senators decreased during Augustus's rule, the senate actually became more democratic in some regards because its membership was drawn more and more from a wider base that even came to include representatives from Spain and Gaul.

As Rome's "first citizen," Augustus became a patron of the arts and regularly brought together Greek and Roman men of learning. He commissioned the poet Virgil to compose an epic poem about Roman leadership, sacrifice, and duty—the *Aeneid*. Augustus lived a modest life with his extended family in a simple house on the Palatine, the hill of Romulus, founder of Rome. He wanted his *domus*, or "household," to serve as confirmation that he lived what he preached as he undertook to redirect Roman society through laws designed to encourage simplicity of living and stabilize marriage and the family.

FAMILY VALUES, ROMAN STYLE

Augustus's first piece of social legislation was a law called the *lex Julia de adulteriis coercendis*, passed in 18 BC. The law made the Roman pastime of adultery a public crime as well as a private offense. Under this new legislation, an unfaithful wife could be divorced by her husband, who could initiate a prosecution against both her and her lover in criminal and civil court. Penalties ranged from punitive monetary awards to banishment and even execution.

A second set of laws—*lex Julia de maritandis ordinibus* (first passed in 18 BC and amended in AD 9)—made it the patriotic duty of every Roman man to marry and have children. With this legislation Augustus intended to strengthen the agrarian family and replenish the Italian stock decimated from the losses of the civil wars. Augustus was disturbed by the numbers of foreigners he saw coming to live and work in Rome and the numbers of slaves who were being freed by their masters. It was a common practice among Romans to free their slaves when they became too old to work in order to avoid having to pay for their upkeep.

Both foreigners and slaves were mixing with Romans to a degree that caused Augustus concern. Some were even intermarrying with

Romans, becoming citizens, and accumulating considerable wealth. More laws were passed prohibiting marriage between ex-slaves and members of the senatorial class and barring ex-slaves and foreigners from holding elective office anywhere in Italy. Nothing, however, prohibited ex-slaves from finding employment in the imperial civil service, and some served in important posts on the administrative staff of Augustus's own household. Over time many immigrants became eligible for citizenship and along with ex-slaves became among the most influential elements in Rome, economically, politically, and socially.

In trying to return Rome to an earlier and simpler time, Augustus was fighting a losing battle. The values of the past no longer had any relevance for Romans awash in money. Trying to promote chastity among unmarried women and fidelity and parenthood among married couples at a time when Roman society was moving, morally at least, in a different direction proved futile. There was considerable resistance to Augustus's laws, and most of it came from the upper classes, who resented what they considered to be outmoded and ridiculous prohibitions regarding sexual behavior, marriage, adultery, and luxury.

Augustus lecturing the Romans on morals and the virtues of simplicity was the equivalent of Gandhi appearing on Wall Street at bonus time to lecture brokers and partners about feeding the hungry of the world. There was public compliance and even praise for his legislation, but it was largely ignored in private. Still, in his memoirs, *Res Gestae,* Augustus wrote with pride, "I restored many good examples of our ancestors that were disappearing from our age and I personally handed on to posterity examples for them to imitate."

In public Augustus presented himself as the upholder of conservative values from a bygone age, but his private life was another matter. Fidelity in marriage was not his strong suit. He divorced his first wife, Scribonia, quite literally as she bore him his first and only child, Julia, in order to take another man's wife, Livia Drusilla. Livia was married to an older Roman aristocrat, Tiberius Claudius Nero, and pregnant with her second child when she began her affair with Augustus. Historians have even speculated that Livia's second son, Drusus, may have been fathered by Augustus while she was still married to her first husband. Throughout his life, Augustus engaged in casual sexual liaisons with courtesans and the wives of prominent Romans, many of whom were procured by Livia, who pandered to his special fondness for deflowering virgins.

Julia, Augustus's only child, proved a great disappointment and public embarrassment when she matured. The man who championed family values could not control the public escapades of his promiscuous daughter. She married three times, each marriage arranged by her father for political purposes. The first marriage was to her cousin Marcellus, the son of Augustus's sister Octavia. When Marcellus died in 23 BC, Augustus married her to Agrippa, his close friend and minister of war, hoping the older man could keep her in check.

When Agrippa died, Augustus married her to his stepson Tiberius. By 2 BC, her antics were such a public embarrassment that Tiberius divorced her and Augustus banished her, along with her equally promiscuous older daughter, to a remote Mediterranean island to live out their lives in isolation. In the very same year, the senate awarded Augustus its highest moral honor: the designation *pater patriae*, "father of the country."

What Julia did give to Augustus through her marriage to Agrippa were five grandchildren, and from the three males among them he drew the first line of candidates for the imperial succession. Augustus introduced them by closely supervised stages into military and political life, giving them positions of increasing responsibility. All of them died young, however, so Augustus turned to the sons of his granddaughters for heirs. In the end, only his stepson Tiberius survived, and succeeded Augustus. Tiberius was smart enough to remain within the guidelines established by Augustus, and during his reign the empire remained stable and prosperous. The emperors succeeding Tiberius were Caligula, Claudius, and Nero. All were related to Augustus, but none ever equaled or even came close to matching him when it came to the skill of governing.

In addition to legislation regarding marriage and morality, Augustus revived Roman religious rites and ceremonies that had been neglected over the years. He outlawed new cults that had infiltrated Rome after Caesar and Antony had conquered the East, and he ordered the restoration of traditional shrines and temples. In reality, Roman religious practices had very little influence on private morality, but Augustus found certain ideas from the early days of the Republic comforting.

The principal belief that guided him was what the Romans called *pax deorum*, their covenant with the gods. Like many good Romans, Augustus believed that the prosperity and well-being of a society could be tied to the observation of *ius divinum*, state-mandated and -directed religious rituals, and to *pietas*, public devotion to the gods. Augustus attributed Roman success, especially in the very early years of the Republic, to the piety of the people, to their willingness in times of crisis to sacrifice their lives and fortunes for the good of Rome, to their essentially conservative nature, and to the simplicity of their lives. He believed that if he could instill in his contemporaries a similar respect for and compliance with traditional religious ceremonies he could ensure the peace and prosperity of Rome through the goodwill of the gods. To further his aims, Augustus became a member of the Roman sacred college of priests and was elected *pontifex maximus*, "head priest," in 12 BC.

As a result of his political position as head of the Roman government, his public piety, and his efforts to restore the traditional religion, a cult of personality soon developed around Augustus. The prosperity of Rome and the peace throughout the empire were linked directly to his leadership. There was a glorification of his personality and promotion of his role as the protector of Rome. Coins were issued bearing his image, and in the eastern provinces shrines were established where the faithful could worship him as a living god, a practice Augustus did not allow in Rome.

Although there was precedent for the worship of a leader among the lower classes of Rome—similar cults had developed around Marius and Caesar—Augustus discouraged it. But the senate, ever mindful of public opinion, proclaimed him *divi filius*, "son of a god." Julius Caesar had been proclaimed divine upon his death, and Augustus accepted the honor because he was Caesar's adopted son. Augustus's birthday became a public holiday, and libations were poured in his honor at banquets.

Even as Augustus was moving closer to deification in his lifetime, he continued in his usual casual manner, refusing divine honors when they were offered by the senate but allowing the worship of his image outside of Rome and Italy as a method of building the unity of the empire. In the East, worship of the leader as a god was a common practice. Persian kings, Egyptian pharaohs, and Hellenistic leaders since Alexander had been deified while they still lived. Caesar and Antony had received divine honors when they campaigned in the East, but this did not always mean that people actually believed their kings were living gods. Contemporary historians tend to view the bestowing of these honors as an act of gratitude or homage. Eventually, the cult of Augustus spread to the western provinces of the empire, and in 12 BC, an altar was built at Lyon and dedicated by Augustus's stepson, Drusus.

The empire had two continual problems while Augustus ruled and for years after: restless barbarians on its borders and never enough money in the imperial treasury to keep everybody happy, especially the army. By the first century AD, most of the ancient world had developed a money economy although some provinces paid Rome in kind, primarily grain or precious metals. Augustus always needed hard currency to keep his armies loyal, his civil service working, and his governors and senior government officials honest or at least reasonably so.

Coins had always been an important component of image building among leaders in the ancient world. Those issued by Rome circulated widely and came to reflect Augustus's idealized view of himself as restorer of the Republic, upholder of Roman liberty, and champion of Roman greatness. Images alluding to legends associated with him and to highlights from his career appeared on coins that were issued to pay Roman soldiers. Those coins reinforced his public image as pater patriae and protector of the empire.

The principal treasury for the empire was located at Rome, and into it the revenues collected from Italy and the provinces were deposited. Authorized by the senate, Augustus took what he wanted to carry out his duties and to fund the expenses of the empire. He developed a tax policy for the empire based on how much his advisers believed would be needed for a particular year. When that amount was established, the official rate was set.

Augustus had money from other sources in addition to the public treasury. He had inherited money from Caesar, he appropriated money and properties from his enemies in the civil wars, and he controlled the wealth of Egypt. Eventually he accumulated so much personal wealth that he was able to make loans and donations to the Roman government in times of need, engaging in a form of deficit financing as he made up government shortfalls out of his own funds. As Rome's richest citizen, Augustus played the role of super-benefactor, especially when it came to meeting the costs of the army and public entertainment.

The empire grew and prospered at a tremendous rate, but there came a time when its limits were reached and the Roman economy began to contract. Costs of government kept rising, especially those associated with supporting the army and providing public entertainment, while revenues declined. Fewer areas of the ancient world were worth the expense and risk of conquest, so returns were meager. Augustus believed that one should "never begin an undertaking unless the expectation of gain outweighs the fear of loss." Rome had already conquered Spain, France, Turkey, and Egypt. Outlying areas such as Germany in the north and Parthia in the east (present-day Armenia, Iran, and Afghanistan) were populated by fierce barbarian tribes and offered little in the way of returns.

After years of dominance, the Roman Empire received its first major shock in AD 9 when three Roman legions, fifteen thousand soldiers, were massacred in the Teutoburg Forest, a wilderness east of the Rhine River. The loss stunned Augustus, who had never before experienced such a defeat, but his response was measured and well thought out. Instead of launching a massive retaliation against the Germanic tribes, which could have resulted in even more Roman losses, he decided to set limits to his empire by establishing a fortified frontier along the Rhine and Danube rivers.

The army made Augustus and its support kept him in power. He recognized early on that no matter how popular he might be with the people or the senate he drew his power from his soldiers. They enforced his will and guarded the frontiers of his empire. In peacetime they built his roads and bridges, aqueducts, canals, and fortifications, but they were expensive to maintain and constantly demanded benefits and bonuses. While Augustus controlled the army, it also controlled him. He had what the Romans called "a wolf by the ears."

Soldiers were recruited from Roman citizens, primarily from Italy but also from Gaul and Spain. All were required to take an oath of loyalty and obedience to Augustus and paid directly by the treasury at Rome. Thus the dangerous financial tie that had existed decades before between commanders in the field like Caesar and Pompey and their armies was severed. The highest-ranking officers were appointed by Augustus, usually from among his relatives and closest friends.

To provide for his personal security, Augustus established the Praetorian Guard, an elite unit stationed primarily in Rome. Members received significantly higher pay and better benefits than the common soldiers in the field, retirement after sixteen years instead of twenty, comfortable quarters, good food, and no fighting barbarians in some remote outpost. The Praetorian Guard was commanded by officers selected by Augustus from the equestrian ranks and later played a key role in the appointing and deposing of the Roman emperors who ruled after him.

At the age of seventy-seven and after more than forty years as Rome's "first citizen," Augustus fell ill. As hard as his Greek doctors tried, they could not find the cause or arrest his decline. Fearing he was being poisoned, he would eat only figs from his garden and drink rainwater collected from his cistern. Augustus died in AD 14, and historians believe he may have been poisoned by Livia, who had become concerned that her son Tiberius might not become the next emperor.

The current travails of Citigroup, AIG, and corporate empires such as General Motors underscore what an extraordinary leader Augustus was. Putting together an empire—geographic or corporate—is impressive. Expanding one's corporate domain in good times is hardly uncommon, but keeping it together in a mortal crisis and strengthening it afterward is an astonishing feat.

Rome could very well have splintered when Julius Caesar was murdered (some three hundred years later, Rome did in fact divide into two parts). Augustus bested his foes and proved his military and political prowess. But he then demonstrated unique administrative talents and sensitive political diplomacy as he pushed through major political and economic reforms.

One reason for Augustus's success as a leader was that unlike so many contemporary politicians and CEOs he had a practical sense of limits. Doing his own version of cost-benefit analysis for Rome's frontiers, he calculated that it was time to stop expanding. He knew instinctively that to push the boundaries of the empire farther simply for his own glory, as Alexander did, would be immensely costly and ultimately self-destructive. In today's world Augustus never would have binged on subprime mortgages, gagged on derivatives, or overleveraged his balance sheet.

Like other leaders we have examined, Augustus had a vision and knew how to inspire. He possessed enormous energy, which he proved capable of focusing for the good of Rome in a disciplined way. But he never lost his appetite for managing detail or let himself fall victim to hubris. He was that managerial rarity—both a first-rate strategist and politician—who never let success warp his judgment or control his behavior.

This book opened with Steve Forbes browsing in a bookstore in Naples, Florida, for something interesting to read about history and leadership. It ends with John Prevas spending Thanksgiving in Key West in the company of two young Coast Guard petty officers and their families discussing what leadership means to them.

The Thanksgiving Day table was laden with the traditional fare: turkey, sweet potato pie, corn pudding, stuffing, mash potatoes, upside-down apple pie, pumpkin pie, key lime pie, and plenty of Cool Whip. Football was blaring from the TV; the kids were chasing the family dog around the house, while the ubiquitous Key West chickens were running wild outside in the yard. There were open Corona bottles everywhere, and it was eighty degrees and sunny, not exactly traditional Thanksgiving weather. The atmosphere in the home of that young petty officer was congenial and welcoming.

Both men are serving on a 110-foot Coast Guard patrol boat that plies the often turbulent waters between Key West and Cuba. Their mission is to interdict smugglers ferrying illegal aliens, drugs, and weapons from Cuba and points south to Miami. Both have been in the Coast Guard for years with considerable experience at sea. So after dinner, in the style of the ancient Greeks, but over beer instead of wine, we held an American version of the classic Socratic symposium. First, I posed the question "What constitutes good leadership for you guys?"

They were eager to respond. A good leader looks out for his men and is willing to go that extra mile for them when things get tough. That can mean bending the rules a little if need be, and in return, those who follow will give unquestioned loyalty and support. It also means turning to those you lead for help when you don't have all the answers. For these petty officers, leadership is a simple formula of reciprocity and cooperation between those who lead and those who follow.

This is the classic style of Xenophon, Hannibal, and Augustus, with a little of Alexander and Caesar mixed in. Xenophon, Hannibal, and Augustus inspired those they led and developed a genuine rapport with them. Alexander and Caesar did as well but added a little material incentive to sweeten the pot.

The worst type of leader, both officers agreed, is the one who thinks he has all the answers. They pointed out the frustration they faced on board ship, often on a daily basis, with executive officers, usually recent Coast Guard academy graduates, who think they have the answer to every question and the solution for every problem. As leaders they lack experience, but often their egos will not allow them to ask for help or rely on their subordinates in difficult situations. The mistake they make is seeing their function as always giving orders, and that type of leadership can have tragic consequences for everybody.

These petty officers had been running a ship at sea for years and faced just about every conceivable situation, from 15-foot seas to armed smugglers and desperate refugees. They found it frustrating to take orders from someone who lacked experience just because he wore a little brass on his collar that rubbed off on his ego.

Also present at dinner that day was the father of one of the petty officers, Rusty Meadows. Rusty left a secure executive position with AT&T in 1984 to start his own architecture and design firm in Washington, D.C. With nothing more than an idea and the desire to be his own boss, he built his company into one of the most successful in the nation's capital doing major projects for the State Department, the Department of Transportation, the World Bank, AOL, Freddie Mac and Fannie Mae, and, ironically enough, the new Coast Guard headquarters in Washington, D.C.

In addition to doing work in the United States, Rusty was among a handful of innovative entrepreneurs who saw the potential in opening up the Middle East for American engineering and design firms. Without knowing a lot about Islam and the ways of doing business in an Arab culture, he went to the Persian Gulf (Dubai), made some mistakes, learned from them, persevered, and landed a string of projects. Then he had to come home and convince his reluctant partners in Washington that they could work in the Middle East and make money. At the height of a robust international market, he pulled off the perfect ending by selling his company to a national architecture firm eager to expand.

Rusty had remained quiet during the initial discussion, preferring to let the young men talk first. When it came his turn he didn't have to think for a moment about what successful leadership means. For Rusty, as we saw with many of our leaders in the prior chapters, there are three essential components—vision, setting direction, and inspiring those who follow you to get there, especially when the going gets rough. Vision means the big picture, knowing where you want to go and what you want to accomplish. But vision, as we have seen throughout our book, is often not enough. You have to follow up on it by laying out the path to accomplishing your goal and then motivating people to believe in you and follow it.

Leadership for Rusty does not mean having the answer to every problem but it does mean providing the vision, the direction, and the support to move a company or a Coast Guard cutter through rough seas. A leader is a navigator and a captain. His role requires dealing effectively with not only his own people on board but competitors or smugglers, embracing inclusion but not accepting insubordination. It means accepting responsibility for your mistakes and learning from them. Leadership also means reaping the rewards. Once again, this view is clearly in line with Cyrus, Xenophon, Hannibal, and Augustus, with just a few overtones of Alexander and Caesar.

● ● ●

What have we learned from the leaders from the ancient world, four empires, and about two dozen contemporary corporate leaders and their companies? Three key points emerge to command our attention:

1. Character is the indispensable foundation upon which good leadership is built.

2. The willingness to consider other opinions and points-of-view shows strength and confidence, not weakness in a leader.

3. It is a fatal mistake to believe that the success of a business is based solely on the skills and charisma of just one individual and then rely on that person exclusively to get the job done.

CHARACTER

While character is no guarantee of success, a leader simply cannot succeed in the long run without it. The lack of it will show through, especially when times get tough. The real challenge of leadership, as we saw with Alexander and Caesar, is to maintain character in the face of success. Leadership brings with it a host of temptations, opportunities for enormous personal gain, adulation, and inflated ego, all of which can become a toxic brew. And while a leader can get away with a sip or two, as we have seen in some of our examples, a prolonged or deep draft can be fatal. This requires an almost daily effort, a focus on keeping the right perspective on one's self, working each day to stay on track.

The ancient Romans recognized the danger and placed a slave in the chariot of each general who returned home in triumph. As the general drove his chariot along the parade route and enjoyed his moment of glory, the slave whispered into his ear, "You are a man, not a god."

Sometimes managing success can become more challenging than achieving it. Cyrus knew that character mattered in a leader, which is why he made honesty the cornerstone of a Persian education. Xenophon relied on it to sustain him through tough times. As we have seen recently in both politics and business, nothing exposes the lack of it in a leader quicker than the stresses and demands for solutions brought on by difficult times and circumstances.

The Persians, Greeks, and Romans all believed character was an indispensable component of leadership, but what exactly is character? How about integrity as a start? A leader who has character is one who is transparent in his actions and if not exactly like Caesar, at least like Caesar's wife, who had to be above even the suspicion or appearance of impropriety or wrongdoing. We saw in an earlier chapter that Caesar divorced his second wife, Pompeia, after she was discovered in a compromising situation, even though he testified in court that he believed she was innocent of any wrongdoing. The point he was making was that her character had to be so far above reproach that the people he counted on for support would not even consider her capable of wrongdoing, much less require her to prove her innocence.

Good character was, as we have seen, never exactly a consistent component of Caesar's own political leadership style except when it came to leading his army. As a military leader he was remarkable for the quality of his character: His men crossed the Rubicon with him because they believed in him and his vision. But in the end, it was the failure of his character in the political realm that brought about his demise. We have found that the best leaders, corporate or political, are those who are willing to put what is right, either for the country or their own company, before self-interests, careers, and portfolio returns. The worst are those who violate their fiduciary responsibilities and like Bernard Madoff take the short-term gains at the expense of those who trust them—shareholders and investors. Being courageous, sincere, and honest are hard qualities to fake. Voters and shareholders have a way of spotting the leaders who lack those qualities—maybe not at first, but eventually it comes out in the wash.

OTHER PEOPLE

Socrates, one of history's earliest gurus on leadership, believed asking the right question was always more important than proposing the right answers. Ask the questions that will stimulate thought among those who look to you for leadership and generate new insights regarding persistent problems. Leadership does not mean always having the right answers, although that does help. It means remaining firmly in control of the process for finding them. Socrates believed that leaders need to be trained to question and probe as they lead. They must understand that wisdom, real wisdom, lies in understanding and accepting the fact that you do not have all the answers and that in the long run you cannot bluff, intimidate, or bully people into thinking that you do. The key is asking the right questions and then moving toward finding solutions within that framework.

Plato, another Greek philosopher, wrote that extraordinary leaders, what he called "philosopher kings," were born with this quality, and it sets them apart from others. Aristotle believed it was something you could learn under the right teacher. But as we saw in an earlier chapter, his star pupil—Alexander—did not turn out as well as he had hoped and had to be done away with. Character certainly matters in a leader, and a good one learns early on that once developed and maintained it will serve as his armor for a lifetime. When a strong authority figure proposes a solution, ex cathedra, the proposal, coupled with his executive status, can actually close off other potentially productive channels of thought and debate among subordinates. Corporations suffer from the same problem when they impose rigid guidelines and standards for their workers.

According to Greek legend, a bandit named Procrustes lived in a cave in the countryside outside ancient Athens preying on unsuspecting travelers. He invited the weary into his cave to rest on his bed. Once on the bed the unfortunate victims were bound to it, and if they were too long for a perfect fit, Procrustes cut off as much as necessary. If the victims were too short they were stretched on a rack to the proper length. In our own time the term *Procrustean bed* has come to symbolize an arbitrary standard to which everyone is expected to conform, and is even a byword for cruelty. Corporations and institutions with a "procrustean" mentality can actually shut down other potentially fruitful paths of inquiry and problem solving through debate and discussion. When confronted with a problem, don't merely rely on how things have traditionally been done—focus instead on how the organization can most effectively tackle the problem utilizing its best intellectual resources. Leaders cannot rely entirely or exclusively on intuition and experience. A good leader fosters an environment that encourages subordinates to come forward with their ideas, perspectives, and opinions on solving problems. That does not mean tolerating insubordination, but it does mean being open to dissenting opinions, evaluating them objectively, discarding what is of little value or is even detrimental, and incorporating what is useful.

As Roger Ailes, chairman and CEO of Fox News, remarked in a recent *U.S. News & World Report* article, "A leader who does not fear making decisions has no fear of openness with his employees. I will listen to everybody and then I will make the decision and take the consequences. Once you have a mission and you have a delivery date it really has to be an act of God to stop you." Even the best executive decisions, made in a vacuum, have little chance of success if the people who make up the organization and have to carry out those decisions don't believe in them.

Any executive can extract minimal compliance from his workforce by employing fear and reward, but a successful leader gets people on board, the way Xenophon did, and brings them together to carry out the mission. A good leader recognizes that mistakes happen, and sometimes they are his, and other times they are due to the failures of subordinates or circumstances. But the important point is that a leader has to confront the issues head on—bring them out into the open quickly and fix them—and, above all, not spin them. Make it right no matter what the cost, and you will win in the long run. Spin them, avoid them, blame others, and all you will do is prolong for a short time your own demise. Character is the strength to step forward and take the heat; ability is being able to fix the problem.

THE HEROIC MYTH

In the ranks of corporate leadership, a crucial mistake is attributing the success of a company solely to the skills and charisma of one individual, its "heroic" CEO. The "myth of leadership" has traditionally been that of an Alexander or a Caesar, the solitary individual at the top whose brilliance, insight, and heroic nature enable him or her to lead the way for the rest. In reality, the most effective leader is not the one leading the parade but the one who can get the job done without drawing a lot of attention to himself, a Xenophon or an Augustus.

Colin Powell is one of the most respected and admired public figures in the world today, and fits the model of the self-effacing leader. He realizes it's about the job, not the person giving the orders. In the preface to his recent autobiography, *My American Journey,* he writes about the importance of establishing a mission and then inspiring those who follow to carry it out. He believes that the basic principles of good leadership can be applied to any field or area of human endeavor, and, like Cyrus, Xenophon, Alexander, Hannibal, Caesar, and Augustus, great leaders articulate their mission in a way that the people who follow them understand what they are being asked to do, why it needs to be done, and how they are going to do it. That is what effective leadership is all about. It was that way over two thousand years ago, and it remains that way today.

ACKNOWLEDGMENTS

The authors extend their thanks to the following people who contributed to making this book happen. First, to our agent, Larry Kirschbaum, and our editor, John Mahaney. Larry was once described in a *New York Times* article as "the nicest man in publishing." To that should be added generous, supportive, patient, and savvy. John Mahaney is one of the best editors in a difficult and demanding business. Metaphorically speaking, he is a sculptor who knows how to pick the right block of marble from all the rest out there and then ever so slowly and methodically shape it into the finished product. We owe him.

Many thanks to Elizabeth Ames, whose editorial and research contributions helped shape the project in its initial stages; Juliette Fairley, who spent countless hours researching the business portions of this book; Merrill Vaughn for invaluable editorial assistance in the preparation of the initial drafts of the manuscript; Jill Mathers for research in the initial stages; Clarita Jones for so amiably handling the repeated requests for more information as the project moved along; Jo Rodgers for editing the final manuscript; Bill Dal Col, who always provides indispensable advice; and Jackie DeMaria and Maureen Murray, without whose assistance Steve would never have been able to do his part for the book according to schedule, and John would have suffered a nervous breakdown.

Professor Jonathan Scott Perry, of the University of South Florida, graciously took the time to proofread the history chapters and offer helpful suggestions that were incorporated into the final draft. Abdullah Ayazi, of Washington, D.C., prepared our maps as he has done for John's prior books and once more did an outstanding job.

And finally, on a very personal note, we would like to acknowledge our wives, Sabina Forbes and Mavis Gibson, for their encouragement and suggestions throughout a long and tedious process that has brought the two of us together as friends.

Needless to say, we take joint responsibility for any errors and omissions that are ours alone. It is our hope that you, our readers, will share our love of history and enjoy this book as much as we enjoyed writing it.

Steve Forbes
John Prevas
June 2009

INDEX

ABOUT THE AUTHORS

STEVE FORBES is a lifelong student of history and an admirer of Winston Churchill. As chief executive officer and editor in chief of Forbes Media, Forbes manages a powerful communications company committed to the principles of entrepreneurial capitalism. On two occasions he has entered the political arena as a candidate for the presidency of the United States. In the mid-1980s, President Reagan named Forbes chairman of the bi-partisan Board for International Broadcasting (BIB) where he served until 1993. In this position, he oversaw the operation of Radio Free Europe and Radio Liberty. Broadcasting behind the Iron Curtain, Radio Free Europe and Radio Liberty were praised by Poland's Lech Wałesa as being critical to the struggle against communism. A widely respected economic prognosticator, Steve Forbes is the only writer to have won the highly prestigious Crystal Owl Award four times. The prize was formerly given by USX Corporation to the financial journalist whose economic forecasts for the coming year proved most accurate. In studying corporations, Steve Forbes has never forgotten what his paternal grandfather believed: If you want to appraise the prospects of a company, take a look at what the "head knocker," the person running the show, is doing. Like his grandfather, Forbes believes that individuals, especially leaders, are infinitely more important than balance sheets in determining the success of an enterprise. Forbes received a B.A. in history from Princeton in 1970.

JOHN PREVAS was born in Baltimore, Maryland, on February 6, 1943. He was educated in history and political science at the University of Maryland where he was awarded his bachelor's degree in 1967 and a master's degree in 1969. He went on to earn a second master's degree in educational psychology at Johns Hopkins University in 1972 and a law degree from Antioch School of Law, Washington, D.C., in 1980. He has studied Latin on the graduate level at both Yale University and the University of Maryland. For thirty years Mr. Prevas had taught Latin, Greek, government, law, and history at St. Mary's College of Maryland, Towson University, and Thomas Stone High School. For the last eight years he has taught Latin and ancient history at Eckerd College in St. Petersburg, Florida.

Mr. Prevas's first book, *Hannibal Crosses the Alps*, was published in 1998 and was based on his extensive research and travels in the French Alps. He spent several summers in Paris studying the Greek and Latin manuscripts pertaining to Hannibal in the Galerie Mazarine in the Institut de France and then undertook to climb all the major passes in the southern French Alps that historians over the centuries have speculated might have been Hannibal's route. He continues to lead groups of students and interested political and business leaders into the Alps each summer to retrace Hannibal's footsteps.

John Prevas has made presentations on Hannibal at Princeton University, Rutgers University, Vassar College, Stanford University, and Meridian House International in Washington, D.C. He has given a number of presentations in France where he was featured in the French magazine *Passion*. He has participated in a documentary on Hannibal filmed in the Alps by the BBC, has appeared on the History Channel, and has spoken on Hannibal at a meeting of United Nations ambassadors in New York and at the Smithsonian.

His second book, *Xenophon's March*, was released in January 2002 and like *Hannibal* is based on the author's manuscript research and retracing of the famous march of Greek mercenaries through some of the most remote mountain areas of eastern Turkey, along the Russian, Iranian, and Syrian borders and the Black Sea. He has lectured on his research and travels to the Turkish Embassy in Washington, D.C., and has spoken on *Voice of America*.

The author's third book, *Envy of the Gods*, is the story of the unraveling and demise of Alexander the Great in the east. The book was published in 2004 and was favorably reviewed in *Kirkus Reviews* and the *New York Times*. In preparation for the writing of the book Mr. Prevas traveled alone to Iran, Afghanistan, Uzbekistan, and Pakistan on his Greek passport, tracing the route of Alexander and his army through those troubled lands. His travels took him from the Zagros Mountains of Iran and the ancient Persian capital of Persepolis, over the Hindu Kush Mountains of Afghanistan, the Khyber Pass, and into the Swat Valley of Pakistan. From the Swat Valley he followed the Indus River to the fringes of the desolate no-man's land known in ancient times as the Gedrosian Desert. In conjunction with the release of his book, Mr. Prevas was interviewed on CNN and by numerous radio stations, and appeared on the Fox News network show *Hannity & Colmes*. He has recently lectured on Alexander at Stanford University, Meridian House International in Washington, D.C., and in France at the Festival du Livre in Aix-en-Provence. He continues to speak about Alexander and Hannibal as leadership figures to business groups around the country as well as at the annual Forbes CEO Conferences.

John Prevas is married to Mavis Gibson, a commercial interior designer in Washington, D.C., and currently divides his time between his residences in Belleair, Florida, and Cannes, France.